D1339610

FORMAL METHODS IN CIRCUIT DESIGN

Cambridge Tracts in Theoretical Computer Science

Titles in the series

FORMAL METHODS IN CIRCUIT DESIGN

V. Stavridou
Royal Holloway and Bedford New College, London

CAMBRIDGE
UNIVERSITY PRESS

Published by the Press Syndicate of the University of Cambridge
The Pitt Building, Trumpington Street, Cambridge CB2 1RP
40 West 20th Street, New York, NY 10011-4211, USA
10 Stamford Road, Oakleigh, Melbourne 3166, Australia

First published 1993

Printed in Great Britain at the University Press, Cambridge

Library of Congress cataloguing in publication data available

British Library cataloguing in publication data available

ISBN   0 521 44336 9   hardback

Contents

List of Figures

ix

List of Tables

Acknowledgements

This book is the result of my research in hardware verification over the past six years. My work in formal methods and hardware started in the Department of Computer Science in the University of Manchester and is continuing at Royal Holloway and Bedford New College in the University of London.

In Manchester I learned to work with formal methods. More importantly I learned how to do research. In both tasks, I was blessed with the friendship, support, kindness and patience of many people. Howard Barringer at the University of Manchester was a constant source of invaluable technical advice and fortitude. He has shaped my thinking on many aspects of computer science and has, in many ways, set the standards of my aspirations. John Cullyer of the University of Warwick (then at RSRE, Malvern) provided the initial impetus that got me started in hardware verification. John Gurd, Doug Edwards and Cliff Jones at the University of Manchester have been instrumental in providing the background which made my work in hardware verification possible. My other friends in Manchester, Graham Gough and Michael Fisher supplied a friendly and warm working environment. The Department of Computer Science was a stimulating place to work which I left with great sadness.

Joseph Goguen of Oxford University has been an inspiration in much of my research work and his friendship and help are gratefully acknowledged. John Tucker and his team at University College Swansea have been instrumental in the writing of this book by providing early reviews and by meticulously checking the draft for errors and inconsistencies. Steven Eker, currently at Rutherford Appleton Laboratory, has done much pioneering work with synchronous concurrent algorithms and OBJ3 and has contributed the Pixel Planes case study. Steven, Ben Thompson and especially Robert Stephens have provided very useful reviews of the material. The text of this book owes much to the thoroughness of these people. Any remaining problems in the text are purely of my own making.

Mark Moriconi and the other people of the Computer Science Laboratory of SRI International in Menlo Park have made me welcome and provided a very productive and stimulating working environment on many occasions during the past five years. The same is true of the Programming Research Group of the Oxford University Computing Laboratory where I spent a sabbatical year working on hardware verification amongst other things.

Ten years ago, Derek Coleman introduced me to formal methods. He has since become my husband and has been a constant source of support and patience during my toils. However, none of this would have been possible without the inspiration and forbearance of Stefanos Stavridis and Alexandra Stavridou, my parents. This book is dedicated to them.

Victoria Stavridou
March 1993

Chapter 1

Introduction

1.1 The perceived need for formal methods

The idea that computers can be used for reasoning as well as calculation was mooted in the 40s by Turing and von Neumann [vN46]. During the 60s and the 70s considerable progress was made in modelling and reasoning about computer programs. Building on the ideas of Floyd and others, Hoare provided a sound basis for program verification by devising his well known logical theory of imperative programs. An impressive array of influential theorem provers were developed and used to verify programs in the 80s [Lin88].

However error free software is only as good as the hardware it is running on. As digital devices are deployed in a growing number of high integrity applications there is increased anxiety about the dependability of such systems. Furthermore, the rapid growth of the VLSI market in the last two decades has meant that manufacturers of commodity VLSI devices are under pressure to deliver increasingly complex, reliable and cost effective products within short time-to-market scales; a product can be rendered unprofitable by a six month introduction delay. Formal techniques have clearly had an impact on the design of safety critical systems as acknowledged by the recent MOD Standard 00–55 [MOD91]. They have also been shown to be commercially advantageous as for example in the production of the Inmos IMS T800 floating point unit [MS87].

So program verification techniques have, in the past ten years or so, migrated into the hardware domain. It can in fact be said that in some ways, hardware verification has been more successful than software verification. It is easy to see why when one reflects on the success stories of software verification - fairly small (a few tens of pages of code) critical parts of programs in security and microcode applications. The common factor between these and hardware designs is that the size of the problems is sufficiently small so that their verification is within the capabilities of existing theorem proving tools. But in hardware the size and importance of a product are not necessarily proportional; the verification of a multiplier circuit could be commercially advantageous whereas the verification of a multiplication program is rightly regarded as a toy problem. Yet another success factor is that the formal theories needed to model hardware at certain levels of abstraction are simpler than those needed for software.

In this book we analyse these and other success factors and their impact on the industrial take up of hardware verification techniques. We thus formulate a set of criteria against which we evaluate various approaches. We also propose and assess an algebraic alternative.

1.1.1   Overview

This book is concerned with the verification and validation of synchronous digital systems. It aims to

1. identify hardware specific requirements,

2. identify the issues affecting wide industrial use,

3. conduct evaluation case studies on various non algebraic formalisms using the above criteria, and

4. propose and evaluate an algebraic approach according to the same criteria.

The work described here is intended to be problem-driven rather than technology-driven.

The next chapter discusses both the hardware specific and the technology transfer requirements on formalisms. In doing so, we refer to the relationship of the hardware/software development processes and analyse two verification experiments – the Viper development and the Inmos work on the T800 and T9000 transputers. We thus establish a set of criteria against which formalisms will be evaluated in the rest of the book.

The third chapter starts with a review of notations and applications and having presented the case study examples, proceeds to present and discuss a number of evaluation studies.

The fourth chapter investigates the term rewriting paradigm and its applications to hardware verification through a case study. It provides some theoretical background and analyses issues such as the equivalence of term rewriting systems and the relative merits of structural and inductionless induction. It concludes with an evaluation of the approach.

Chapter 5 proposes, demonstrates and evaluates the OBJ3 paradigm for the specification of synchronous digital systems. The approach is investigated for a number of device categories ranging from switch level descriptions to synchronous concurrent algorithms.

The sixth chapter discusses the use of OBJ3 as a theorem prover by presenting the logical framework and the associated methodological issues. The viability of the OBJ3 approach is demonstrated in the following chapter where a number of case studies integrating specification, simulation and proof within a single formalism are presented.

The closing chapter summarises the results of our analysis of the hardware domain and the results of our case studies. It also reflects on the OBJ3 paradigm and proposes future work and its intended impact on the hardware development process.

It is likely that this book will be useful for three groups of people:

- Undergraduate and postgraduate students seeking an introduction to the field of hardware verification.

- Postgraduate students and other research workers interested in the equational approach to the specification and verification of hardware.

- Hardware designers who want to find out ways in which formal methods can be used to supplement existing best practice.

1.2 Preliminaries

Throughout this book, we will be relating formalisms to the various stages of the design and development of digital systems. It is therefore important to characterise and define our understanding of the development process. This is done in this section which also identifies the development stages that are relevant to the subject matter of this book.

1.2.1 Defining the development process

Development involves the refinement of some kind of object from an inital one to a final one. We write $O_1 \xrightarrow{D} O_2$ to indicate that object O_2 has been derived from O_1 using derivation D. This D may be a formal or an informal transformation. It is intended that the derivation of O_2 from O_1 represents an improvement over O_1 in the sense that O_2 is closer to the final object of the development activity. In what follows, we will use the term *model* to denote a view or an abstract representation of an object.

The development of a system encompasses three classes of models and their relationships; requirements specification (R), design specification (S) and implementation (I). If D is a derivation relation between two such models (that is one is derived from the other by a series of formal or informal transformations), then one intuitive way (there are of course others) of defining the development process Dev is

$$Dev \stackrel{\text{def}}{=} R_{1...i} \xrightarrow{D_{RS}} S_{1...j} \xrightarrow{D_{SI}} I_{1...k}$$

where $R_{1...i}, S_{1...j}, I_{1...k}$ represent model refinements through the development. $R_{1...i}$, for instance, is an abbreviation for $R_1 \xrightarrow{D_{R_1 R_2}} R_2 \xrightarrow{D_{R_2 R_3}} \ldots \xrightarrow{D_{R_{i-1} R_i}} R_i$. R_i, S_j, I_k are the final refinements of the requirements, the specification and the implementation respectively.

For such a development to be correct we require that D is an *improvement* relation. An improvement is a relation between models p and q, denoted $p \sqsubseteq q$, if for any purposes, the observable behaviour of q is as good as or better than that of p; more precisely, if q satisfies every requirement satisfied by p and maybe more. Here are some examples of improvement:

- If p and q are watches and p is splash-proof and q is water-resistant to 10m, then $p \sqsubseteq q$.

- If p and q are predicates on the natural numbers and $p(0) = true$ (p is only defined for 0) and $q(0) = true$ and $q(1) = false$ (q is defined for 0 and 1), then $p \sqsubseteq q$.

- If p and q are programs in a procedural language and q terminates more often than p and/or gives a more determinate result, then $p \sqsubseteq q$.

The improvement relation is always defined with respect to some property of interest. In almost all work on reification and refinement, the property of interest is nondeterminism (for example [Mor90]). But often other properties, such as speed and size (for programs) or cost (for consumer products) are of primary interest. Jacob in [Jac91] gives an excellent account of various properties of interest and associated notions of improvement.

We define the observable behaviour of a model to be the set of direct and indirect observations we can make with respect to the properties of interest. In the case of sequential programs, the set of observations consists of the values of variables before and after execution. If our programs are concurrent, the set of observations includes complete sequences of state pairs representing changes due to actions of the processes making up the program. Formally, the improvement relation is defined by:

$$p \sqsubseteq q \stackrel{\text{def}}{=} observations(p) \subseteq observations(q)$$

where $\sqsubseteq$ is necessarily reflexive and transitive (a preorder[1]). Each development stage removes some freedom from a model by adding new constraints. At each stage, the resulting model can be shown to be contained in (or to imply) the model of the previous stage.

If p and q operate on different data spaces they cannot be compared directly. This is not the case when p and q are watches but consider the case of source and target programs in compilers; the source uses identifiers to denote variables whereas the target uses registers and RAM locations. If r is a mapping from the data space of q to that of p, then p and q can be compared before and after the translation:

$$r : Q \rightarrow P$$
$$p \sqsubseteq r(q)$$

where P and Q are the data spaces of p and q respectively. Now the correct development process can be restated as

$$Dev \stackrel{\text{def}}{=} R_{1...i} \sqsubseteq T_{SR}(S_{1...j}) \sqsubseteq T_{IR}(I_{1...k})$$

where $T_{SR} : S \rightarrow R$ and $T_{IR} : I \rightarrow R$ translate between the data spaces of (S, R) and (I, R) respectively and

$$T_{SR}(S_{1...j}) \quad denotes \quad T_{SR}(S_1) \sqsubseteq T_{SR}(S_2) \sqsubseteq \ldots \sqsubseteq T_{SR}(S_j)$$
$$T_{IR}(S_{1...k}) \quad denotes \quad T_{IR}(I_1) \sqsubseteq T_{IR}(I_2) \sqsubseteq \ldots \sqsubseteq T_{IR}(I_k).$$

In what follows, the term *designer* is used to denote the person(s) effecting any stage of the development process. The term *system* is used to denote a hardware or software or hybrid computing entity. We use the term *correctness* as an abbreviation for *correctness w.r.t. the specification*.

1.2.2   The meaning of verification

Given the above formalisation, verification is perceived as the means of establishing that $\xrightarrow{D_{RS}}$ and $\xrightarrow{D_{SI}}$ are indeed improvement relations. Three approaches can be distinguished:

1. **Proof oriented development** whose task is to establish a logical theory of the relation $\sqsubseteq$. This assumes the existence of provably equivalent semantics for the models involved in the development process and must include enough theorems to enable the designer to select correct target constructs for each source construct, eventually arriving at a provably correct final implementation. This is the approach taken for instance in [Hoa90b] where a provably correct compilation scheme is constructed

---

[1]A partial order if we are interested in semantics as well as syntax.

using sound sets of axioms and theorems relating source and target language programs. In this case, providing enough theorems enables the compiler to choose amongst a number of alternative target constructs in order, for instance, to produce optimised code. Correctness is implicit in the case of proof oriented development; the implementation is axiomatically correct since it is derived from the requirements by a series of sound and correctness preserving transformations. Questioning the correctness of such an implementation is akin to questioning the correctness of, say, a chemical formula such as $NaOH + HCl \rightarrow NaCl + H_2O$.

2. **Verification** whose goal is, given all the components of a specific *Dev*, to establish via formal argument (proof) that $\sqsubseteq$ is indeed an improvement relation on the components of *Dev*. This is a weaker case of proof oriented development since it only establishes a minimal theory of $\sqsubseteq$ and it seeks to prove that specific instances of R, S and I are derived by a series of improvements.

3. **Validation** shares the goals of verification except that it seeks to achieve them via rigorous as well as formal argument (testing and proof). This approach in fact embodies existing best practice as exemplified by the examples analysed in the next chapter.

This book is primarily concerned with verification and validation. We will see that incursions of one into the other are in fact necessary.

1.2.3 The scope of verification

It is often said that the use of formal techniques in the production of systems should be viewed as a means of delivering enhanced quality rather than establishing correctness. This difference of perception is crucial and needs to be particularly highlighted in the case of high integrity systems. We believe that formal methods can help deliver correctness (w.r.t. some requirements) and therefore enhanced quality; but correctness is not the end of the story.

As pointed out by Cohn [Coh88a, Coh89], correctness involves two or more models of a system (designer intentions and fabricated chip), where the models bear a tentative but uncheckable and possibly imperfect relation to both the requirements and the implementation. Even under the best possible circumstances, when we have an accurate interpretation of the requirements, at best, we can assert that the model of the implementation satisfies these requirements. We can no more guarantee the correct operation of the actual system in situ, than we can guarantee that every experiment involving the previously mentioned chemical formula will unconditionally produce a molecule of salt and a molecule of water. The success of the experiment will depend on factors ranging from communication, training, and behaviour to the performance of mechanical, electrical and chemical components both within the system and its operational environment.

We require that systems are not only correct but that they are *dependably* so. There are many terms associated with dependability, and considerable international effort has been expended to standardise these. The accepted definition of the overall concept is [Lap91]:

Dependability is that property of a computing system which allows reliance to be justifiably placed on the service it delivers.

The life of a system is perceived by its users as an alternation between proper and improper service. Delivery of proper service (service which adheres to specified requirements) is normally termed *correctness*. Therefore a "correct" system is not necessarily a dependable system. Dependability is an overall property which entails other aspects such as safety, reliability and availability. Laprie [Lap91] defines these terms as follows:

Safety is a measure of the continuous delivery of service free from occurrences of catastrophic failures.

Reliability is a measure of the continuous delivery of proper service (where service is delivered according to specified conditions) or equivalently of the time to failure.

Availability is a measure of the delivery of proper service with respect to the alternation of proper and improper service.

Formal methods address correctness issues and these form the substance of this book. We do not address other dependability aspects here although safety, reliability and availability should be modelled and measured independently of verification, using techniques such as probabilistic analysis and testing. However, it is worth pointing out that confusion often arises between the above concepts which are, in fact, distinct. For instance, a safe system is not necessarily reliable (an airplane in flight may be safe for only some of the time), a reliable system is not necessarily correct (the autopilot may reliably compute an incorrect course) and a safe system is not necessarily available (the safest airplane is one that never leaves the ground).

1.2.4   The relationship between proof and testing

The realm of mathematics is relatively simple and orderly; the real world is not. It is therefore important that well behaved mathematical denotations are not confused with the physical artifacts they represent. The behaviour of physical objects must be established in practice as well as in mathematical theory through extensive testing in the operational environment. Moreover, testing is relevant to real world artifacts and their mathematical counterparts since in many cases we lack proof construction mechanisms and resources. These observations can be generalised in the following empirical rule:

Some proof complements extensive testing
and
some testing complements extensive proof.

The first conjunct forms the premise of post-development validation and characterises current pioneering attempts to supplement comprehensive testing with proof in order to achieve quality improvements.

The second conjunct affirms the standard mathematical practice of attempting proof only once a reasonable hypothesis (tentative theorem) has been established through observation and dynamic analysis.

1.3 Industrial take up of formal methods

The safety critical industry has made significant steps towards the adoption of formal methods and there have been some success stories in the non safety critical sector. The development of new technology has been impressive in the last decade. But in spite of this progress, wide industrial uptake has proceeded at a very slow pace and formal methods have not yet produced significant impact on every day designer practice [BS92b]. Progress is especially disappointing when compared to other new technologies such as CAD, CASE, expert systems or object oriented programming. So what is going wrong?

Today formal methods exist primarily as a collection of notations and experimental tools which tend to be non scalable and poorly engineered. Proof oriented development is by and large a (non trivial) research exercise (see [B+89]). In other words, we have plenty of impressive research results but relatively little "fit for purpose" technology. More fundamentally, industry's main goal is productivity, measured over the time to market phase of the lifecycle. This is not directly addressed by formal methods (even though the Inmos experience shows that formal methods can improve productivity) whose main goal is quality. Quality is often an industrial subgoal although higher quality can result in improved productivity (measured over conception to decommission) because of reduced maintenance costs. Furthermore, a proportion of the formal methods research community has been inward-looking and has not therefore been able (or willing) to explore ways of working with and improving best practice. Finally, formal methods require mathematical expertise which is simply not available in an industry where many practitioners have limited formal education in computer science and mathematics.

But, as already mentioned, hardware applications seem more promising than software ones. In this book we explore the hardware design process and attempt to identify ways of improving it through the effective use of formal methods. These technology transfer success factors will form the reference point against which the existing and the proposed hardware specification and verification approaches will be evaluated.

Chapter 2

Requirements

2.1 Introduction

In early 1991 Hewlett–Packard announced three 9000 Series 700 PA-RISC workstation computers. For a time, these machines gave HP the competitive edge in terms of price and performance in the workstation market. The order of complexity of these machines is daunting; for instance, the CPU contains 577,000 transistors, the floating point coprocessor 640,000 transistors and the memory and I/O controller is of the order of 185,000 transistors [G+92]. The product design cycle for the 700 series from inception to system release was 18 months [DW92]. It is instructive to observe that the design and implementation of these machines were undertaken with the following objectives in order of priority:

- Time to market

- Performance

- Product cost

- Development cost

First silicon in all parts had no critical bugs; in fact the first CPU chip booted the operating system four minutes after it was installed in the processor board [DW92]. The entire design of the Series 700 chips was validated using simulation with the HP ChipBuster toolset [A+92].

To maintain competitiveness in the high performance area, manufacturers such as Hewlett–Packard must offer continual performance and cost improvements as the basic technologies evolve. The industry trend for performance growth has historically been a doubling of high-end performance levels every 12 to 18 months. The challenge to any new technology such as formal methods is to become sufficiently relevant to this industrial reality. Being useful in this context implies that formal methods must offer advantages over and above current practice which, in the case of the HP Series 700 validation effort at least, seems to have been extremely effective.

In this second chapter we investigate the VLSI engineering domain in order to establish a set of criteria for industrial relevance and applicability of formal methods. The evaluation of various formalisms which have been used and/or suggested for reasoning about digital

9

systems will be carried out against these criteria. This is achieved by establishing and analysing a set of requirements given the state of the art in VLSI engineering. In the course of this, we identify areas where formal methods can make a contribution and a number of open research questions.

The terms *formalism* and *notation* are used interchangeably in this and the following chapters and they refer to mathematical or logic frameworks within which systems can be specified and verified. The term *tool* will be used to denote software that provides machine support to notations. Tools will include compilers, simulators, theorem provers, proof checkers and proof assistants.

2.2   Successful industrial take up

The prerequisite for industrial uptake of formal hardware verification/validation technology is a formalism which can adequately deal with the pertinent aspects of digital systems. However, the existence of such a formalism is not sufficient; the relevant technology must also be able to address the problems of the digital systems industry and must do so in a way that is commercially advantageous. A simple economic model of new product development and commercialisation [Rei83] shows that:

- In both high growth (20% growth rate, 12% annual price erosion, 5 year product life) and low growth markets (7% growth rate, no price erosion, 10 year product life) overrunning development costs by 50% has less than a 4% impact on profits before tax.

- In a high growth market with short product life cycles, shipping a product six months late can reduce its lifecycle profits by 33%. In slow growth markets with long product lifecycles, late shipment creates only a 7% decline in these profits.

- In many cases, the single most important factor is cost. A product cost overrun of only 9% resulted in a devastating 45% decrease in profits in a slow growth market, while a similar overrun in a fast growth market reduced profits by as much as 22%.

It is possible to deduce from the above that even if the use of formal methods incurs higher development costs, this is unlikely to be the predominant factor. The critical considerations to a greater or lesser extent (depending on market growth rates) are development speed and final product cost. Is it, therefore, evident that

formal methods can deliver cheaper products rapidly?

We recognise that given the current technology, the use of formal methods is more likely to slow down rather than speed up the process. It is however the case that in specialised markets such as the high integrity sector, other factors such as product quality may be the overriding concern. A further consideration must be whether

formal methods can enhance product quality.

Therefore,

$$industrial\ uptake\ =\ provision\ of\ suitable\ formalism\ +$$
$$well\ defined\ migration\ path\ into\ existing\ best\ practice\ +$$
$$commercial\ advantage.$$

In the rest of this chapter, we set about identifying what makes a formalism suitable for hardware specification and verification and what are the technology transfer success factors. We do this by examining current industrial practice, by reflecting on the prominent formal methods experiments of the Viper microprocessor and the Inmos transputers and finally by analysing the hardware features that commonly require specification and verification. These results, which we collectively call *requirements*, enable the construction of the evaluation platform used in the rest of this book.

2.3 Requirements capture

2.3.1 Technology transfer factors

Although our primary interest is VLSI engineering, we believe that a comparison of the software and hardware development processes is very revealing in the context of understanding VLSI technology transfer factors. It is also true that although VLSI and software engineering have traditionally been viewed as separate disciplines, not only do they share many process development aspects [SD84], but even apparently dissimilar structures such as mutually recursive software modules and circuit feedback loops are in fact alike. We will often therefore refer to software engineering practices for insights into VLSI engineering.

If formal techniques are to have an impact on the VLSI engineering process, such a process must exist and be well defined. We feel that such a process exists but is in many ways less mature (with one notable exception that we mention later) than the software engineering process. Furthermore, the "VLSI lifecycle" is not well established as in the case of software, although it would be very similar.

We have seen a generalised formulation of the design process in the introductory chapter of this book. The entity refinements, $R_1 \ldots R_i, S_1 \ldots S_j, I_1 \ldots I_k$, and the improvement relation $\sqsubseteq$ can be further characterised by levels of abstraction (system, switching network, geometry) and properties of models (behavioural, structural, physical). Taking this idea further we can depict the development process as a graph shown in figure 2.1. We will return to this graph later on.

2.3.1.1 Levels of abstraction

Let us now see how this framework is used in the case of VLSI design. The highest, *conceptual* level of abstraction is generally informal and typically consists of verbal descriptions augmented by charts and graphs. This level includes high level algorithmic descriptions. The *architectural* level is a formalisation of the first informal level and includes block diagrams. Typical of architectural level descriptions is the PMS notation [Sie74]. The next level down is the *register transfer level* which is concerned with the transfer of information between architectural entities. The transition from the architectural to the register transfer level is usually accompanied by a change in orientation from systems properties

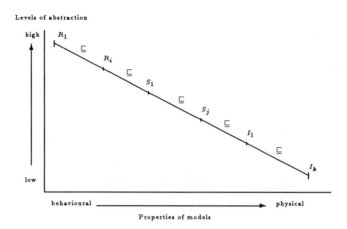

Figure 2.1: Development process graph

to a particular VLSI chip design. Computer hardware description languages such as CDL
[Chu74], DDL [Die74] and others, exemplify this level.

The next lower level is the *logic* level – the mainstay of TTL technology which details
combinational elements and state preserving elements. At the next level down, the *circuit*
level, descriptions are in terms of gates and devices. The concern throughout these two
levels is the mapping of system level components to physical hardware elements.

The last two levels contain the *geometry* level of the design [MC80]. At the *flexible*
geometry level the design is described, as a minimum, in terms of planar topology (captured by, say, stick diagrams), containing orientations and relative positions of primitives.
At the lowest layout *mask* level, physical sizes and absolute locations are set and this
description (for instance, in CIF) normally forms the input to the fabrication process.

The levels of abstraction are summarised in figure 2.2[1].

2.3.1.2   Properties of models

The VLSI design properties associated with each level of abstraction are *behavioural,*
structural, and *physical.* Within the category of behavioural properties, a further distinction is made between *functional, performance,* and *temporal* properties. Functional
properties address the logical correctness of a design at a given level of abstraction (or
what a design does). Performance behaviour is a subset of what in software terms is qualitative behaviour such as testability, modifiability, efficiency, flexibility and so on (or *how*
well a design does). The third type of property, that is the temporal aspect, addresses
the dynamic behaviour of the design (*when* and in what order do the actions occur).

Structural model properties include the hierarchical definition of components in terms
of subcomponents and connectivity information. Physical model properties address the
actual layout of the design on a chip area.

These properties are summarised in figure 2.3.

---

[1]For an alternative abstraction structure see [SBN82].

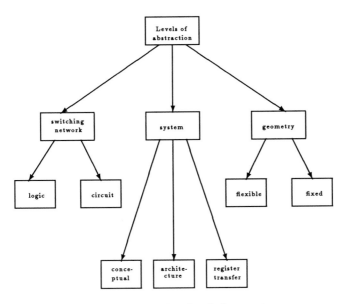

Figure 2.2: The levels of abstraction

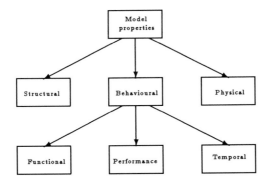

Figure 2.3: Properties of models

2.3.2 Aspects of VLSI engineering

Here, we make some general remarks about the state of the art in VLSI engineering. Many of these comments are only relevant in the case of mass produced hardware and do not apply in the specialised safety critical domain.

In contrast with software design, the primary qualitative category in VLSI design is performance. That is, the question of *how well* a design does is currently largely equivalent to *how fast* in the VLSI domain. This discrepancy is perhaps due to the relative youth of VLSI and to the fact that designs are currently dominated by technological constraints. If this is true, we can expect that the notion of quality in the VLSI domain may soon become closer to software where quality includes not only performance but reliability, modifiability, testability and flexibility. If formal methods yield qualitative design improvement, then the question that has to be asked in the short term is;

> *can formal methods deliver faster chips?*

It is not obvious whether or how formal methods can directly help in this area although it could be argued that they have an indirect impact in so far as they can aid the design of asynchronous, and therefore, faster designs. [BM88b] reports on some interesting results in this direction.

2.3.2.1 Maintenance

One of the less disputed issues on the use of formal methods is that they can drastically cut maintenance costs. Despite the *de facto* truth of the importance of time to market scales, this is a very important benefit as currently 60% of the cost of software systems is incurred at the maintenance stage [SD84]. Software maintenance primarily consists of major/minor enhancements and correction of latent faults, that is faults which remained undetected during testing and have produced errors which in turn cause operational system failures. What is the equivalent in the VLSI domain? Superficially, it appears that there is no equivalent since chips are not "patched" after fabrication. However, software maintenance often requires backtracking to earlier steps in the development process when for instance it becomes obvious that the failure is not the result of a coding fault but the result of a flawed design decision. The analogy in VLSI occurs when there is a need to build a chip with slightly different functionality or improved performance. Currently, because of the lack of tools allowing design backtracking, the only feasible modifications are minor enhancements (typically speed) and error corrections, whilst major enhancements require an entire redesign. The question is therefore;

> *can formal methods aid VLSI design backtracking?*

We believe that the answer is yes, provided that the notation(s) used are flexible and have well defined interfaces when more than one is used during system development[2]. This is in fact an area where formal methods can have maximal impact leading to commercially advantageous design practices.

Since this seems a promising technology migration path, it would be appropriate to investigate the provision of tool support facilitating design backtracking and design time

---

[2]It is likely that different notations will be used for different development phases and it is, therefore, important to formally justify the transition from one notation to the next.

testing. Most current software approaches to the development of automated tools supporting the design process aim at collecting useful tools in a "toolkit" or "workbench". While each tool is individually useful for a particular task, the integration of tools is not a primary consideration. A more fruitful approach is the development of an integrated CAD system to support the design process as it progresses through each phase. Such a system would be built around a central pool of design information and would facilitate both mapping the design between levels of abstraction and evaluating model properties at each level, effectively assuming the rôle of a digital system oriented IPSE. The feasibility of integrating a formalism in such an integrated CAD system will be one of our main evaluation criteria.

2.3.2.2 Reuse

Reuse is the notable exception mentioned earlier in this chapter in connection with the maturity of the VLSI lifecycle. Whereas software reuse is a major issue in software engineering (despite the emergence of various paradigms such as parameterised, modular and object oriented programming), VLSI reuse is very well established. Not many VLSI engineers would set about designing and fabricating custom multiplexors or D/A/D converters when they need such components. However, the average programmer routinely produces custom code for traversing binary trees and sorting linked lists. This situation can be explained by the fact that chip fabrication is much more involved than code production and that VLSI interfaces are simple and well defined (number of pins, pin purpose) whereas the software interfaces are complex and still the matter of much debate in the area. Reuse is then a particularly well developed craft in VLSI. This leads to the question:

> *Do formal methods support VLSI reuse?*

The answer depends on particular formalisms and their tool infrastructure such as support for existing and evolving component libraries through the provision of a suitable CAD interface. Consequently, the ability of a formalism to support primitive component libraries will also feature strongly in our evaluation studies.

2.3.2.3 Process maturity

The maturity of the design process is recognised as an important factor for successful technology transfer [HKC89]. The more mature the process the greater the impact of advanced techniques such as formal methods. It is therefore important to assess the maturity of VLSI engineering.

Most industrially used VLSI design tools are physically oriented and are based on descriptions at the geometry level [MC80]. In this respect, the evolution of the software development process has shifted from the assembly/machine level to algorithmic languages such as Algol and Pascal. It is interesting that there is considerable resistance amongst expert VLSI designers to the development and use of fully automated layout systems since they will be inherently less efficient than custom layouts. Similar resistance was encountered when FORTRAN was first introduced and extra attention was paid to optimising the code generated by FORTRAN compilers in order to mitigate this resistance. But as the introduction of compilers and later operating systems had a dramatic effect on productivity and the scope of designs, super optimisation is no longer an issue. In the VLSI domain however, and despite some encouraging work [BC86, Bro91], silicon compilers and silicon operating systems are still largely referred to as "mythical" [SD84].

The final maturity indicator of the VLSI design process is the collection of labour intensive stages. In the VLSI domain, manual transformations are required at the lower right portion of our development process graph in figure 2.1. This is extremely labour intensive because of the complexity of the designs and the critical chip area considerations. In software, the labour intensive efforts occur at the upper left portion of the graph between the conceptual/functional and algorithmic/structural transformations. As chip space becomes less critical, higher level switching network constructs may become the building blocks of VLSI design, and indeed evidence to this can be found in [Tho90]. However, it must be noted, that the VLSI industry will probably be "locked in" due to the vast investment in existing technology just as the software industry is locked in Cobol and FORTRAN.

In conclusion, it appears that the VLSI design process is less mature than the software design process and thus presents a challenge to formal methods technology transfer. It is all the more important, therefore, that formal methods should be targetted towards well defined stages of the development process such as reuse and contribute to weak areas such as design backtracking.

2.3.2.4   The demise of the microprocessor?

Thomas [Tho90] strongly argues that the traditional embedded microprocessor will be replaced by application specific integrated circuits (ASICs) during the next 20 years as fabrication techniques and design tools make them easily affordable. Given the disadvantages of embedded microprocessors (performance mismatch, complexity, size, weight, power consumption, heat dissipation) Thomas's vision does not seem unrealistic. What, then, are the implications of a massive market shift to ASICs for VLSI engineering?

Apart from the clear implications for design languages and synthesis tools, such a shift will also have profound effects on VLSI designers who will have to acquire the software designer's ability to handle both greater complexity and increased abstraction. This enforced maturity of VLSI engineering will mean that labour intensive efforts will concentrate on the gap between the conceptional/functional and algorithmic/structural transformation, the areas where today formal techniques have maximal impact in the case of software. Furthermore, the cost effectiveness of custom designs will mean that design reuse and backtracking will become more prominent in the development cycle and therefore formalisms supporting reuse and facilitating backtracking will be desirable. Moreover, the qualitative speed requirement, which is not readily answered by formal methods, will become a less important constraint as the ASIC technology itself yields far more efficient circuits. It would seem that if technology does bring about the changes that Thomas anticipates, formal methods will have an even greater rôle to play in VLSI engineering.

2.3.3   Hardware aspects

Having discussed the technology transfer factors and the nature of VLSI engineering, we now switch our attention to the pertinent hardware aspects that formalisms must address, such as the nature of the circuits designed today and some of the factors that influence the design process. Current engineering practices are discussed further in [MC80, Dav88] amongst others.

The field of digital design is diverse and contains a large variety of design styles and techniques. Some designs are logically simple but require complex analog interface circuitry. Other designs have a functional behaviour which would be impossible to determine from a circuit description since the function is predominantly dependent upon information stored in ROM or RAM. It is similarly difficult to decide what level of precision is required to describe a design accurately. A VLSI chip design description can include such diverse information as geometric descriptions, chemical characterisation and description of the package and its electrical properties. The hard task is to know what is important for a particular chip and what can be ignored.

The behavioural specification of sequential digital designs presents a similar problem. It is insufficient to view a legal behaviour as one which takes a sequence of inputs and produces a sequence of outputs. There is inherently no relationship between inputs and outputs that does not also include *state*. The number of possible states may be combinatorially huge and the problem gets worse when other important aspects of system behaviour, such as time and electrical properties, are included. It is therefore important to avoid *overspecification*.

2.3.3.1 Design specification components

Functionality The design must receive a sequence of logical inputs and produce the correct set of logical outputs. It would be desirable to specify functionality either by enumeration (e.g. truth tables) or as a transfer function. However, enumeration is tedious and feedback means that behaviour cannot be characterised by a simple transfer function.

I/O characterisation This is the interface specification and deals with three sets of requirements:

- **Logical**. Inputs are grouped in logical subsets with defined value subranges and a mapping between logical values and valid electrical levels.

- **Temporal**. Sets of inputs may be constrained by the time of stability and value change.

- **Electrical**. A variety of electrical requirements, such as current levels and rise and fall times, are necessary for the interface to interact with the environment in the specified way.

Cost The system cost will be constrained in various ways, for example materials, board area, manpower, weight, power requirements etc.

Speed Most systems must meet performance criteria. Speed is the predominant quality factor.

Power The total system should stay within its power budget in all phases of its operation. This also has obvious implications for heat dissipation.

Volume In some applications, size is an important limiting factor.

Packaging The nature of the design may be constrained to a certain packaging format.

Reliability Some systems are designed with reliability specifications.

A formal or even a usable informal specification cannot possibly encompass this breadth of information. If overspecification is to be avoided, only pertinent aspects must be included. Every specification must contain functional and interface requirements but other attributes may be primary considerations in some applications (e.g. power consumption and weight on space craft). Thus the producer of a formal design specification is faced with two problems:

- Which of the above requirements should be in the specification?

- In what way should the requirements be expressed?

The former question is put to all specifiers, formal or not, and the answer depends on cumulative expertise. The latter presents problems for some aspects for which formal notations are either not available or not appropriate. Functionality and I/O characterisation are, subject to model granularity and expressiveness, expressible formally although, in some circumstances, a traditional engineering model, such as control theory, may be more appropriate for interface specifications. Speed, power and reliability requirements cannot be formally expressed at present for the lack of appropriate hybrid mathematical models although much current work [ZHR90, Sor90, Nor90, THS92] is focussing on these problems. Cost, volume and packaging fall outside the premise of formal methods and are best dealt with by different (continuous/probabilistic) branches of mathematics.

2.3.3.2   VLSI circuitry

Circuit components are as diverse as the design itself. A circuit will contain all the following aspects:

Analog circuits Analog circuitry exists in every chip and as circuit sizes shrink, its rôle is becoming more important because of the area and speed advantages. In some cases, functional requirements can only be met by using analog components.

Digital circuits These can be *combinational* in which case functionality can (within reason) be specified with transfer functions or enumeration (but general structures such as PLAs may present problems) or *sequential* for which state encoding is required.

Temporal discipline Traditionally systems have been *synchronous*, that is synchronised by a global clock, where non clocked inputs to clocked components must be stable at the clock edge. Although this practice simplifies many electrical aspects, clock skew and distribution on large chips are serious problems. Because of these difficulties, *asynchronous* designs which have the advantage of speed (as systems do not have to be clocked to the speed of the slowest component) are beginning to be more popular despite the corresponding increase in design complexity.

Board level designs have the added problem of programmed functionality, signal conditioning and power distribution.

Some of these aspects are inherently difficult to describe and it is common practice to specify the set with an almost equally large set of descriptive techniques. The challenge to formal specification notations is the ability to deal with these aspects which are routinely dealt with by most good designers in the short term, and the provision of adequate expressive power in a single semantically consistent representation for all aspects in the long term. Currently, synchronous and asynchronous designs of combinational and sequential devices can be formally specified within certain size and structure limitations. Analog devices are not usually studied in connection with formal methods although some work in this direction does exist [Sho83, Seu90]. Whilst there is an urgent need for more accurate formal models, it is clear that there are severe limitations on how far this can be taken; as Cardelli points out [Car82] specifying and verifying the properties of an armchair using quantum mechanics is hard. Nonetheless expressive power will be an important consideration in the evaluation of formalisms.

The conclusion is that designers of formal notations must do as VLSI designers – do their best to come as close as they can to actually achieving these goals. The hard part is not just the development of proof techniques. It is at least as hard to properly describe the right aspects of a design and to specify the correct behaviour.

It must also be borne in mind that digital designers do not need verification systems for straightforward designs where experience suffices and safety is not an issue. They need such systems for counterintuitive designs, especially those requiring new techniques, outside their experience. It is important that the basic approach to specification and verification be scalable to the realistic systems that designers are striving to produce today. The scalability of approaches will be another of our evaluation criteria.

2.3.4 Practicing formal methods – two examples

Having discussed the principles involved in the design of hardware, let us now examine two diverse instances of practical experimentation with formal techniques in an attempt to investigate why and how were the techniques used. In the first case, the Viper microprocessor, qualitative aspects are primary, whereas in the second case, the Inmos transputers, the overriding concern is the time to market factor.

2.3.4.1 Viper

Viper (Verifiable Integrated Processor for Enhanced Reliability) was the first "real" microprocessor subjected to formal verification – Hunt's FM8501 (PDP-11 like) [Hun85] and Gordon's computer (PDP-8 like) [Gor83b] although verified and now manufactured, were never intended for serious use. This fact, coupled with its Ministry of Defence parentage, makes Viper a high profile hardware verification experiment. In [Cul85], Cullyer outlines the reasons behind the chip's development, namely MOD control of chip design, manufacture and marketing. The constraints on the architecture and manufacture on Viper can be summarised under the heading of "simplicity" [Ker84]. This is understandable as simplicity is a very sensible requirement for systems used in safety critical applications; it is also fortunate because in this instance it made formal verification experiments possible. Simplicity coupled with the need for quality are potentially fertile ground for the use of formal methods. Whether this can be stretched to Thomas's belief that *you should not build anything that is not simple enough for formal methods* is doubtful; technology and progress always carry implicit risks.

Returning to the Viper experiments, let us examine what happened[3]. In the first in-stance, Cullyer and Pygott [Cul84, Pyg85, CP85] produced an LCF–LSM specification of the chip which was animated by translating LCF–LSM primitives to Algol 68. In [Coh88b, Coh88a], Cohn presents proofs in HOL [Gor85] relating the top level specifi-cation with the host machine (state machine) and the block level description of Viper (register transfer level description). The block level itself, is still very abstract as one has to go through the gate and electronic levels before arriving at the manufactured chip. The proof relating the top level functional specification with the host machine revealed a type error, a confused definition and an incomplete check [Coh88b] whilst the (only partially completed) block level proof did not reveal any problems. Neither proof was of direct concern to the fabricators of Viper chips and indeed, the fact that the first batch of chips from one of the manufacturers contained errors cannot be attributed to the flaws discov-ered by Cohn. The chips and the associated nomenclature appeared a long time before the conclusion of the formal verification work. It is clear therefore that formal verification in the case of Viper was a *design quality assurance* exercise. The associated costs were prohibitive and therefore the next generation of the chip, Viper2, was not subjected to similar hardware verification (although other verification techniques have been used).

The lessons from the Viper experiment can be summarised as follows:

- The dependability of the chip was enhanced at a price, although no measurements are available.

- Formal methods can certainly help deliver *slower* chips because efficient but complex structures are hard to verify.

- Although no comparative figures were available, it is difficult to imagine that the formal verification work produced a cheaper chip. As the model for new product development which we discussed at the beginning of this chapter shows, development cost has relatively little impact on the viability of new products. What can be devastating, however, are delays in the development cycle. Pygott [Pyg92] argues that the Viper verification work did introduce precisely these unacceptable delays.

- The formal verification work is not directly utilised in the development of Viper2 (which is very similar to the original with the addition of a multiply instruction) so there is no evidence of the work aiding design backtracking.

- The experiment has certainly shown that HOL is scalable even if painfully so [Coh88a]. Pygott [Pyg92] calculates that the Viper verification work took 18 person months. He also suggests that theorem proving of this nature is tedious rather than complicated and therefore is not an activity that is likely to be attractive to suitably trained mathematicians.

- Pygott [Pyg92] also reports that communication between the hardware designers and the people doing the verification was problematic since the mathematicians had no intuition about the design and the designers found it difficult to trace the

---

[3]A detailed, critical review of the Viper verification work can be found in [BH90]. [Coh89] discusses the context, meaning and limitations of the Viper proofs.

problems discovered by the theorem prover back to the design level. This raises the important question of who should do the proofs; mathematicians or hardware designers? Based on the Viper experience it would appear that ultimately it must be the responsibility of the design team.

Viper is famous not only for the use of formal verification during its development but also for the controversy surrounding the extent to which it was proven correct [Mac91]. As we have seen the context of the Viper formal verification work was one of design assurance. This means that the proofs were still being done after the chip had reached the market place accompanied by nomenclature claiming that it had been proven free of design defects. The ensuing dispute, which very nearly landed the UK Ministry of Defence in the High Court accused of "negligent misrepresentation", is a stark reminder that there are fundamental disagreements and misunderstandings about the meaning of "proof" when applied to physical as opposed to mathematical artifacts. Although the debate on the meaning of proof is bound to continue, it is plainly the case that accounts of formal verification, especially when safety critical systems are concerned, must not only include descriptions of what has been proved, but perhaps more importantly, they must contain a clear statement of what has *not* been proved. Finally, as MacKenzie notes [Mac91], the central issue, which has frequently been submerged in the storm of publicity, is that no "bug" has been found in Viper chips. Indeed their design has been subjected to an unprecedented degree of scrutiny, checking, simulation and mathematical analysis.

2.3.4.2 Inmos T800/T9000 Transputers

Shepherd and May [MS87, She90] report on a further formal methods experiment. In this case, the Occam transformation system [Gol88] was used to translate high level Occam implementations of the IMS T800 floating point unit instructions into low level Occam microcode descriptions. This work therefore amounts to microcode rather than hardware verification. The Inmos work is important and is included here because it originates from standard microprocessor industry rather than the safety critical sector. May and Shepherd report in their findings that the microcode correctness was established in far less time than would be needed by an adequate amount of testing and that this has enabled Inmos to produce the chip well ahead of schedule with a high degree of confidence in the microcode. In other words, the use of a formal approach resulted in commercial benefit both in terms of quality and more importantly in terms of time to market timescales.

Although detailed information about the T800 work is scarce (for commercial reasons) it is possible to draw some conclusions:

- The dependability of the unit was enhanced. May [MBS92] reports that four years after the introduction of the T800 two bugs have been discovered in the FPU microcode, both in areas that were not covered by the formal methods work.

- There is no evidence that the use of the transformation system resulted in a faster chip.

- The verification work produced a (value added) chip within short and commercially advantageous time to market scales.

The T800 FPU work earned Inmos and the Programming Research Group of Oxford University Computing Laboratory the 1990 Queen's Award for Technological Achievement.

In 1989 Inmos embarked on the design of a new transputer now launched as the T9000. The T9000 was to be compatible with the T800 and since the former is a much more complex processor than the latter, a number of verification problems emerged. [MBS92] describes the formal verification work on the T9000 virtual channel processor (VCP) and [Ros92] discusses the verification of the T9000 pipeline. The fact that Inmos had used formal methods successfully in the past clearly gave a much needed impetus (as discussed by May in [MBS92]) for deploying the technology once again on a more complex problem. Collective expertise such as this plays a significant rôle in the adoption of any new technology. However, despite past positive experiences with the methods, May reports that bringing together engineers and mathematicians on the T9000 project was a continuing challenge. The T9000 work is not yet reported complete but it is possible to highlight some aspects.

- Inmos have found that since processor subcomponents are often specified and designed within many different notations, it is essential that different design descriptions can be consolidated and checked against each other [MBS92].

- Design backtracking would seem to be a major issue given the compatibility requirements between the T9000 and the T800. It is not however obvious that formal methods have been useful in this context since complete formal specifications of the two processors do not exist (which is not surprising given their complexity). The fact that a new set of tools has had to be developed for the T9000 work is also symptomatic of the inability to benefit in a concrete way from the previous work on the T800.

- Roscoe [Ros92] describes the Inmos approach to effective use of formal methods in their design activities as one of "identifying windows of opportunity" for the technology. Although such an approach is necessarily *ad hoc* and cannot lead to established design methodologies improved by formal methods, it does however clearly delineate what is possible with current technology and how to make optimal use of it. Such an "opportunistic" approach is obviously the necessary first step towards well organised and understood design technology. A similar, successful approach using HOL on selected aspects of complex microprocessors is described in [BCF92].

2.4   Requirements analysis

In this section we examine the impact that certain hardware properties have on the applicability of various formal notations. We discuss formal hardware models, the specification requirements of sequential devices and summarise wider issues such as specification/reasoning ratios and integration.

2.4.1   Formal hardware models

The "accuracy" of hardware verification (that is how sure we can be that a verified circuit will work correctly) depends not only on proofs and proof tools but also on the proximity of the circuit model used in such proofs to physical reality. Many circuit models do not fully reflect the complex electrical and temporal properties of VLSI and consequently, within such models, it is possible to formally verify a chip which operates incorrectly or deduce clearly wrong circuit properties.

Transistors do not always behave like switches; the actual behaviour of a CMOS n–transistor is that it conducts when its gate voltage is higher, by some threshold, than the voltage on its source. If, for instance, transistors are modelled as switches it can be easily shown [CGM86] that a "correct" XOR gate does in fact behave incorrectly. Furthermore, widely used formalisms such as HOL do not capture all relevant aspects of bidirectionality. [MNP87] shows that it is possible to deduce obviously wrong properties about a verified CMOS inverter (the proven property implies that the circuit would still function correctly if it were "turned around" which is clearly not the case).

There are other aspects of circuit design which are not handled by the models of commonly used hardware verification methods, for instance transistor gate capacitance (in NMOS devices) and charge sharing. Gate capacitance is dealt with in [Gor81] for example, using the register transfer model, but not in a way in which it could be combined with charge sharing or bidirectionality. Nonetheless, such formalisms are very important, as long as it is remembered that if the semantics of the model do not correctly describe all behavioural aspects of a device, then a proof of correctness in that model no longer guarantees that the device behaves correctly. Such compromises are necessary in order to achieve tractable verification techniques.

Formalisms which adequately model the physical properties affecting the computational behaviour of a device exist, but are not widely used largely because of the inefficiency involved in manipulating detailed models. Bergstra and Klop [BK83] have given an axiomatic semantics for restoring logic circuits both statically and dynamically. Bryant [Bry81, Bry84] defined a switch level model which describes the logical behaviour of MOS devices in terms of characteristics such as dynamic and static storage, charge sharing, bidirectional pass transistors etc. Winskel [Win86] has defined a much more accurate, compositional, CCS derived notation where capacitances and resistance are contained within the model. Musser has also proposed an improved model [MNP87] which can describe properties such as bidirectionality by representing wires as a data structure containing value, strength, capacitance and charge.

Despite the complexity introduced in proofs of correctness in models supporting physical device behaviour, certain aspects such as bidirectionality must be considered if the proof is to be of any value at all. Another, perhaps more hopeful approach is to work within two models, one simple and one more accurate. If the two models are formally related it may then be possible to ensure that assertions which hold of a circuit according to the simple model (for which verification is tractable) are correct with respect to the more accurate model. Work in this direction is reported in [Win87, Win86] and [ZH91].

2.4.2 Behaviour through time

2.4.2.1 State Transition Machines

Every module of a logic system can be represented by the general model of the state transition machine. This model contains the elements required to describe the module behaviour in terms of its inputs, outputs and time. Figure 2.4 shows the general model

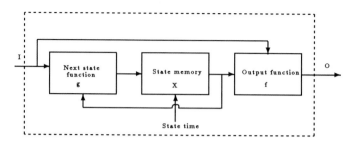

Figure 2.4: Generalised state machine

with the *next-state function*, the *state* and the *output function*. The *state* of a machine is the memory of sufficient past history to determine future behaviour. In terms of the state machine, this means sufficient information to determine both an output and a next state if the present inputs are known. This memory element is usually made from a group of flip flops forming the state register. A state register consisting of n flip flops allows 2^n possible states.

Each state of a machine has a next state determined by the *next state function*. The *state time* is normally determined by a periodic input to the state register. At the end of each state time the next state becomes the present state. The next state function, g depends upon the present state X, and the inputs I. If the basic state time is represented in terms of a unit t (e.g. seconds) and k is a counting integer, then $X(kt)$ represents the state at the discrete time kt. Therefore the next state function can be defined as follows:

$$X((k+1)t) = g(X(kt), I(kt))$$

The *output function* generates a set of outputs O from the state and input information for each state. As with the next state function it consists of a transform operation f :

$$O(kt) = f(X(kt), I(kt))$$

The general state machine model encompasses various classes of machine behaviour, the simplest being combinational machines which have no state memory or next state function and are thus fully described by the output function alone.

2.4.2.2   Specifying Time Dependency

We define *time dependency* in a specification as that part of the behaviour of a system that must be defined with reference to some external periodic event such as a clock. The next state function definition in the previous section is an example; it must be defined with reference to the state time kt. It is this requirement to specify and reason about behaviour through time that differentiates general state machines from combinational devices such as binary adders, etc.

Formalisms used for specifying and verifying the behaviour of such machines must be able to express and reason about time dependency. Furthermore, the choice of time representation crucially affects the expressive power and associated reasoning overheads of

a notation. In general, expressive power and reasoning complexity are inversely proportional.

Time dependency can be *explicit* in the specification as in the definition of the next state
function g above and in higher order logic specifications through higher order functions,
or *implicit* as in temporal logic through the use of temporal operators. In order to define
a unit delay element with input I and output O in HOL [Gor85] we specify the predicate:

$$Del(I, O) = (\forall t).O(t + 1) = I(t)$$

where t is the external periodic event. In temporal logic the same unit delay is specified
by the sentence:

$$\Box((\bigcirc O) = I)$$

Here, the time dependency is hidden by the temporal $\bigcirc$ (next) operator. Both these
examples record behaviour with reference to a single external event, the clock tick. The
behaviour of the system is not defined *between* the clock ticks because we have no way of
partitioning the clock pulse and looking at the behaviour at time $t/2$.

The state machine cycles through its states, reaching a stable condition during every
state time kt. The state and, consequently, the next state and the outputs are defined
only during the *stable period* of the state time. The other component of the state time is
the *transition period* which is determined by circuit delays. In order for the state machine
to be definable, the stable state time must be greater than the transition time. The
transition period is a function of the gate settling times. In order, therefore, to be able to
express some requirements (for example that the transition period must be strictly less
than the duration of the clock pulse) we must be able to partition state time.

These observations also apply in the case where behaviour must be recorded with reference to more than one external event such as the behaviour of a system with multiple
clocks. Such time division is possible in notations which have been developed for use with
reactive systems, for example real time temporal logic [Ost89], timed CSP [DJS90] and
Lustre [TP91] amongst others. Systems with multiple clocks are treated with retimings
in [Har89]. Many ideas originating from reactive systems theory [Pnu86] are relevant to
the specification and verification of asynchronous digital systems.

2.5 Summary and evaluation criteria

Evaluating a formalism on its academic merit is probably impossible and certainly contro-
versial. Moreover, the evaluation exercise itself is necessarily subjective. In order to have
a sensible comparison approach we have set a goal, namely the industrial applicability of
hardware specification/verification techniques and we analysed the factors affecting their
use. We believe that we have introduced some measure of objectivity in the comparison
process. Needless to say, this does not absolve us of subjectivity during the comparative
exercise which we describe in the following chapter.

The pertinent factors identified in this chapter are summarised as follows:

1. Can formal methods deliver cheaper VLSI devices quickly?

2. Can formal methods enhance product quality?

3. Can formal methods deliver faster chips?

4. Can formal methods aid VLSI design backtracking?

5. Do formal methods support VLSI reuse?

6. Are formal notations expressive enough to capture all engineers want to say?

7. Are formal techniques scalable?

8. Are formal notations/tools usable by engineers?

9. Is there a well defined technology migration path?

Some of these issues (1, 3) are questions which require further research and cannot be answered in this book. We can however refine some of them to the following criteria:

Expressive power is important because it affects the range of devices that can be specified, the ability of engineers to express physical device properties and requirements and the scalability of formal approaches.

Readability of the notation is very significant for two reasons. First it is desirable that the verification of hardware is ultimately performed by the design team rather than "bought-in" mathematicians. Second, even if the proofs are done by mathematicians, they still need an appropriate communication medium with the chip designers and clearly a readable notation is desirable in this context.

Machine supported verification is critical for cost and time effectiveness of formal approaches as well as their scalability, usability and their reliability in that it reduces the risk of errors introduced by manual transformation and proofs.

Direct or indirect simulation without manual transformations is desirable as it allows design experimentation and blends well with existing design procedures.

Interfacing to VLSI tools is necessary for usability and effectiveness. The IPSE software argument applies equally well to hardware.

Reasoning overhead is directly related to expressive power to which it is inversely proportional and affects effectiveness, scalability and usability. High reasoning overheads necessitate sophisticated machine support and proof management facilities.

Efficiency of formal methods tools is normally the main obstacle in terms of scalability, usability and time and cost effectiveness.

User friendliness of the notation and the user interface of associated tools is important for usability.

Levels of expertise required to use a notation and tool efficiently is again a serious stumbling block in scalability, usability and time and cost effectiveness. Digital designers may be trained in some aspects but they will never become mathematicians or logicians.

These are the criteria that will be used in the rest of the book for evaluation and comparison purposes. It must be borne in mind that some of these are necessarily subjective factors of the experimental study that follows; for instance user friendliness and required expertise levels.

Chapter 3

Case Studies

3.1 Introduction

As we shall shortly see, a plethora of formalisms have been proposed and used in conjunction with digital system verification. This chapter aims at understanding the complexities, strengths and weaknesses of some of the notations, in a unified framework. Hands on experience with the various notations affords insights which cannot be obtained by literature searching alone. Our strategy consists of working with incrementally "harder" test cases which are used to investigate the characteristics of each formalism. Here we report on our experiences with various notations on two device categories; purely combinational circuits and sequential circuits (state machines).

We thus evaluate a number of approaches and discuss their relative merits. Although this piece of work cannot encompass the entire spectrum of notations, and is therefore of necessity incomplete, we hope that the outcome is a useful chart of the current state of the art.

The rest of the chapter is organised in four sections. The next section contains a compact literature guide together with a classification method. We then present our evaluation framework and comment upon the chosen notations and examples. The following section contains the results of our controlled experiments with a range of formal systems. The chapter concludes with a summary and a discussion of our findings.

3.2 Literature guide

Given the abundance of formalisms which have been proposed for the specification and verification of hardware systems, two facts become obvious:

1. One can write lengthy literature surveys. This is not what is intended here. We mention other work fairly comprehensively but briefly; we do, however, dwell on a number of approaches later on in this chapter. The interested reader is referred to the comprehensive work of McEvoy and Tucker [MT91] as well as the compact guide by Camurati and Prinetto [CP88].

2. In spite of the above disclaimer, it is useful for our purposes to impose some structure on the set of notations in order to facilitate comparisons of like with like. Although this is a fuzzy distinction, for classification purposes, we can view formalisms as

- *behavioural*, where we define a set of properties that the system behaviour should possess and check whether the desired properties can be deduced from this set, or

- *modelling*, where we construct a model of the system under investigation and proceed to check whether this model exhibits the desired properties.

The following section contains work which is not mentioned elsewhere in this book[1]. In particular, work on temporal and equational logic, model checking, term rewriting, OBJ3 and computer hardware description languages (CHDLs) is omitted.

3.2.1   Programming languages and variants

Sheeran has developed μFP (a variant of Backus's FP [Bac78]), a functional programming language for describing regular arrays [She84, She83, She85]. Each μFP construct has a corresponding layout equivalent and feedback is modelled using the special μ operator. Sheeran has subsequently proposed Ruby [She91] where the functions of μFP are replaced by relations.

νFP [PSE85] is another adaptation of FP which is primarily used for the design and evaluation of hardware algorithms. νFP functions have corresponding planar topology equivalents.

Boute [Bou86] has developed a theory of digital systems which is based on transformational reasoning and a functional programming style to support this reasoning. The functional programming language SASL [Tur79] is augmented with a simple type description language which is used to describe digital systems at all levels. Boute's recent work includes the functional CHDL Glass [Seu90] which can be used to describe digital and analog devices.

Suzuki [Suz85] has used Concurrent Prolog for simulation and formal verification of hybrid systems. Tiden [Tid88] has a Prolog enhanced with unification in finite algebras which is used to perform symbolic verification of switch level circuits. Leeser [Lee88] has used Prolog for specifying the structure of circuits whilst timing properties are expressed in temporal logic. CHIP, a Prolog extended with constraint handling has also been used in the design and verification of digital devices [SND88].

Johnson and Boyer [JB88] report on the use of Daisy, a general purpose functional list processing language for modelling and manipulating transistor level hardware.

As we have seen, Occam and its associated culture have been used successfully in the Inmos hardware verification work. Roscoe [Ros92] describes further applications of the language to VLSI design and formal specification.

3.2.2   General logics

Higher order logic was first used for specifying and verifying hardware by Hanna [HD85] who developed the VERITAS theorem proving system. More recently, Hanna and his team have produced the VERITAS–90 system which implements a higher order logic with dependent types [HD92]. Paulson's Isabelle theorem prover [PN90] is used by Rossen to

---

[1]For lack of space, we also omit work on the use of formal methods in VLSI synthesis, an important area which has been gathering substantial momentum.

implement an axiomatic definition of Ruby [Ros91]. Busch [Bus91, Bus92] uses LAMBDA [FFFH89], a theorem prover implementing a constructive higher order logic for automating proof based transformations of hardware models. Mendler [Men91] has used the LEGO proof checker [Pol88] which supports the encoding of natural deduction style logics in order to carry out constrained proofs with an extension of the calculus of constructions [CH88, Luo88]. The Nuprl [C+86] proof development system which is based on constructive type theory was used by Aargaard and Leeser to prove the correctness of a boolean simplification system [AL91] and a non trivial section of a floating point adder [Lee92]. The same team has used Nuprl for synthesis. Bickford and Srivas [BS92a] have used Clio, a theorem prover for a higher order, polymorphic functional language, to carry out extensive verification of the Cayuga family of processors. PVS [ORS92] is a prototype verification system implementing a strongly typed higher order logic with predicate subtypes. PVS has been successfully used to prove the equivalence of a pipelined and an unpipelined microprocessor design.

First order logics have also been used extensively in the area. Wagner first attempted to apply the predicate calculus to the verification of hardware in 1977 [Wag77]. Barros and Johnson use first order predicates to describe some classes of commonly used asynchronous circuits [BJ83]. [CMP91] reports on the use of the resolution based OTTER theorem prover [McC89, Mar92] to verify combinational and sequential circuits. Shostak has used the STP theorem prover to verify analog and asynchronous circuits using verification conditions on graphs modelling hardware [Sho83].

3.2.3 Hardware specific calculi

A number of hardware specific calculi have also been developed and used. Some of these are supported by theorem proving or other checking tools. Milne has designed Circal [Mil83, MP88], a notation based on the dot calculus which can be used for specifying and analysing circuit behaviour. An early, seminal work was done by Barrow who developed VERIFY [Bar84], a Prolog program for checking the correctness of finite state machines. Silica Pethecus, developed by Weise [Wei84] can be used to prove the functional correctness of NMOS switch level designs. Paillet [Pai86] uses operative expressions to describe specifications and implementations of synchronous register transfer circuits. STREAM, a data flow language, has been designed by Delgado Kloos [Klo87] to describe circuits at the register transfer, gate and switch levels. Brookes [Bro84] has derived a semantics for VLSI by applying fixed point reasoning to a directed graph model. Cardelli has proposed net algebras where networks are described by expressions in many sorted algebra [Car82]. Finally, Tucker *et al* have used the theory of synchronous concurrent algorithms [Tho87] for the specification and design of VLSI architectures [Har89, HTT88a].

3.3 The framework

The verification principles behind all notations are similar. In general, formal checks involve proving that a certain implementation satisfies the specification in a certain way. The specification, implementation and properties are expressed as *assertions* in the given logic. Specific instances of theorems state facts such as:

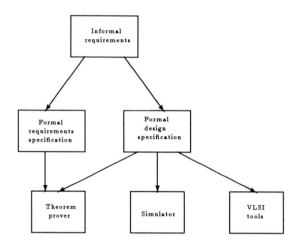

Figure 3.1: A conceptual design framework

- A high level (abstract) design is *equivalent* to the structural composition of lower level (concrete) components, for example an incrementer, a multiplexor and some register primitives when wired up in a specific way, produce the behaviour of a loadable counter.

- An implementation *implies* the specification, which is a weaker version of equivalence proofs. Such proofs are very common as the specification is often intentionally underdetermined for flexibility's sake. For example, if an incrementer, a multiplexor and some register primitives are wired up in a specific way, then the resulting circuit will behave as a loadable counter.

- A specification *implies* a property that the system should exhibit, for instance that a binary adder does indeed produce the mathematical sum of its inputs.

Formal checks such as these represent the core of current standard practice which mainly consists of a *posteriori* verification. However, as we have seen, formal techniques have a much wider scope of application in the design process, and indeed their potential benefits can be maximised in a design framework such as the one illustrated in figure 3.1. In this context, the formal system specification serves a dual purpose. It is first used for simulation purposes in order to ensure that the design exhibits the desired behaviour. Once a fair degree of certainty about the suitability of the design is attained, a theorem prover is used to make formal checks on the specification. A consequence of this approach for the evaluation exercise that follows is that candidate notations must be considered both on an individual basis and as pairs ⟨*specification/simulation language, theorem prover*⟩.

Another implication of the framework is that the specification notation must be executable (directly or indirectly) in order to allow investigative simulation before embarking on resource-intensive verification. Since the specification notation is executable, it is tempting to abandon the traditional simulators associated with CHDLs [Cam88, SBE88], although in practice specification languages are neither engineered with emphasis on hard-

Specification Languages	Logics	Theorem Provers
UMIST OBJ	Equational logic	REVE
OBJ3	Equational logic	OBJ3
ML	PPLAMBDA	Cambridge LCF
ML	Higher order logic	HOL
Boyer–Moore Lisp	Boyer–Moore logic	Boyer–Moore
ELLA		
SML	Temporal logic	mcb, dp

Table 3.1: Formalisms under investigation

ware peculiarities nor are they sufficiently efficient. Ongoing research aims at harnessing the benefits of both families of notations by providing well defined, automated interface mechanisms between them. The same is true of graphical capture design systems and specification languages [NS86].

Finally, the framework of figure 3.1 supports validation as well as verification. This reflects the inapplicability of formal techniques for some aspects of hardware design as well as the need to incorporate formal methods in existing best practice.

3.3.1 The notations

The evaluation approach used here is based on a detailed comparative study of alternative approaches using two examples illustrating various aspects of digital systems. A careful distinction must be drawn between such test cases and the establishment of benchmarks. The various notations and systems have historically evolved with particular classes of devices and levels of abstraction in mind. Therefore, while it is possible to define evaluation criteria, it is not straightforward to construct a set of benchmarks which can be used to measure the *goodness* of notations. The test cases here should not be interpreted as benchmarks.

The systems investigated here are listed in table 3.1. The classification of Lisp and ML as specification languages, reflects their rôle in the framework of figure 3.1. For reasons similar to those relating to the use of declarative instead of imperative languages for software development [Bac78], here we consider mainly the former. We defer the discussion of the equational approach until later on where it will be expanded upon at length and it will be evaluated against the same criteria.

The results of the case studies are presented in pairs (wherever possible) of ⟨*specification / simulation language, theorem prover*⟩. The same simulation tests are used for all specification languages, and the theorem provers attempt to prove the same theorem. In general, the specification text requires amendments before it can be passed to the theorem prover, because the components of the pairs were not designed as cooperating tools. The theorem provers under investigation support different logics and associated inference mechanisms. They also represent radically different approaches to theorem proving, ranging from highly interactive proof construction to automatic proofs.

The Boyer–Moore, REVE and LCF systems were evaluated on a VAX 7800 whereas

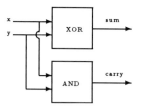

Figure 3.2: Half adder

the HOL, OBJ3, temporal logic and SML studies were carried out on a diskless Sun 3/75 with 8 Mbytes of RAM. ELLA was investigated on a VAX 11/750. For brevity's sake we do not include all the specification texts and proof scripts in the book. The full set can be found in [Sta90b, Sta90a].

3.3.2   The examples

The test cases used are introduced below.

1. n-bit wide parallel binary adder (purely combinational logic).

2. Twisted ring counter (state transition machine).

The adder was chosen for its simplicity and because it displays hierarchical and regular structure which allows the use of inductive arguments in the proofs. The second example was chosen for its generality and breadth which exercises the expressive power of the notations. Not all systems were evaluated with respect to both examples. Instead, the interesting aspects of the problem determine the set of notations that can be usefully investigated. For instance, temporal logic is clearly not an appropriate formalism to use for the n-bit adder, as the temporal aspects of the circuit's behaviour are not of interest. Furthermore, in order to avoid repetition, the exposition here is limited to one example (the most interesting) per notation.

3.3.2.1   The Adder

The basic building block is the half adder of figure 3.2 which consists of an AND and an XOR gate. The full adder is made up of two half adders and an OR gate as shown in figure 3.3. The n-bit adder consists of a cascade of n full adders with the output carry of the $(i-1)^{th}$ unit connected to the input carry of the ith unit as shown in figure 3.4.

3.3.2.2   The Counter

Ring counters are typically used as special sequence generators rather than for performing a counting task. An important application area is time-state-pulse generation which is widely used for CPU timing control. Ring counters can "hang" [Fle80]; that is, enter an unused (illegal) state from which they will not return to the main counting sequence unless forcibly reset. Unused states may be entered either during power-up or because

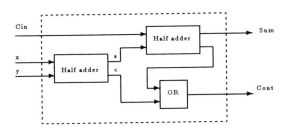

Figure 3.3: Relationship between full and half adder

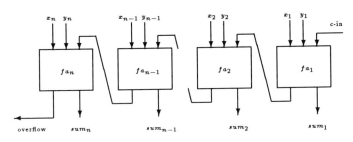

Figure 3.4: N-bit wide parallel binary adder

of signal noise during normal circuit operation. The counter has a single external input which is used to reset the circuit, and 3 output lines which deliver the count as shown in figure 3.5. The circuit can be implemented with D type flip flops using well known techniques. Our design produced the twisted ring counter implementation of figure 3.6. Figure 3.7 shows the generated sequence.

The claim is that this implementation satisfies the two following requirements:

1. The designed circuit does indeed perform a counting function. The main counting sequence of figure 3.6 is given by a simple shift operation which complements the most significant bit and appends it to the least significant bit.

2. The circuit is self-correcting; that is, having entered an illegal state it will revert to a legal one within a finite number of clock cycles:

   (a) If the circuit enters illegal state 010 then if no reset signal occurs at time t, then the circuit will enter legal state 100 at time $t + 1$.

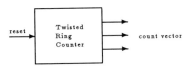

Figure 3.5: The specification of the counter

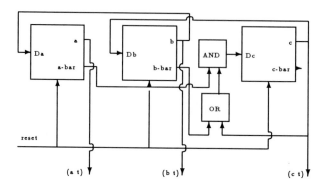

Figure 3.6: Three-bit twisted ring counter

A	B	C
0	0	0
0	0	1
0	1	1
1	1	1
1	1	0
1	0	0
0	0	0

Figure 3.7: A three-bit twisted ring counter sequence

(b) If the circuit enters illegal state 101 then if no reset signal occurs at times t and $t + 1$, then the circuit will enter legal state 100 at time $t + 2$.

These requirements form two proof obligations, the former being that the implementation must imply the specification, and the latter being that the implementation must possess self-correcting properties.

3.4 The experiments

3.4.1 ELLA

Computer hardware description languages (CHDLs) were the first textual descriptive techniques to be used in the design of hardware. A multitude of CHDLs have been used for this purpose and the interested reader is referred to [Lew77] which contains a thorough review. ELLA, which we examine here, and VHDL [VHD87] have emerged as the contemporary contenders. The popularity of CHDLs as design description tools, has practically enforced the need for formally based notations to provide the same degree of features and facilities if they are to be accepted by digital designers.

Although here we concentrate on ELLA, primarily because of its current importance, there have been other attempts to harness the combined benefits of CHDLs and formal notations. Dasgupta [Das81, Das83] has used an architecture description language, S_A^*, for specifying computer architectures which are then verified using the Floyd–Hoare inductive assertion method. Uehara *et al* [USMK83] have developed a temporal logic based verifier for DDL descriptions. Eveking [Eve81, Eve86] has used CONLAN assertions to verify hardware using Dijkstra's predicate transformer technique. Pygott [Pyg88] reports on the use of the NODEN HDL for hardware verification. This work is particularly interesting since its direction has been influenced by the experiences of the Viper verification work.

In fact, one of the most encouraging signs of formal methods research blending with existing best practice, has been the recent activity on using formal techniques in conjunction with CHDLs. The main approach consists of providing a formal semantics for the chosen CHDL and using mechanised reasoning on design descriptions. [BGG+92] describes work on the semantic embedding of ELLA, VHDL and SILAGE subsets in HOL. [Goo90, BGM91, B+91, Goo91] discuss the formalisation of the semantics of various subsets of ELLA. [LFMM92] reports on the use of a substantial subset of VHDL which has been given formal semantics and used in conjunction with the SDVS theorem prover. Borrione, Pierre and Salem in [BPS92] report on work on VHDL in a similar direction. Other related efforts include the work described in [BHY92, HB92] on using an HDL with Boyer–Moore as well as our own work on FUNNEL, a new CHDL that we discuss later on.

ELLA is a relatively new (circ. 1982), wide-spectrum, orthogonal CHDL with emphasis on functional description style. As such it contains no assignment statements or other imperative features. ELLA is unusual in that it has no built-in signals. Instead functions can have inputs and outputs of any user defined type. The fact that the language is strongly typed allows early detection and removal of logical errors with the consequential gain in design productivity. In general, ELLA embodies mature technology and is well served by an array of tools comprising a simulator, a support environment (EASE) and an interface to other CAE systems (ELLANET).

The language allows abstract and concrete specifications by supporting both implicit and explicit descriptions. For instance an XOR gate can be defined explicitly as follows:

```
FN XOR = (bool: x y) -> bool:
BEGIN
   MAKE AND:a1 a2,
        INV:i1 i2,
        OR:o1.
   JOIN x -> i1,
        y -> i2,
        (i1, y) -> a1,
        (x, i2) -> a2,
        (a1, a2) -> o1.
   OUTPUT o1
END.
```

Whereas this description contains connectivity information, the implicit definition of the same gate below, avoids this level of detail:

```
FN XOR = (bool: x y) -> bool:
(OR (AND(NOT(x),y), AND(x,NOT(y))) ).
```

This abstract specification style is possible because the compiler of the language implicitly manages the MAKEs and JOINs.

ELLA functions cannot be recursive. This clearly presents difficulties when intuitively recursive structures such as the n-bit adder are modelled. Here is a 4-bit adder with the recursive call unfolded:

```
FN BA4 = (bool: x1 y1 x2 y2 x3 y3 x4 y4 ci add) -> [5] bool:
(AND(add,SUM(FA(x1,y1,CARRY(FA(x2,y2,
                       CARRY(FA(x3,y3,
                       CARRY(FA(x4,y4,ci)))))))))),
AND(add,SUM(FA(x2,y2,CARRY(FA(x3,y3,
                       CARRY(FA(x4,y4,ci))))))),
AND(add,SUM(FA(x3,y3,CARRY(FA(x4,y4,ci))))),
AND(add,SUM(FA(x4,y4,ci))),
CARRY(FA(x1,y1,CARRY(FA(x2,y2,
               CARRY(FA(x3,y3,
               CARRY(FA(x4,y4,ci)))))))))).
```

ELLA functions cannot be higher order either. Therefore, modelling timing dependency requires the use of signals consisting of strings of values. The macro construct allows the definition of functions over integers and ELLA types, and can be used to model recursive structures. The macro definition of the adder is shown below:

```
MAC REC_ADDER{INT n} = ([n]bool: x y, bool:ci) -> ([n]bool, bool):
BEGIN
   LET oneadd = FA(x[1],y[1],ci).
   OUTPUT IF n=1
          THEN ([1]oneadd[1], oneadd[2])
```

```
      ELSE (oneadd[1] CONC
            (REC_ADDER{n-1}(x[2..n], y[2..n], oneadd[2]))[1],
            (REC_ADDER{n-1}(x[2..n], y[2..n], oneadd[2]))[2])
      FI
END.
```

The macro must be instantiated before it can be used for simulation as shown below:

```
FN ADD4 = ([4]bool: x y, bool:ci) -> ([4]bool,bool):
REC_ADDER{4} (x, y, ci).
FINISH.
```

Although ELLA has a special-purpose simulator, surprisingly, simulation speeds were not impressive for our examples. Camilleri [Cam88] comes to the same conclusion, having compared ELLA to ML.

Despite its applicative nature, ELLA does not have a formal semantics yet. It is not therefore possible to formally verify systems directly. Cullyer and Pygott [Cul84, CP85] have performed formal checks on the Viper specification, by manually translating ELLA into the object language of LCF–LSM. The manual translation has not been verified although a practical method of checking the equivalence of ELLA specifications to ELLA implementations was developed and used by Pygott [Pyg85] in this context. Current research [BGHT90, Goo90, BGM91, B+91, Goo91, BGG+92] aims at providing a formal semantics for ELLA and it should then be possible to provide formal verification support for the language.

In conclusion, although ELLA has, to a certain extent, bridged the gap between CHDLs and formal specification languages (and consequently has a user acceptance problem), it was not suitable for a formal development approach when this evaluation was carried out, the main problem being the lack of formal semantics. This assessment will obviously change when the language is given semantics especially in view of its already available integration facilities.

3.4.2   ML and Cambridge LCF

ML and Cambridge LCF are not compatible in the spirit of our evaluation framework. Although ML was designed as the metalanguage (in this case a language of proof generating commands or *tactics*) of the LCF system [GMW79], the ML description is of very little use as input to the theorem prover. This is so because the object language of LCF (in which specifications must be expressed) is very different from its metalanguage.

In the tradition of functional languages, ML supports strong typing, polymorphism and higher order functions. The behaviour of the adder is defined as

```
fun adder(c-in,l,nil) = if (c-in eq f) then l else inc(l) |
    adder(c-in,nil,l) = if (c-in eq f) then l else inc(l) |
    adder(c-in,bit1::rest1,bit2::rest2) =
        sum(fulladder(bit1,bit2,c-in))::
        adder(carry(fulladder(bit1,bit2,c-in)),rest1,rest2) ;
```

where :: is the cons operator and | is choice. Simulation tests are carried out with the **test** operator:

```
fun test(n1,n2) =
    bin-to-nat(adder(f,nat-to-bin(n1),nat-to-bin(n2))) ;

test(2213,21) ;
> val it = 2234 : int
```

The theorem prover used here is Cambridge LCF, a direct descendant of Edinburgh LCF which was originally intended for reasoning about denotational semantics and functional programs. CLCF added many technical improvements to ELCF, but it was originally developed in order to augment the logic with $\vee, \exists, \Longleftrightarrow$ and predicates. LCF–LSM [Gor83a] is a system built on top of CLCF by adding terms loosely based on CCS. It has been used to verify realistic devices [Gor83b, GH85, CP85] but is now obsolete. LCF stands at the opposite end of the spectrum of automatic theorem proving, when compared with systems such as the Boyer–Moore prover. It may be viewed, more accurately, as an environment for constructing machine checked proofs.

- The logic is *PPλ* which is essentially a typed λ-calculus together with fixed point induction. It is based on a logic designed by Dana Scott for proving theorems about computable functions [Sco69]. Data types are interpreted as domains, allowing reasoning about partial functions, lazy evaluation, fixedpoints of functionals and denotational semantics. It supports the natural deduction style of proofs with introduction and elimination rules for each logical connective.

- All sorts have a partial ordering and a bottom element (UU).

- Inference rules are encoded into *tactics* thus supporting goal-directed (backward) proofs.

A disadvantage of partial functions is having to prove the totality of functions before they can be used. Additionally, proofs tend to become cluttered with extra cases because of the bottom element. Proving the adder theorem involves solving the following goal:

```
set_goal([],"!x y c-in. ~x == (UU:(tr)vector) /\
                        ~y == (UU:(tr)vector) /\
                        ~c-in == (UU:tr) ==>
           (bin-to-nat(adder(c-in,x,y))) == bin-to-nat(x) +
                                            bin-to-nat(y) +
                                            bit(c-in)");;
```

where ! is the universal quantifier $\forall$, ~ is the negation predicate and **tr** is the predefined sort for booleans.

The proof uses the *subgoal* package to break up the original goal into a set of subgoals which are solved individually using inference rules and tactics. The proof trace in this case was 18 pages long. In general, since proof construction is a highly interactive activity, the user must be able to guide the proof. This offers a high degree of confidence in the correctness of the proof, but on the other hand can be tedious and requires a lot of user expertise. In conclusion:

1. In order to make effective use of LCF, the user must be experienced in both proof mechanisms and the system;

2. the very restricted set of pre-proved facts, together with the added complication of dealing with the bottom element cases, can make relatively simple proofs tedious;

3. the proof management facilities (subgoal package), especially in view of the highly interactive nature of the system, are not satisfactory.

The LCF proof of the adder theorem took 3 person weeks. Most of this time was devoted to familiarisation with the system. This fact is indicative of the amount of training required to make effective use of the system. LCF has been practically superseded by HOL and therefore our experiments were restricted to the n-bit adder.

3.4.3 HOL

The first use of higher order logic for hardware verification was reported by Hanna in [HD85]. HOL [Gor85] is a machine-oriented formulation of higher order logic based on Church's lambda calculus [Chu40] extended with the type discipline of the LCF logic PPλ. Higher order logic extends the predicate calculus in three important ways:

1. Variables are allowed to range over functions and predicates.

2. Functions can take functions as arguments and yield functions as results.

3. The notation of the λ-calculus can be used to write terms which denote functions.

HOL has been studied extensively in connection with hardware verification by the Cambridge hardware verification group and others. Behaviours are expressed as relations and reasoning about them is carried out in a natural deduction system.

Since behaviours can be represented by a mixture of relations and functions, it is not possible to execute HOL specifications directly. As previously pointed out, simulation is an essential part of the design process and therefore this is a shortcoming of HOL. The same is identified in [Cam88] where a partial, semi-automatic translator from HOL relations to ML [HMM86, CHP86] functions is described. Although we have previously used ML for simulating HOL designs, this is not considered satisfactory because not all relations can be translated to functions and therefore the possibility of introducing inconsistencies in the transformation between the two notations cannot be ruled out.

Although we have studied both the adder and the counter in HOL, we limit the presentation here to the latter. The specification of the twisted ring counter is shown below:

```
let TRC_DEF = new_definition('TRC_DEF',
              "TRC(reset:^sig,out:^vsig) =
                  !t:^time.
                  out (t+1) =
                      ((reset t) =>
                      (BITV F (BITV F (BITV F BTM))) |
                      (SHIFT (out t)))");;
```

where BTM denotes the empty list, BITV denotes the cons operator, SHIFT is the shift operation performed by the counter, ! is the universal quantifier, _=>_|_ is the if then else operator and ^ incorporates an existing expression into a new one. The data types used are defined by:

```
let time = ":num";;
let sig = ":^time -> bool";;
let vsig = ":^time -> (bool)vector";;
```

A predicate `DTYP_DEF` specifying the behaviour of a D type flip flop can now be formally defined:

```
let DTYPE_DEF = new_definition('DTYPE_DEF',
    "DTYPE(d:^sig,reset:^sig,q:^sig,q_bar:^sig) =
        (!t:^time.
        (reset t => (q (t+1) = F) | (q (t+1) = d t))) /\
                  (!t. (q_bar t = NOT (q t)))");;
```

Similarly, the next state decoder predicate is defined as:

```
let NXT_STATE_DECODER = new_definition('NXT_STATE_DECODER',
    "NXT(a:^sig,b:^sig,c:^sig,out:^sig) =
        !t:^time. (out t = (a t) /\ ((b t) \/ (c t)))");;
```

The expressive power of HOL is obvious in compositional specifications; composite behaviours are obtained from simpler components by taking their conjunction. Internal lines are existentially quantified. Thus, the twisted ring counter implementation in figure 3.6 can be defined as follows:

```
let TRC_DEF = new_definition('TRC_DEF',
            "TRC(reset:^sig,out:^vsig) =
            ?a b c a_bar b_bar c_bar nxt.
            DTYPE(b,reset,a,a_bar) /\
            DTYPE(c,reset,b,b_bar) /\
            NXT(a_bar,b_bar,c,nxt) /\
            DTYPE(nxt,reset,c,c_bar) /\
            VECTOR(a,b,c,out)") ;;
```

where ? is the existential quantifier and the predicate `VECTOR` defines the behaviour of a component which constructs a vector of boolean values.

```
let VECTOR_DEF = new_definition('VECTOR_DEF',
            "VECTOR(a:^sig,b:^sig,c:^sig,out:^vsig) =
            (!t:^time.
            (out t =
            (BITV (a t) (BITV (b t) (BITV (c t) BTM)))))");;
```

A typical fact proved by HOL is that the implementation satisfies the implementation:

```
TRC_IMP(reset,out) ==> TRC(reset,out)
```

Such theorems are established by forward proof. The run time of this proof was 10 minutes 17 seconds and the proof script was 8 pages long. The experiment took 3 person weeks.

It is important to bear in mind that HOL represents the opposite end of the machine-assisted theorem proving spectrum in comparison with approaches such as Boyer–Moore; it is an environment where proofs can be safely constructed, *not* a theorem prover. The advantage is that such a proof checker can handle complex proof obligations under user guidance. But this also means that trivial proofs are long and tedious. In the case of HOL this problem is exacerbated by unrefined system features such as the naive rewriting tactics and the poor proof management facilities.

In summary, HOL affords a very expressive notation and an environment where substantial proofs can be constructed. It is also perhaps the most widely studied system for hardware verification, with a number of impressive results in its repertoire ([Joy87, Coh88b, Coh88a, Her92, BCF92]). The system suffers however from unrefined features which could be improved – for instance the rewriting tactics could be replaced by a general term rewriting engine such as the one used in [GW88] or [C+88]. Even so, it is hard to see how HOL could be integrated in a design environment without *maximal* impact on designer practice, given the lack of simulation facilities and the level of expertise required in order to use the system effectively.

3.4.4 Propositional Temporal Logic and dp

Temporal logic [Pnu77] is a formal notation for specifying and verifying concurrent and reactive systems. Temporal logics allow behavioural specifications with reference to a time domain. The notion of time is modelled through the temporal operators □ "always in the future", ◇ "sometime in the future" and ○ "at the next time in the future". It is this inherent ability to reason about the ordering of events in time without introducing time explicitly, that renders temporal logic particularly relevant for the specification of state machines.

Temporal logic systems can be classified according to the way in which they consider time. In a discrete model, the past is always linear, while the future may be either a unique world or a set of possible worlds. In the former case, time is linear in the future and such a logic is called *linear*; in the latter, time branches in the future and the logic is called *branching*. In linear logics the system has a unique evolution path along time, whereas in branching logics the system has a set of possible evolution paths.

Propositional temporal logic consists of the temporal plus the standard propositional operators. Although here we use such a simple propositional linear time logic, interval temporal logic [HMM83, SMSV83] is particularly interesting for hardware verification (for a comprehensive survey of temporal and other program logics see [FB86]). ITL is an extension of linear time temporal logic based on intervals where propositions are asserted on a sequence of states. These intervals provide a convenient framework for introducing quantitative timing details. They are also used to characterise state transitions by properties relating the initial and final values of variables. The ○ operator is used to simulate the passing of real time units, where each concrete state change forced by ○ corresponds to ticks of an imaginary clock. Applications of ITL to hardware problems are described in [Mos83] and an ITL enhanced Prolog is discussed in [FTMo85]. Although propositional instances of these logics are decidable we are not aware of any form of mechanised verification support.

There have been a number of other attempts at using temporal logics for the specification and verification of hardware. Bochman has used a linear, discrete logic to perform reachability analysis [Boc82]. Fujita *et al* developed a hardware verification approach based on linear temporal logic and Prolog [FTMo83]. Malachi and Owicki have used temporal specifications to describe properties of self timed systems [MO81]. The SDVS theorem prover [LFMM92] is based on a specialised temporal logic whose formulae are called *state deltas*. SDVS has been used to carry out non trivial proofs, including the verification of the microcode for the C/30 production computer.

Programming languages based on temporal logic exist [Mos84] and it is possible to execute certain temporal logics (the PTL specification below is executable). However, no facility was available to us for doing this at the time this evaluation was carried out. Mechanised checks on the behaviour of the twisted ring counter (the only appropriate example in this experiment) have been carried out using the decision procedure dp presented in [Gou84]. The formula describing the implementation of the counter is shown below:

```
G(~fin &
  (0q1 = d1 & ~r ) &
  (0q2 = d2 & ~r ) &
  (0q3 = d3 & ~r ) &
  (d1 = q2) &
  (d2 = q3) &
  (d3 = ~q1 & (~q2 | q3))
 )
```

where dn and qn are the input and output respectively of the *nth* flip flop and r is the reset input to the counter. ~ is negation, & is conjunction, G is the $\square$ operator and 0 is the $\bigcirc$ operator. Given this behaviour, we can prove that it implies a set of desirable properties, such as, the counter recovers from illegal state 010 in one time cycle:

```
 G(~fin &
  (0q1 = d1 & ~r ) &
  (0q2 = d2 & ~r ) &
  (0q3 = d3 & ~r ) &
  (d1 = q2) &
  (d2 = q3) &
  (d3 = ~q1 & (~q2 | q3))) &
  (~q1 & q2 & ~q3 & G~r)
   >
   0(q1 & ~q2 & ~q3)  .
```

where > is implication and fin is a proposition that is true only at the last moment of time. Since the version of the decision procedure we used allows finite models, including G(~fin) in the formulae ensures infinite models.

A formula is validated by the decision procedure by attempting to create a model for its negation; if such a model does not exist then the formula is valid. The validity of the formulae above was established automatically and without difficulty. Proof execution times were minimal (1.4 seconds for the formula above). The time spent in familiarisation with the system plus encoding and proving these properties was also minimal – 1 person day. Specification encoding was trivial due to the expressive power of temporal logic. Using Gough's decision procedure [Gou84] was effortless and fast.

In summary, the combination of temporal logic to express behaviour through time easily, with the existence of automated decision procedures makes the notation very suitable for the verification of state machines. One should however, be acutely aware of the efficiency limitations of decision procedures when large or complex formulae are involved. An alternative approach, model checking, is discussed in the next section. It would also be desirable to add the ability to animate specifications perhaps along the lines of [Mos84, Gab87]. A further weakness of the approach is the need to produce descriptions in a notation which is not familiar to digital designers.

3.4.5 SML and mcb

Finite state machine languages such as SFD-Algol [Par66] and Esterel [BC84] provide a programming language notation for describing state machines. A hardware implementation of Esterel has been successfully used to generate provably correct circuit implementations of programs on field programmable gate arrays [Ber92]. The language used here is SML [BC86] which contains many of the standard control structures found in high level imperative programming languages as well as parallel composition and compression. SML programs are not unlike hardware description language programs. This experiment concentrated on the twisted ring counter. The text for the counter is shown below:

```
program trc;

input RESET;
output 01 = true, 02, 03 = true ;

    procedure copy(in,out)
        if (in) then raise(out) else lower(out) endif;
    endproc

    procedure dtype(in,out)
        loop
        if RESET then
                lower(out)
            else
                copy(in,out)
            endif;
        endloop
    endproc

    parallel
        dtype(02,01)
    ||
        dtype(03,02)
    ||
        dtype(!01 & (!02 | 03),03)
    endparallel
endprog
```

! is negation, **&** is conjunction, | is disjunction and || is parallel composition. The **raise** statement activates and **lower** deactivates its variable. The parallel construct provides a form of synchronous parallelism; each statement examines the inputs and the current state and determines what changes should be made to the output state at the next clock transition. In our example the output vector is initialised to 101.

The output of the SML compiler is a finite state machine in FSM intermediate format (FIF). FIF is accepted as input by the afc program which produces a ROM, PAL or PLA implementation of the state machine. afc can also produce output which is compatible with the Berkeley VLSI tools. The Moore machine corresponding to the twisted ring counter is shown below:

```
NAME = trc;
STATES = 8;
CUBES = 15;
INPUTS = RESET.H;
MOORE-OUTPUTS = 01.H, 02.H, 03.H;
#0 101
1 2
0 1
#1 010
1 2
0 3
#2 000
1 2
0 4
#3 100
X 2
#4 001
1 2
0 5
#5 011
1 2
0 6
#6 111
1 2
0 7
#7 110
1 2
0 3
#END
```

The FIF output can also be used in conjunction with a temporal logic model checker in order to formally verify various properties of the state machine. The architecture of the model checking approach is shown in figure 3.8. Thuau and Pilaud [TP91] use a similar approach where the synchronous declarative language Lustre [CHPP87] is compiled onto a state machine which is then verified with the LESAR model checking tool. Here we use mcb [Bro86] a model checker for Computation Tree Logic [EC81], a branching time temporal logic, to prove the sample property of the counter shown below. The predicate legal checks the legality of a state and AG is analogous to the linear time operator □ and AX corresponds to ○.

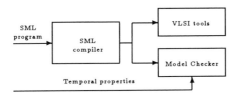

Figure 3.8: The model checking approach

```
legal() := ~( ~O1 & O2 & ~O3 | O1 & ~O2 & O3).

AG(((~O1 & O2 & ~O3) & AG ~RESET) -> (AX (O1 & ~O2 & ~O3))).
```

The model checker determines whether a formula is true or not by traversing the state graph and searching for a counter example. If such an example exists, the checker will always find it, thus providing a very useful specification debugging aid. The complexity of the algorithm is linear in the number of states of the Moore machine, but exponential in the number of inputs and outputs.

Efficiency measurements [GB88] certainly support the view that model checking is an improved alternative to decision procedures for providing mechanised verification of temporal properties. Once the state machine is generated, any number of properties can be checked against it, without the need for recompilation which is the case with decision procedures. However, model checking also suffers from state explosion. Recently, the size of circuits that can be handled by model checking has increased substantially [CBG+92]. Instead of enumerating states, *symbolic* model checking uses representations based on binary decision diagrams (BDDs) [Bry86]. Clarke reports that symbolic model checking has been successfully used to verify systems with over 10^{20} states.

The small scale of the example in this case study does not allow supporting the case for or against model checking. Encoding the specification in SML was easy and the proofs were fast, the whole experiment requiring about 1 person day of effort. What is clear is that the approach of Clarke *et al* which was followed here, is well suited for use in an integrated design environment because it supports both familiar engineering notation and interfacing with standard VLSI tools. This approach also exemplifies the use of two different formalisms in the design cycle; in this case a finite state machine language and a temporal logic. Finally, although the approach does not support simulation directly, the provision of such a facility seems straightforward.

3.4.6   Lisp and the Boyer–Moore theorem prover

The Boyer–Moore theorem prover is based on a quantifier-free first order logic with equality [BM79, BM88a]. The object language of the theorem prover is a form of pure Lisp which is used for simulating behaviours whose properties are later formally verified. This means that in order to use a single specification text both for simulation and verification, the simulation language had to be constrained to the Boyer–Moore Lisp subset which amongst other restrictions does not allow higher order functions. This has important implications for the specification of time dependency in state machines. Although only

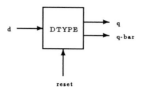

Figure 3.9: D type flip flop

the twisted ring counter experiment is discussed here, the adder case study is presented in [SBE88].

Boyer–Moore has been studied extensively in connection with hardware verification. Apart from the work of Hunt which we mention below, there has been a variety of applications. [VVCM92] presents a description methodology for parameterised modules in the Boyer–Moore logic which has been used to verify a module library of the CATHEDRAL silicon compiler suite. [KK92] illustrates the use of Boyer–Moore for modelling and verifying timing conditions. PREVAIL [BPS92] is a proof environment for VHDL descriptions which selectively uses Boyer–Moore for proving the equivalence of architectures. Hunt has done some early seminal work with Boyer–Moore in the verification of the FM8501 [Hun85]. He has since used the prover to verify another microprocessor, the FM8502 [Hun89]. More recently, Brock, Hunt and Young have used their HDL in conjunction with Boyer–Moore to prove the correctness of a substantial 32-bit general purpose microprocessor, the FM9001 [HB92, BHY92].

In higher order notations, the requirement to define time dependency is satisfied by the use of temporal operators or second order predicates. In Boyer–Moore Lisp, components cannot be modelled as functions whose inputs and outputs are themselves functions of time. A component is defined by observing the changes it causes to input and output lines (*ports*) which are externally visible. In other words, a component is modelled by specifying the behaviour of its interface to the outside world. The component consists of a collection of ports together with some functions amongst them. For instance the D type flip flop of figure 3.9 is defined by the following ports and functions:

Ports d, reset, q, q-bar

Functions (defun q(n)
      (if (reset (sub1 n))
         nil
         (d (sub1 n)))))

    (defun q-bar(n)
      (not (q n)))

The **reset** and **d** inputs are determined by the environment and can either be set to some constant function or be functions of some other ports. Composition of components is straightforward since the resulting system is also viewed as a collection of ports plus the functions between them. The twisted ring counter implementation of figure 3.6 consists of D type definitions such as the ones above, plus the input functions.

Ports d1, d2, d3, reset, q1, q2, q3, q1-bar, q2-bar, q3-bar

Functions (defun q1(n)
      (if (reset (sub1 n))
         nil
      (d1 (sub1 n))))

   (defun q1-bar(n)
    (not (q1 n)))

   (defun q2(n)
    (if (reset (sub1 n))
        nil
      (d2 (sub1 n))))

   (defun q2-bar(n)
    (not (q2 n)))

   (defun q3(n)
    (if (reset (sub1 n))
        nil
      (d3 (sub1 n))))

   (defun q3-bar(n)
    (not (q3 n)))

   (defun d1(n)
    (q2 n))

   (defun d2(n)
    (q3 n))

   (defun d3(n)
    (and (q1-bar n) (or (q2-bar n) (q3 n))))

The disadvantage of this approach is that asynchronous external events such as interrupts and resets cannot be modelled. Hunt [Hun85] achieves this by enriching the structure of the "oracle" elements. The oracle is an extra list argument to a recursive function representing the execution of the machine. Every time the function calls itself, a **car** operation is applied to the oracle, thus emulating the occurrence of some external event and advancing the system state. The simulation results show that Lisp is an acceptable alternative to traditional HDL simulators.

Having restricted the study to Boyer–Moore Lisp for simulation purposes, we would have liked to use the simulation text as input to the theorem prover. However, this was not possible because the *Principle of Definition* which only admits total recursive functions does not allow the definition of *mutually recursive* functions. Clearly the definitions of the q3 and d3 functions above are mutually recursive, as indeed are most definitions of components with feedback loops. Further manipulation is therefore necessary in order to produce a specification acceptable by the principle of definition. This can be achieved by collapsing the definition of **d3** in **q3** (unfolding the recursion) which yields the total recursive function shown below:

```
(defn q3(n)
  (if (greaterp n 2)
      (if (reset (sub1 n))
          f
          (and (not (if (reset (sub1 (sub1 n)))
                        f
                        (if (reset (sub1 (sub1 (sub1 n))))
                            f
                            (q3 (sub1 (sub1 (sub1 n)))))))
               (or (not (if (reset (sub1 (sub1 n)))
                            f
                            (q3 (sub1 (sub1 n)))))
                   (q3 (sub1 n)))))
      f))
```

q1 and **q2** are also redefined in terms of **q3** by substitution:

```
(defn q2(n)
  (if (greaterp n 0)
      (if (reset (sub1 n))
          f
          (q3 (sub1 n)))
      f))
```

```
(defn q1(n)
  (if (greaterp n 0)
      (if (reset (sub1 n))
          f
          (q2 (sub1 n)))
      f))
```

Since time is modelled by natural numbers it is necessary to include the predicate (**greaterp n m**) in the above definitions for verification purposes.

Such manual transformations are not satisfactory because the process may introduce errors and inconsistencies. Furthermore, the specification is no longer clear and intuitive since all structure has been removed in collapsing the functions. It does not, however, appear to be difficult to extend the rewriting engine of the theorem prover in order to, at least, automate the unfolding of function definitions when mutually recursive functions are involved. It is not obvious whether such unfoldings are always possible.

The inference rules of the Boyer–Moore logic consist of the propositional calculus, induction and instantiation. The proof process consists of creating an environment containing the relevant definitions (which must satisfy a well-founded ordering, hence the principle of definition) and proving various necessary lemmas until the target theorem can be proved. The verification of the counter proceeds by introducing the predicate **legal**:

```
(defn legal(n)
  (not (or (and (equal (q1 n) f)
```

```
                (and (equal (q2 n) t)
                     (equal (q3 n) f)))
         (and (equal (q1 n) t)
              (and (equal (q2 n) f)
                   (equal (q3 n) t))))))
```

A sample of proven property, showing that the counter recovers from illegal state 010 in one time cycle follows:

```
(prove-lemma from-010-to-100 (rewrite)
   (implies (numberp n)
            (implies (and (equal (q1 n) f)
                          (and (equal (q2 n) t)
                               (equal (q3 n) f)))
                     (and (equal (q1 (add1 n)) t)
                          (and (equal (q2 (add1 n)) f)
                               (equal (q3 (add1 n)) f))))))
```

The proof script for this property was 2 pages long. The experiment required approximately 4 person weeks.

Although a fair amount of time was devoted to discovering a satisfactory way of modelling time dependency in the first order Boyer–Moore logic, most of the effort in this experiment concentrated on "training" the theorem prover. Boyer–Moore is automatic in the sense that once the instruction to prove a lemma has been given, the user may no longer interfere with the proof. When a proof fails, the user must peer through the output of the system and decide that either some intermediate lemma is required, or the proof fails because the proposed theorem is not valid. This is difficult as it involves examining large amounts of output (in excess of 39 pages for this example). In this context, it is extremely desirable to have some feedback about the reasons of the failure to aid proof debugging. The need for user guidance of the proofs has been recognised by the Computational Logic Inc (CLInc) team and a user interface package which allows interaction with the prover has been implemented.

Although the work of Hunt and others [Hun85, Hun89, HB92, BHY92] at CLInc (notably the verification of the CLInc "short stack") has demonstrated that Boyer–Moore can be used successfully for non trivial hardware verification cases, we found that the system can only be used effectively by expert users with a thorough knowledge of the built-in heuristics. In contrast with HOL, a novice can initiate a non trivial proof very quickly; but in common with HOL, he/she can seldom complete it with the same facility.

3.5 Discussion

We have considered a relatively small number of formalisms and tools and we have restricted our experiments to two small and conventional examples in order to conclude the evaluation in the time available. Whilst recognising the limitations of the experiments and the subjectivity of some of the evaluation criteria which were established in the preceding chapter, we feel that these findings are worthwhile and can be of use both to those

	Boyer–Moore	ELLA	LCF	HOL
Expressive Power	fair	fair	high	high
Verification	automatic	N/A	proof checker	proof checker
Simulation	yes	yes	no	no
CAD interface	no	yes	no	no
Reasoning framework	propositional calculus plus induction	N/A	natural deduction plus induction	natural deduction plus induction
Reasoning overheads	low	N/A	very high	high
User friendliness	fair	good	poor	poor
Performance	good	fair	good for large examples	good for large examples
Required expertise	low	low	high	high

Table 3.2: Evaluation summary – Adder Case Study

wishing to undertake further comparative study and to those who wish to apply formal specification and reasoning to the design of digital systems.

The Boyer–Moore paradigm of automatic theorem proving works well for examples for which the built-in induction heuristics are appropriate. For complex examples, automatic proof becomes hard and uncontrollable. Proof checkers in the style of LCF and HOL are cumbersome even for small examples. Substantial proofs are controllable but no less tedious. Temporal logics, and in particular the model checking technique for reasoning about behaviours, work very well for medium size examples (to the order of 100,000 states) and are currently becoming practical for large systems. Although CHDLs such as ELLA are not currently usable as mathematically precise notations, they may well be the most appropriate descriptive tools once they are provided with formal semantics.

We have summarised our results in tables 3.2 and 3.3. The former relates to the adder case study and the latter to the twisted ring counter. When referring to these tables, it must be borne in mind that the findings refer to the individual case studies carried out here with the available tools at the time. They should not, therefore, be taken as universally true or applicable. Although these experiments were repeated with term rewriting and OBJ3, we defer that discussion until the following chapters.

It is impossible (and probably absurd) to judge a system on its academic merits. These results should be interpreted considering the criteria (and their classification as objective or subjective) established in the preceding chapter of this book.

Although all the systems have shortcomings and are not industrially viable as they stand, improvements and integration are both possible and desirable for the following

	TL	SML	HOL	Boyer–Moore
Expressive Power	high	high	high	fair
Verification	automatic	automatic	proof checker	automatic
Simulation	no	yes	no	yes (manual transformations)
CAD interface	no	yes	no	no
Reasoning framework	decision procedure or model checking	model checking	natural deduction plus induction	propositional calculus plus induction
Reasoning overheads	low	low	high	fair
User friendliness	fair	good	poor	fair
Performance	good for small examples	good for small examples	good for large examples	good for small examples, deteriorates quickly
Required expertise	fair	fair	high	fair

Table 3.3: Evaluation summary – Counter Case Study

reasons:

- There are substantial levels of investment in existing technology both in software and hardware as well as human resources.

- Hardware designers cannot be reasonably expected to become experts in logics, proof theory and the peculiarities of various theorem provers.

- Formal techniques cannot successfully tackle all aspects of system development (for example simulation, timing analysis, analog behaviour).

- It is important that a system under development can be taken through all the design stages without leaving a particular CAD environment, in order to avoid loss of efficiency and discrepancies introduced by manual transformations.

In the words of Martyn Thomas [Tho89]:

Formal methods are the way of the future because they offer far greater certainty throughout the development process and they should be viewed as a way

of strengthening this process by formalising many of the informal processes
which are currently employed.

Chapter 4

The Term Rewriting Approach

4.1 Introduction

With this chapter we begin our study of the algebraic/equational paradigm for the specification and verification of digital systems. The term rewriting approach, which is considered here, combines algebraic semantics with term rewriting. The coalescence of these techniques has in the past primarily been used for algebra and software engineering. Term rewriting has been used by a number of people in the hardware domain, for verification purposes only. Our motivation comes from the desire to harness the elegance and simplicity of equational logic for *both* the specification and verification of digital systems. We will use UMIST OBJ [GCS89] for specification and REVE [Les83] for verification. We have used UMIST OBJ here as it was the only available OBJ tool at the time. In the following chapters we will enlarge this aspect by working with OBJ3 [GW88].

We begin by briefly presenting the theoretical background of term rewriting techniques which underpin the algebraic approach to hardware, continue with specification and verification aspects and conclude this chapter with a survey of relevant work and a discussion of the methods. We also present our evaluation according to the criteria we established in chapter 2 and used in chapter 3.

Term rewriting is a large subject area and therefore we will concentrate here on some background definitions and techniques that are needed to understand the rest of the material in the book. We present the concepts in a way similar to Huet and Oppen [HO80]. In particular we do not deal with order sorted, conditional or associative-commutative term rewriting systems. For further insights into term rewriting including the advanced topics above, the reader is referred to [HO80, Jou87, DJ89]. We also note that the theoretical material in the following section is presented in summary form. For a comprehensive introduction to universal algebra and algebraic specification we recommend Meinke and Tucker [MT92] and Ehrig and Mahr [EM85].

4.2 Equations and rewrite rules

Equations, that is formulae of the form $M = N$, occur frequently in mathematics, logic and computer science. They may be used to *state properties* that hold between objects or they may be used as *definitions*. When equations are regarded as oriented left-to-right rewrite rules they can also be used to *compute*. For example, consider the following rewrite rules which define addition on the natural numbers:

$$add(n, 0) \ = \ n$$
$$add(n, succ(m)) \ = \ succ(add(n, m))$$

We can use this definition to compute, say, $add(succ(0), succ(0))$ into $succ(succ(0))$.

Computing with equations and reasoning about equations are closely related; for instance a set of equations may be compiled into a set of rewrite rules which may in turn be used to reduce expressions to normal form. Equational reasoning, that is the substitution of arbitrary terms by variables and the replacement of equals by equals, is sufficient for dealing with equations which state properties. However, reasoning about equations considered as definitions requires more than just equational reasoning; some form of inductive argument is also needed.

4.2.1   Many sorted algebras

Given a nonempty set of *sorts* S, we define a language θ of types obtained by composing sorts. We restrict ourselves to first order theories and assume that a type is just a sequence of sorts and is denoted by $t = s_1 \times s_2 \times \ldots \times s_n \to s$ (where $n \geq 0$). A *signature* over S consists of a set Σ of *operators* (mappings) together with a typing function $\tau : \Sigma \to \theta$. A Σ–*algebra*, or *algebra*, is a pair $\langle A, \mathcal{F} \rangle$ such that A is an S–indexed family of sets and $\mathcal{F}$ is a Σ–indexed family of functions with:

- $\mathcal{F}_F \in A_s$ if $\tau(F) = s$ and

- $\mathcal{F}_F \in A_{s_1} \times A_{s_2} \times \ldots \times A_{s_n} \to A_s$ if $\tau(F) = s_1 \times s_2 \times \ldots \times s_n \to s$.

A_s is called the *carrier* of sort s in the algebra. When no ambiguity arises, we denote an algebra by its family of carriers. For instance, we talk about the algebra A above and use F to denote the corresponding operator $\mathcal{F}_F$.

We now define special types of algebras, whose carriers consist of finite ordered trees, labelled with operators from Σ. These Σ–algebras are useful in defining terms. With every operator $F \in \Sigma$ we associate a tree consisting of one node labelled F. The family of sets of trees $T(\Sigma)_s$ for $s \in S$ can then be recursively defined as follows:

- If $\tau(C) = s$ (constant) then the tree with one node labelled C and no successors is an element of $T(\Sigma)_s$.

- If $\tau(F) = s_1 \times s_2 \times \ldots \times s_n \to s$ and $M_i \in T(\Sigma)_{s_i}$ for all $1 \leq i \leq n$, then the tree with one node labelled F and n successors $M_1 \ldots M_n$ is an element of $T(\Sigma)_s$. The corresponding algebra $T(\Sigma)$ is called the *term algebra* and $T(\Sigma)_s$ is the set of *ground terms*[1] of sort s.

We also define an S–indexed family of sets V. Elements of V_s are the *variables* of sort s. $\Sigma \cup V$ denotes the signature composed of Σ plus every V_s considered as a set of constants of sort s. The algebra $T(\Sigma \cup V)$ is called the *free Σ–algebra* generated by V, and its carrier $T(\Sigma \cup V)_s$ is the set of *terms*[2] of sort s.

---

[1]Ground terms are often called "closed" relative to Σ in the literature.
[2]Or "open" relative to Σ.

Given two algebras A and B, a mapping $h : A \to B$ (an abbreviation for an indexed family of sort preserving mappings $h_s : A_s \to B_s$) is a Σ-*homomorphism*, or *homomorphism*, iff for all $F \in \Sigma$ with $\tau(F) = s_1 \times s_2 \times \ldots \times s_n \to s$ the predicate $h_s(F_A(a_1, \ldots, a_n)) = F_B(h_{s_1}(a_1), \ldots, h_{s_n}(a_n))$ holds[3]. If $A = B$ then Σ-homomorphisms are called Σ-*endomorphisms*.

The universal property for the free Σ-algebras states that given a Σ-algebra A, any A-assignment $v : V \to A$ can be extended in a unique way to a Σ-homomorphism from $T(\Sigma \cup V)$ to A. The assignment v provides values for variables whereas its extension, which is defined recursively over the structure of terms (as in [EM85] for example), provides values for terms. In the literature, the extension is often denoted $\overline{v}$. We use v to denote both the assignment and its extension. Σ-endomorphisms from $T(\Sigma \cup V)$ to itself are called *substitutions*.

If $\langle A, F \rangle$ is a Σ-algebra, a transitive, reflexive, symmetric and sort preserving relation $\equiv$ on elements of A is called a Σ-*congruence*[4] over A iff it satisfies the following substitutivity condition:

$$(\forall F \in \Sigma)(\forall a_1, b_1, \ldots, a_n, b_n \in A).a_1 \equiv b_1 \wedge \ldots \wedge a_n \equiv b_n \Rightarrow F(a_1, \ldots, a_n) \equiv F(b_1, \ldots, b_n)$$

If $\equiv$ is a Σ-congruence on A, then for $a \in A$, $[a]$ denotes the *equivalence class* of a with respect to $\equiv$, and is defined as:

$$[a] = \{b \in A \mid b \equiv a\}$$

We now define quotient algebras which are useful when constructing algebras with special properties later on in this section. Let $\equiv$ be a Σ-congruence on an S-sorted algebra A. The *quotient algebra* $A/_\equiv$ of A by the congruence $\equiv$ is the Σ-algebra with the S-indexed family of carriers $A/_\equiv = \langle (A/_\equiv)_s \mid s \in S \rangle$ where $(\forall s \in S).(A/_\equiv)_s = A_s/_{\equiv_s}$. The elements of the quotient algebra are defined as follows:

- If $\tau(C) = s$ (constant) then $C_{A/_\equiv}$ is the congruence class generated by C, that is $C_{A/_\equiv} = [C]$.

- If $\tau(F) = s_1 \times s_2 \times \ldots \times s_n \to s$ and given any $a_1, \ldots, a_n \in A_s$, $F_{A/_\equiv}([a_1], \ldots, [a_n]) = [F(a_1, \ldots, a_n)]$.

Finally, given two congruences, $\equiv^\phi$ and $\equiv^\theta$, we say that $\equiv^\theta$ is a *finer* congruence than $\equiv^\phi$ iff $\equiv^\theta \subseteq \equiv^\phi$. The *finest* congruence on A, denoted $\equiv^{min}$, is finer than every Σ-congruence on A.

4.2.2 Equations and varieties

A Σ-*equation*, or *equation*, consists of a pair of terms $\langle M, N \rangle$ where M and N belong to the free algebra $T(\Sigma \cup V)_s$. Equations are denoted $M = N$. In equations, variables are implicitly universally quantified.

Given an algebra A and an equation $M = N$, $M = N$ is *valid* in A (or A is a *model* of $M = N$), denoted by $A \models M = N$, iff for every A-assignment $v : V(M) \cup V(N) \to A$,

---

[3] The homomorphism definition for constants is obvious and therefore omitted here.

[4] We define congruence relations in the single sorted case for the sake of clarity. The definition for the many sorted case is straightforward. For every $s \in S$ we index congruences as $\equiv_s$.

where $V(M)$ and $V(N)$ are the sets of variables in terms M and N respectively, it is the case that $v(M) = v(N)$. In other words, M and N denote the same element of the carrier A_s no matter how the variables of M and N are interpreted as elements of A. A is a model of a set of equations if every A–assignment validates every equation in this set.

Given a set of equations $\mathcal{E}$, the *variety* $\mathcal{M}(\Sigma, \mathcal{E})$ or simply $\mathcal{M}(\mathcal{E})$ is the class of all models of $\mathcal{E}$. That is, $A \in \mathcal{M}(\mathcal{E})$ iff $A \models E$ for all $E \in \mathcal{E}$.

The *validity problem* in a class C of algebras is, given an equation E over $T(\Sigma \cup V)_s$, decide whether or not E is valid in all algebras in C, denoted $C \models E$. When $C = \{A\}$ and E is a ground equation, the validity problem is called the *word problem* for A.

4.2.3   Proof theory

An *equational theory* $=_\mathcal{E}$ generated by a set of equations (*axioms*) $\mathcal{E}$, is the finest Σ–congruence over $T(\Sigma \cup V)$, $\equiv^{min}$, containing all pairs $\langle \sigma(M), \sigma(N) \rangle$, where $M = N \in \mathcal{E}$ and σ is an arbitrary substitution.

Birkhoff's completeness theorem [Bir35],

$$\mathcal{M}(\mathcal{E}) \models M = N \Longleftrightarrow M =_\mathcal{E} N$$

states that the equational calculus is sound and complete. In other words, the equation $M = N$ is true in the variety $\mathcal{M}(\mathcal{E})$ iff it can be obtained from the equations in $\mathcal{E}$ by substitutions and by replacing equals by equals. So two terms are equivalent iff they can be shown to be equivalent in a finite number of proof steps. Whenever $\mathcal{E}$ is a recursive set of axioms, this gives us a semi-decision procedure for the validity problem in the variety. Restated more formally, proof steps in the equational calculus consist of applications of the following inference rules:

1. **Reflexivity.** Each equation $M = M \in \mathcal{E}$ is deducible.

2. **Symmetry.** If equation $M = N$ is deducible from $\mathcal{E}$, then so is the equation $N = M$.

3. **Transitivity.** If the equations $M = N$ and $N = O$ are deducible from $\mathcal{E}$, then so is the equation $M = O$.

4. **Substitution.** If equation $M = N$ is deducible from $\mathcal{E}$ then so is the equation $\sigma(M) = \sigma(N)$ for every substitution $\sigma : T(\Sigma \cup V) \to T(\Sigma \cup V)$ such that $v(M) = v(N)$.

Birkhoff's theorem and the inference rules of equational logic will be restated in the context of using reduction as deduction in chapter 6.

An equation $M = N$ is *satisfiable* in an algebra A iff there is an A–assignment $v : V(M) \cup V(N) \to A$ such that $v(M) = v(N)$. An equation $M = N$ is satisfiable in the variety of $\mathcal{E}$ iff there exists some algebra $A \in \mathcal{M}(\mathcal{E})$ such that $M = N$ is satisfiable in A.

Signatures with booleans contain the distinguished sort *boolean* and the distinguished constants *TRUE* and *FALSE* of sort *boolean*. Given a signature Σ with booleans, the set of equations $\mathcal{E}$ is *consistent* iff $TRUE \neq_\mathcal{E} FALSE$.

4.2.4 Initial algebras and the word problem

The *initial* algebra $I(\Sigma, \mathcal{E})$ or simply $I(\mathcal{E})$, generated by a set of equations $\mathcal{E}$, is defined as the quotient of the term algebra $T(\Sigma)$ by the congruence $=_{\mathcal{E}}$ restricted to ground terms. When $\mathcal{E}$ is empty the initial algebra coincides with the term algebra $T(\Sigma)$. There is a unique Σ–homomorphism from $I(\mathcal{E})$ to any algebra in the $\mathcal{E}$–variety of all its ground instances, $\mathcal{M}(\mathcal{E})$ [GTW78]. It is known [HO80] that the validity problem over $I(\mathcal{E})$ is the same as the validity problem in $\mathcal{M}(\mathcal{E})$ and this is the reason for the importance of the initial model as a *standard* one.

Equational reasoning is complete for the word problem in the initial algebra (only ground terms). In other cases, $I(\mathcal{E}) \models M = N$ may be solved by inductive reasoning but in general no inductive schema is strong enough to solve the validity problem in the initial algebra [HO80].

4.2.5 Unification

Unification is one of the basic algorithms used in computational logic and plays a central rôle in the inference rules of *resolution* [Rob65] and *paramodulation* [RW69]. The unification problem is the satisfiability problem in the term algebra $T(\Sigma \cup V)$. Given two terms $M, N \in T(\Sigma \cup V)$, M and N are $\mathcal{E}$–unifiable iff there exists a substitution $\sigma : V \to T(\Sigma \cup V)$ such that $\sigma(M) =_{\mathcal{E}} \sigma(N)$. The set of such substitutions, denoted by $\mathcal{U}_{\mathcal{E}}(M, N)$, are called $\mathcal{E}$–unifiers.

We are generally interested in finding not only whether two terms are unifiable, but also the set of all their unifiers. This is best explained by an ordering on substitutions, which is itself the extension of the instantiation ordering on terms. The *instantiation* or *subsumption* preorder $\preceq_{\mathcal{E}}$ is defined over terms in $T(\Sigma \cup V)$ by

$$M \preceq_{\mathcal{E}} N \iff (\exists \sigma : V \to T(\Sigma \cup V)).\, N =_{\mathcal{E}} \sigma(M)$$

We now want to extend $\preceq_{\mathcal{E}}$ to substitutions. Let X be any finite subset of V. The preorder $\preceq_{\mathcal{E}X}$ on substitutions is defined by:

$$\sigma \preceq_{\mathcal{E}X} \sigma' \iff (\exists \rho : T(\Sigma \cup V) \to T(\Sigma \cup V)).(\forall x \in X).\sigma'(x) =_{\mathcal{E}} \rho(\sigma(x))$$

Now let M and N be two terms of the same sort and $X = V(M) \cup V(N)$. Let Y be any finite set of variables containing X, that is $X \subseteq Y \subset V$. A set of substitutions S is a *complete* set of $\mathcal{E}$–unifiers of M and N away from Y iff:

1. $(\forall \sigma \in S).\, \mathcal{D}(\sigma) \subseteq X \,\wedge\, I(\sigma) \cap Y = \emptyset$

2. $S \subseteq \mathcal{U}_{\mathcal{E}}(M, N)$ (soundness)

3. $(\forall \sigma \in \mathcal{U}_{\mathcal{E}}(M, N)).\, (\exists \rho \in S)\, \rho \preceq_{\mathcal{E}X} \sigma$ (completeness)

where $\mathcal{D}(\sigma) = \{x \in V | \sigma(x) \neq x\}$ and $I(\sigma)$ is the set of variables introduced by σ. The set S is said to be *minimal* iff $(\forall \sigma, \sigma' \in S)\, \sigma \neq \sigma' \Rightarrow \sigma \not\preceq_{\mathcal{E}X} \sigma'$. Minimal complete sets of unifiers do not always exist. When they do, they are unique, up to the equivalence generated by $\preceq_{\mathcal{E}X}$.

One-way unification (when unification is permitted in only one of the terms) is called *matching*. We say that σ is an $\mathcal{E}$–match of M and N iff $\sigma(M) =_{\mathcal{E}} N$.

4.2.6   Term rewriting systems

Using equations as rewrite rules over terms is the basis of both decision procedures based on normal forms and abstract interpreters for directed equations considered as a programming language.

A *term rewriting system* over Σ is a set of directed equations $\mathcal{R} = \{\lambda_i \to \rho_i | i \in I\}$ such that $(\forall \lambda \to \rho \in \mathcal{R}).V(\rho) \subseteq V(\lambda)$. The reduction relation $\to_\mathcal{R}$ associated with $\mathcal{R}$ is the finest relation over $T(\Sigma \cup V)$ containing $\mathcal{R}$ and closed by substitution and replacement, that is:

- $M \to_\mathcal{R} N \Rightarrow \sigma(M) \to_\mathcal{R} \sigma(N)$, and

- $M \to_\mathcal{R} N \Rightarrow P[u \leftarrow M] \to_\mathcal{R} P[u \leftarrow N]$

where $P[u \leftarrow M]$ denotes the term P in which we have replaced the subterm at occurrence u by M. From now on, we use $\to$ for $\to_\mathcal{R}$. $\to^*$ denotes the transitive-reflexive closure of $\to$ and we use $\longleftrightarrow$ for its symmetric closure. Note that $\longleftrightarrow^*$ is the same as the $\mathcal{R}$ equality $=_\mathcal{R}$ when $\mathcal{R}$ is considered as a set of equations.

The fundamental difference between equations and term rewriting rules is that equations denote equality (which is symmetric) whereas term rewriting systems treat equations directionally as one-way replacements. Further, the only substitutions required for term rewriting rules are the ones found by matching.

The completeness of using rewrite rules to make deductions equationally is expressed by the *Church–Rosser* property. $\mathcal{R}$ is Church–Rosser iff:

$$(\forall M, N).\ M =_\mathcal{R} N \Longleftrightarrow (\exists P).M \to^* P \land N \to^* P$$

A term M is in *normal form* relative to $\mathcal{R}$ iff there is no N such that $M \to N$. We say that N is an $\mathcal{R}$–*normal form* of M iff $M \to^* N$ and N is a normal form relative to $\mathcal{R}$.

When $\mathcal{R}$ is Church–Rosser, the normal form of a term is unique when it exists. A sufficient condition for the existence of such a normal form is the termination of all rewritings. That is, $\mathcal{R}$ is *noetherian* or *finitely terminating* iff there exists no M for which there exists an infinite chain of reductions issuing from $M : M_1 \to M_2 \to \ldots \to M_i \to \ldots$ where $\forall i.M_i \neq M_{i+1}$.

Let $\lambda \to \rho$ and $\lambda' \to \rho'$ be two rules in $\mathcal{R}$ (where variables have been renamed so that λ and λ' share no variables). Given a non variable occurrence u in λ such that λ/u (that is the subterm of λ at occurrence u) and λ' are unifiable with minimal unifier σ, the pair $\langle \sigma(\lambda[u \leftarrow \rho']), \sigma(\rho) \rangle$ is *critical* in $\mathcal{R}$. If $\mathcal{R}$ is finite, there are only finitely many such critical pairs and they can be effectively computed using standard unification algorithms [HO80].

When $\mathcal{R}$ is a finite set of rules which is Church–Rosser and noetherian, the equational theory $=_\mathcal{R}$ is decidable since $M =_\mathcal{R} N \Longleftrightarrow M \downarrow = N \downarrow$ where $M \downarrow, N \downarrow$ denote normal forms obtained from M by an arbitrary sequence of reductions. Confluence is undecidable for arbitrary term rewriting systems. The decidability of confluence for ground term rewriting systems is an open problem. Confluence is, however, decidable for noetherian systems [HO80]. A confluent and noetherian term rewriting system is called *complete*. Termination of arbitrary term rewriting systems is undecidable. The problem is however decidable for ground systems [HL78].

4.2.7 Compiling canonical forms

Let $\mathcal{E}$ be a finite set of equations. If there exists a complete term rewriting system $\mathcal{R}$ such that[5]

1. $(\forall (M = N) \in \mathcal{E})\ M \downarrow = N \downarrow$, and

2. $(\forall (\lambda \to \rho) \in \mathcal{R})\ \lambda =_{\varepsilon} \rho$,

then $M \downarrow$ is a normal form of M for the theory $=_{\varepsilon}$ in the sense that $(\forall M, N \in T(\Sigma \cup V))\ M =_{\varepsilon} N \Longleftrightarrow M \downarrow = N \downarrow$. This gives us a decision procedure for the validity problem in $\mathcal{M}(\mathcal{E})$ and of course a decision procedure for the word problem in $I(\mathcal{E})$. The well known Knuth–Bendix completion algorithm [KB70], which attempts to generate $\mathcal{R}$ satisfying the two conditions above given an $\mathcal{E}$, is as follows:

$\mathcal{E}_i$ is a set of equations and $\mathcal{R}_i$ a term rewriting system where i is a natural number. Initially, let $\mathcal{E}_0 = \mathcal{E}$, $\mathcal{R}_i = \emptyset$ and $i = 0$.

1. If $\mathcal{E}_i = \emptyset$ stop with answer $\mathcal{R} = \mathcal{R}_i$. Otherwise select $M = N \in \mathcal{E}$ and let $M \downarrow$ and $N \downarrow$ be normal forms for M and N respectively, using the current system $\mathcal{R}_i$. If $M \downarrow = N \downarrow$ then let $\mathcal{E}_{i+1} = \mathcal{E}_i - \{M = N\}, \mathcal{R}_{i+1} = \mathcal{R}_i$, increment i by 1 and go to 1. Otherwise go to 2.

2. Choose nondeterministically one of the following:

   (a) If $V(M \downarrow) \subset V(N \downarrow)$ then let $\lambda = N \downarrow, \rho = M \downarrow$

   (b) If $V(N \downarrow) \subset V(M \downarrow)$ then let $\lambda = M \downarrow, \rho = N \downarrow$

   If neither (a) or (b) applies, stop with failure. Otherwise, let $\mathcal{E}'_i = \{\lambda' = \rho'|\lambda' \to \rho' \in \mathcal{R}_i$ and λ' or ρ' contains an instance of λ as a subterm$\}$. Then let $\mathcal{R}'_i = \mathcal{R}_i - \mathcal{E}'_i \cup \{\lambda \to \rho\}$ and go to 3.

3. If $\mathcal{R}'_i$ is not noetherian, stop with failure. Otherwise, let $\mathcal{R}_{i+1} = \mathcal{R}'_i$ and $\mathcal{E}_{i+1} = (\mathcal{E}_i - \{M = N\}) \cup \mathcal{E}'_i \cup \{P = Q$ where $\langle P = Q \rangle$ is a critical pair of $\mathcal{R}_{i+1}\}$. Increment i by 1 and go to 1.

The algorithm is nondeterministic because of the various choices. It may stop with success, stop with failure or loop forever. The algorithm shown here is only applicable to many sorted equational systems. Similar algorithms exist for the order sorted case which is relevant to OBJ3 systems [GKK88]. Some research has also been done in generalising the Knuth–Bendix algorithm to conditional rewrite systems [Kap84].

4.2.8 Separable equational theories

Let Σ be a signature with booleans and an operator $\#$ with $\tau(\#) = s \times s \to boolean$. $\mathcal{E}$ is s–separable iff

1. $(x \# x = FALSE \in \mathcal{E})$ for $x \in V_s$, and

2. $(\forall M, N \in T(\Sigma)_s).M \neq_{\varepsilon} N \Rightarrow M \# N =_{\varepsilon} TRUE$.

---

[5]Bergstra and Tucker [BT80] show that such complete systems exist under certain conditions.

The following theorem (due to Huet and Oppen [HO80]) gives us a semi-decision procedure for the validity of some equations $M = N$ in the initial algebra $I(\mathcal{E})$.

Theorem 1 *Let $\mathcal{E}$ be a consistent, s–separable set of equations and M, N be two terms of sort s. Then $I(\mathcal{E}) \models M = N$ iff $\mathcal{E} \cup \{M = N\}$ is consistent.*

This theorem allows us to limit induction to a single proof of s–separability and consequently permits proofs by pure equational reasoning that would normally require induction. This is the basis of the so called *inductionless induction* (proof by consistency) proof technique which we will use later on in this chapter. The practical value of the technique is limited since consistency is not even recursively enumerable. It is however useful for decidable theories for which consistency is also decidable.

This technique can be used in conjunction with the Knuth–Bendix algorithm. When the completion algorithm terminates, it may be used to decide the consistency of a theory and may therefore be used for solving the validity problem in the initial algebra of certain separable equational theories. This use of the completion algorithm is different in spirit from its use in generating complete forms for an equational theory. Generating a complete term rewriting system for a theory is very costly in terms of efficiency but it only needs to be done once. Future proofs will consist simply of reductions to normal form. On the other hand, each proof in $I(\mathcal{E})$ requires using the completion algorithm and its associated costs (such as termination proofs) even if $\mathcal{E}$ is itself completed. However, disproofs (contradictions) may be obtained even when the completion algorithm does not terminate; as soon as $TRUE = FALSE$ is generated as a critical pair we know that the theory is inconsistent.

After this introduction to the terminology, we are ready to examine the term rewriting approach to the specification and verification of hardware.

4.3   Specifying with UMIST OBJ

We will limit our discussion to the n-bit parallel adder. As outlined in the previous chapter, the specification will be used for both simulation and verification. The aim is to prove that the circuit produces the mathematical sum of its inputs.

4.3.1   UMIST OBJ as a formalism for hardware description

The UMIST OBJ system [GCS89] implements an executable subset of the algebraic specification language OBJ3 which was developed by Goguen *et al* over a number of years. OBJ3 as described in [GW88] was not fully implemented or available for distribution when the work reported here was carried out. We have therefore used UMIST OBJ for this part of the work and we will make the transition to OBJ3 in the next chapter.

The UMIST OBJ development effort has concentrated on producing a widely available and portable version of the language rather than adding functionality to OBJ3, the aim being to allow early and wide experimentation with the language in software engineering projects. The language is a subset of OBJ3 without subsorts, parameterisation and order sorted rewriting. In common with the executable subset of OBJ3 it has denotational semantics given by initial algebras and operational semantics given by term rewriting.

Although UMIST OBJ was meant for use in writing and executing algebraic specifications of programs, in common with other declarative languages, it also provides a convenient notation for expressing circuit behaviour. As we have seen, hardware components that can be modelled as functions from inputs to outputs are readily expressible in notations supporting functional definitions. In UMIST OBJ devices are modelled as abstract data types. Additionally, UMIST OBJ has a number of features which are helpful when specifying hardware.

- Mixfix syntax enhances readability and the ability to define functions through case analysis eliminates the need for selector operations which give rise to strange encodings (e.g. car and cdr combinations in Lisp).

- UMIST OBJ is executable and therefore allows direct animation of specifications.

- A notation used for hardware specification must support composition and decomposition since these are very important concepts in system design. UMIST OBJ supports these through its modular structure and abstraction mechanisms.

- By encoding the basic Boolean algebra rules in a UMIST OBJ program, the term rewriting semantics of the language can be used for circuit optimisation. Due to the inaccuracy of hardware models currently in use, there are a number of difficulties involved in this process. [Clo85] further discusses circuit optimisation using reduction techniques and identifies particular problems.

4.3.2 The adder specification

As the width of the adder is not specified, the inputs and the output are modelled using vectors of bits. To eliminate the need for traversing the vectors before additions, the least significant bit is held at the head of the vector. UMIST OBJ specifications are structured in modules called **objects**.

```
OBJ Vector
SORTS vector
OPS nil : -> vector
    _._ : BOOL vector -> vector
JBO
```

This object can be enriched with the operations which implement mappings from vectors of bits onto natural numbers and vice versa. These operations are used for simulation and for formulating the adder correctness theorem later on.

```
bin-to-nat : vector -> nat
( bin-to-nat(nil) = 0 )
( bin-to-nat(b . v) = bit(b) + (2 * bin-to-nat(v)) )
```

where **nat** is the sort for natural numbers with the usual operations and operator **bit** provides a mapping from bits to natural numbers:

```
bit : BOOL -> nat
( bit(T) = 1 )
( bit(F) = 0 )
```

nat-to-bin maps natural numbers onto vectors of bits:

```
nat-to-bin : nat -> vector
( nat-to-bin(0) = nil )
( nat-to-bin(succ(n)) = not(even(succ(n))) .
                        nat-to-bin(succ(n) div 2) )
```

Finally, the operator inc adjusts the input bit vector so that its natural number representation is incremented by 1:

```
inc : vector -> vector
( inc(nil) = T . nil )
( inc(T . v) = F . (inc(v)) )
( inc(F . v) = T . v )
```

The basic building block of the n-bit adder is the half adder which consists of an AND and an XOR gate. The circuit produces a sum and a carry output which are paired using sort pair with selectors sum and carry.

```
OBJ Half-Adder
SORTS pair
OPS mkpair : BOOL BOOL -> pair
    halfadder : BOOL BOOL -> pair
    sum : pair -> BOOL
    carry : pair -> BOOL
VARS x,y,s,c : BOOL
EQNS ( halfadder(x,y) = mkpair(x xor y, x and y) )
     ( sum(mkpair(s,c)) = s )
     ( carry(mkpair(s,c)) = c )
JBO
```

where the _xor_ operator is trivially defined as

```
_xor_ : BOOL BOOL -> BOOL (COMM)
( F xor x = x )
( T xor x = not(x) )
```

The full adder is made up of two half adders and an OR gate.

```
OBJ Full-Adder / Half-Adder
OPS fulladder : BOOL BOOL BOOL -> pair
VARS x,y,c-in : BOOL
EQNS ( fulladder(x,y,c-in) =
mkpair(sum(halfadder(sum(halfadder(x,y)),c-in)),
       carry(halfadder(x,y)) or
       carry(halfadder(sum(halfadder(x,y)),c-in))) )
JBO
```

The n-bit adder consists of a cascade of n full adders with the output carry of the $(i-1)^{th}$ unit connected to the input carry of the ith unit.

```
OBJ Adder / Full-Adder Vector
OPS adder : BOOL vector vector -> vector
VARS bit1,bit2,c-in : BOOL
     v1,v2 : vector
EQNS ( adder(F,nil,v2) = v2 )
     ( adder(T,nil,v2) = inc(v2) )
     ( adder(F,v1,nil) = v1 )
     ( adder(T,v1,nil) = inc(v1) )
     ( adder(c-in, bit1 . v1, bit2 . v2) =
     sum(fulladder(bit1,bit2,c-in)) .
     adder(carry(fulladder(bit1,bit2,c-in)),v1,v2) )
JBO
```

This specification of the adder can be used to perform simulation. The tests are carried out using the auxiliary operator **test**.

```
test : nat nat -> nat
( test(n1,n2) =
bin-to-nat(adder(F,nat-to-bin(n1),nat-to-bin(n2))) )
```

The input carry c-in is set to F to indicate that an addition is about to take place. A typical test and result are shown below.

```
run test(2345,456) nur
AS nat : 2801
```

4.3.3 Specifying behaviour in time

Despite the combinational nature of our example here, we make some comments on sequential devices for which specifications involving time are essential. Specifying such devices or systems usually involves higher order functions, since input and output lines are modelled as mappings from times to values. UMIST OBJ does not support higher order functions. Therefore, we need an alternative way of expressing properties involving time. We will first examine the concept of *histories* in this context. In the next chapter we will show how the parameterisation facilities of OBJ3 can be used to emulate second order functions.

The basic idea here is that a line can be modelled by its *history*. Such a history is simply a sequence of *instances*. Every time the clock ticks, the next instance in the history of the line is generated. An instance can be defined as a triple ⟨*name, value, time*⟩. This concept of history is similar to Lucid histories [AW77]. In UMIST OBJ we have:

```
OBJ Name
SORTS name
OPS l1,l2 : -> name
JBO
```

which generates some names for lines. Instances are defined as follows:

```
OBJ Instance / Name
SORTS instance
```

```
OPS
    mkinstance : name BOOL nat -> instance
    name? : instance -> name
    value : instance -> BOOL
    time  : instance -> nat
VARS
    l : name
    val : BOOL
    t : nat
EQNS
    ( name?(mkinstance(l,val,t)) = l )
    ( value(mkinstance(l,val,t)) = val )
    ( time(mkinstance(l,val,t)) = t )
JBO
```

Thus time is modelled with natural numbers.

```
OBJ History / Instance
SORTS history
OPS
    empty : -> history
    _._    : instance history -> history
JBO
```

Now we can define operations that look into the history of a line and retrieve some information:

```
OBJ Operations / History
OPS
    last : history -> BOOL
    nth  : nat history -> BOOL
VARS
    l : name
    val : BOOL
    t,n : nat
    h : history
EQNS
    ( last(mkinstance(l,val,t) . h ) = value(head(h))
                                   IF not(h==empty) )
    ( nth(succ(n),mkinstance(l,val,t) . h) = val
                                   IF succ(n) == t )
    ( nth(succ(n),mkinstance(l,val,t) . h) = nth(n,h)
                        IF (succ(n) < t) and not(h==empty) )
JBO
```

where **last** returns the value of the line at time $(t-1)$ and **nth** returns the value at time $(t-n)$. Note that the definitions are partial. A one unit delay can now be specified as

```
OBJ Delay / History
OPS
    delay : history history -> history
```

```
VARS
    l : name
    val : BOOL
    t,n : nat
    h,h' : history
EQNS
    ( delay(mkinstance(l,val,t) . h, h') =
                        mkinstance(l,val,t+1) . h' )
JBO
```

Effectively a hardware device is modelled through the instances it causes to the history of its I/O lines (its traces). Although this approach is adequate for defining simple circuits, descriptions of more complex systems are very complicated and riddled with detail. More fundamentally, in general, it is not clear how to compose primitive components into larger ones without the ability to define higher order functions[6]. We, therefore, feel that histories in the context of UMIST OBJ do not provide an effective way of specifying behaviour through time.

4.4 Verifying with REVE

UMIST OBJ equations are sentences in many sorted equational logic. It is therefore possible to reason about the adder specifications formally. In order to use term rewriting as a decision procedure for the equational theory defined by a specification, the corresponding term rewriting system must be shown to be complete. As we have seen, a term rewriting system is complete iff it has the Church–Rosser property and is finitely terminating [HO80]. UMIST OBJ specifications, however, are not subject to such completion checks. Consequently, before the OBJ specification can be used for formal reasoning, a complete term rewriting system must be constructed from the equations in the specification. Practically this means that we must use a completion procedure such as the Knuth–Bendix algorithm [KB70] which we presented earlier on. Knuth–Bendix is supported by the REVE theorem prover [Les83]. In particular, the version used here (2.4) supports completion of equational theories modulo associative–commutative operators but does not allow conditional equations or rules.

REVE is single sorted and has no hierarchical structure. The user builds an equational theory $\mathcal{E}$ in the system and can then apply Knuth–Bendix with various termination orderings, attempt automatic termination proofs, reduce terms, compute normal forms, find unifiers for two terms, find critical pairs between rules and so on. The objective is to generate a complete rewriting system $\mathcal{R}$ corresponding to $\mathcal{E}$ such that equational reasoning or consistency proofs can be attempted. REVE is an automatic theorem prover in the sense that once a proof has started no user interaction is possible (apart from the ability to orient equations manually).

The semantics of OBJ specifications are given by initial algebras defined by the set of equations. Using just the initial model compromises the completeness property of equational logic and thus, we can no longer prove an equation valid (or invalid) in the

---

[6]We note that if the components are defined by primitive recursion over a suitable algebra then composition can be effectively done [ST92]. The result is also primitive recursive.

initial algebra by mere equational reasoning; some kind of induction is necessary. REVE supports *proof by consistency* or *inductionless induction*, in particular the Huet–Hullot induction in equational theories with constructors [HH82]. As we have seen, this permits proofs of equations without explicit induction.

4.4.1   UMIST OBJ specifications as input to REVE

The UMIST OBJ specifications cannot be fed directly into REVE for completion. The following syntactic and semantic amendments are required:

1. OBJ's = must be replaced by REVE's ==;

2. Variable names must be changed to begin with the letters x,y,z,w to conform with REVE's naming conventions;

3. Outer parentheses must be stripped from OBJ equations;

4. Sorting information, signatures and variable declarations must be removed from the OBJ text;

5. Conditional equations must either be removed or replaced by a set of unconditional ones.

Items (2) and (4) above underline the fact that REVE is not many sorted whereas UMIST OBJ is. A consequence of this is that REVE will accept and will attempt to work with semantically ill defined terms thus creating an unnecessarily large search space. Item (5) is even more important. Most specifications contain conditional rules and it is not always straightforward or even possible to replace these by unconditional ones. Introducing an `if_then_else_` operator does not solve the problem in most cases because no suitable termination reduction ordering on the terms can be found and the Knuth–Bendix algorithm keeps on generating longer and longer rules without terminating. Hence, the absence of a completion procedure for conditional equations in the version of REVE used here, was a serious obstacle in proving the correctness of the adder circuit.

4.4.2   A practical view of the decision procedure

The text of the OBJ specification is shown below after having been changed to conform with the constraints of the previous section.
System $\mathcal{E}_1$

```
1.        and(x, F)  == F
2.        and(x, T)  == x
3.        xor(x, x)  == F
4.        xor(x, F)  == x
5.        or(x,T) == T
6.        or(x,F) == x
7.        1 == succ(0)
8.        2 == succ(succ(0))
```

```
9.       x + 0 == x
10.      x + succ(y) == succ(x + y)
11.      x * 0 == 0
12.      bin-to-nat(nil) == 0
13.      bin-to-nat(x.y) == bit(x) + 2 * bin-to-nat(y)
14.      carry(mkpair(x, y)) == y
15.      sum(mkpair(x, y)) == x
16.      x * succ(y) == (x * y) + x
17.      (x+y)*z == (x*z) + (y*z)
18.      inc(nil) == T.nil
19.      inc(F.x) == T.x
20.      inc(T.x) == F.inc(x)
21.      halfadder(x, y) == mkpair(xor(x,y),and(x, y))
22.      adder(F,x,nil) == x
23.      adder(T,x,nil) == inc(x)
24.      adder(F,nil,x) == x
25.      adder(T,nil,x) == inc(x)
26.      adder(z, x . xva, y . yvb) ==
         sum(fulladder(x,y,z)).adder(carry(fulladder(x,y,z)),xva,yvb)
27.      fulladder(x,y,z) ==
             mkpair(sum(halfadder(sum(halfadder(x,y)),z)),
                 or(carry(halfadder(x,y)),
                     carry(halfadder(sum(halfadder(x,y)),z))))
28.      bit(F) == 0
29.      bit(T) == succ(0)
```

As we have seen, deciding whether an arbitrary term rewriting system is complete is undecidable (because the finite termination of such a system is undecidable) [HO80]. Therefore, the Knuth–Bendix procedure might loop forever when attempting to complete a system which has no equivalent terminating and Church–Rosser system. In REVE Knuth–Bendix is used both for deciding whether a system is complete and whether an equation (proposition) is valid in an equational theory (by using the inductive extension of the algorithm as presented in [HH82]). However, the Knuth–Bendix procedure is a computationally intensive process. When the equational theory contains associative–commutative operators (+, *, and and or in this particular system), the algorithm is even more inefficient. The situation is made worse because the user has no control over the search strategy that REVE uses. Undecidability coupled with inefficiency mean that, in practice, once the algorithm has been running for some time, the user cannot tell whether the set of rewrite rules is genuinely not canonical and Knuth–Bendix is in a non terminating loop or the algorithm is just taking a long time discovering the equivalent canonical system. This then means, that although the algorithm might eventually terminate for complete systems and valid equations (if that is, the correct reduction ordering has been found), its use is not practical for most problems in the hardware verification domain.

4.4.3   Knuth–Bendix as inference rules

A way of overcoming the above difficulty, is to construct alternative but *equivalent* sets of rules to the original. Then completion and proof of properties can be attempted again on

a new system. These systems must be simpler than the original in the sense that Knuth–
Bendix is presented with a simpler task. The process of finding such systems amounts
to performing some of the steps of the decision procedure manually. Furthermore, if the
notion of completion is formalised within the framework of a proof theory [BDH87, DJ89],
then these steps can be regarded as applications of the appropriate inference rules. The
notion of completion can be formalised within the framework of proof theory as follows.
The objects of the proof calculus are pairs $\langle \mathcal{E}, \mathcal{R} \rangle$ where $\mathcal{E}$ is a set of equations and $\mathcal{R}$ is
a set of rewrite rules. The proof theory consists of the following inference rules:

- Orienting an equation.

$$\frac{(\mathcal{E} \cup \{s = t\}, \mathcal{R})}{(\mathcal{E}, \mathcal{R} \cup \{s \rightarrow t\})} \quad if \quad s > t \tag{4.1}$$

- Adding an equational consequence.

$$\frac{(\mathcal{E}, \mathcal{R})}{(\mathcal{E} \cup \{s = t\}, \mathcal{R})} \quad if \quad s \leftarrow u \rightarrow t \tag{4.2}$$

- Simplifying an equation.

$$\frac{(\mathcal{E} \cup \{s = t\}, \mathcal{R})}{(\mathcal{E} \cup \{u = t\}, \mathcal{R})} \quad if \quad s \rightarrow u \tag{4.3}$$

- Deleting a trivial equation.

$$\frac{(\mathcal{E} \cup \{s = s\}, \mathcal{R})}{(\mathcal{E}, \mathcal{R})} \tag{4.4}$$

where $\mathcal{E}$ is a set of equations, $\mathcal{R}$ is a set of rewrite rules, $>$ is a reduction ordering, $\rightarrow$
is the reduction relation and $\leftarrow$ is the inverse of the reduction relation. If P is a proof
theory, we write $(\mathcal{E}, \mathcal{R}) \vdash_P (\mathcal{E}', \mathcal{R}')$ to indicate that $(\mathcal{E}', \mathcal{R}')$ can be obtained from $(\mathcal{E}, \mathcal{R})$
by one or more applications of the inference rules of P. A (possibly infinite) sequence
$(\mathcal{E}_0, \mathcal{R}_0), (\mathcal{E}_1, \mathcal{R}_1, \ldots)$ is called a P–derivation if $\forall i > 0, (\mathcal{E}_{i-1}, \mathcal{R}_{i-1}) \vdash_P (\mathcal{E}_i, \mathcal{R}_i)$.

Here are some examples of applying these inference rules. Multiplication in the rewrite
system $\mathcal{E}_1$ of the previous section is redundant since it is defined in terms of addition. The
equations defining multiplication (11, 16 and 17) can be removed and all occurrences of *
replaced by + terms. This is achieved by orienting the equations defining multiplication
and using the resulting rewrite rules to simplify equation 13 yielding equation 12 in the
system $\mathcal{E}_2$.

System $\mathcal{E}_2$

1.	`and(x, F) == F`
2.	`and(x, T) == x`
3.	`xor(x, x) == F`
4.	`xor(x, F) == x`
5.	`or(x,T) == T`
6.	`or(x,F) == x`
7.	`1 == succ(0)`
8.	`2 == succ(succ(0))`
9.	`x + 0 == x`
10.	`x + succ(y) == succ(x + y)`
11.	`bin-to-nat(nil) == 0`
12.	`bin-to-nat(x.y) == bit(x) + bin-to-nat(y) + bin-to-nat(y)`
13.	`carry(mkpair(x, y)) == y`
14.	`sum(mkpair(x, y)) == x`
15.	`inc(nil) == T.nil`
16.	`inc(F.x) == T.x`
17.	`inc(T.x) == F.inc(x)`
18.	`halfadder(x, y) == mkpair(xor(x,y),and(x, y))`
19.	`adder(F,x,nil) == x`
20.	`adder(T,x,nil) == inc(x)`
21.	`adder(F,nil,x) == x`
22.	`adder(T,nil,x) == inc(x)`
23.	`adder(z, x . xva, y . yvb) ==`
	`sum(fulladder(x,y,z)).adder(carry(fulladder(x,y,z)),xva,yvb)`
24.	`fulladder(x,y,z) ==`
	`mkpair(sum(halfadder(sum(halfadder(x,y)),z)),`
	`        or(carry(halfadder(x,y)),`
	`           carry(halfadder(sum(halfadder(x,y)),z))))`
25.	`bit(F) == 0`
26.	`bit(T) == succ(0)`

The task of the completion procedure can be further simplified by enhancing the set of equations with some of the critical pairs that the algorithm would otherwise have to produce itself. Note that since REVE is unsorted, Knuth–Bendix cannot use equations for generating critical pairs selectively, on the basis of typing information available in the OBJ specification. The completion procedure is, therefore, unnecessarily time consuming. Manual generation of critical pairs also allows removing these equations whose consequences have been replaced by equations generated from the appropriate critical pairs. Therefore equations 18 and 24, defining the behaviour of the half and the full adder respectively, can be replaced by their consequences as shown in equations 10 to 13 and 14 to 21 in system $\mathcal{E}_3$ later on. An example of deriving such a critical pair equation is shown below, where equation 10 is derived in 6 steps as follows:

1. Unifying the left hand sides of equations 1 and 18 produces the critical pair

```
halfadder(and(x,F),y)
mkpair(xor(and(x,F),y),and(and(x,F),y))
```

2. Orienting equation 1 and using it to simplify the critical pair

```
halfadder(F,y)
mkpair(xor(F,y),F)
```

3. Adding the critical pair equation to the system

```
halfadder(F,y) == mkpair(xor(F,y),F)
```

4. Unifying the critical pair equation with equation 3 produces another critical pair

```
halfadder(F,xor(x,x))
mkpair(xor(x,x),F)
```

5. Orienting equation 3 and using it to simplify the critical pair

```
halfadder(F,F)
mkpair(F,F)
```

6. Adding the new critical pair equation to the system

```
halfadder(F,F) == mkpair(F,F)
```

The rest of the equations are derived in a similar way. The system $\mathcal{E}_3$ below, shows the simplified equations for the **halfadder** and the **fulladder**. Note also that since **and, or, xor** are no longer required their definitions can be removed from the system (equations 1 to 6 of $\mathcal{E}_2$).

System $\mathcal{E}_3$

```
1.      x + 0 == x
2.      x + succ(y) == succ(x + y)
3.      bin-to-nat(nil) == 0
4.      bin-to-nat(x.y) == bit(x) +  bin-to-nat(y) + bin-to-nat(y)
5.      carry(mkpair(x, y)) == y
6.      sum(mkpair(x, y)) == x
7.      inc(nil) == T.nil
8.      inc(F.x) == T.x
9.      inc(T.x) == F.inc(x)
10.     halfadder(F,F) == mkpair(F,F)
11.     halfadder(F,T) == mkpair(T,F)
12.     halfadder(T,F) == mkpair(T,F)
13.     halfadder(T,T) == mkpair(F,T)
14.     fulladder(F,F,F) == mkpair(F,F)
15.     fulladder(F,F,T) == mkpair(T,F)
16.     fulladder(F,T,F) == mkpair(T,F)
17.     fulladder(F,T,T) == mkpair(F,T)
18.     fulladder(T,F,F) == mkpair(T,F)
19.     fulladder(T,F,T) == mkpair(F,T)
```

```
20.      fulladder(T,T,F) == mkpair(F,T)
21.      fulladder(T,T,T) == mkpair(T,T)
22.      adder(F,x,nil) == x
23.      adder(T,x,nil) == inc(x)
24.      adder(F,nil,x) == x
25.      adder(T,nil,x) == inc(x)
26.      adder(z, x . xva, y . yvb) ==
         sum(fulladder(x,y,z)).adder(carry(fulladder(x,y,z)),xva,yvb)
27.      bit(F) == 0
28.      bit(T) == succ(0)
```

In fact, this last system is the one that can be successfully used to prove the theorem about the correctness of the adder, which can be formulated as follows:

```
bin-to-nat(adder(x,y,z)) == bin-to-nat(y) + bin-to-nat(z) + bit(x)
```

where + is associative and commutative. The completed set of rules below shows the proved theorem as rule 29.

System $\mathcal{R}_1$

```
1.       0 + x -> x
2.       bin-to-nat(nil) -> 0
3.       carry(mkpair(x, y)) -> y
4.       sum(mkpair(x, y)) -> x
5.       inc(nil) -> T . nil
6.       inc(F . x) -> T . x
7.       inc(T . x) -> F . inc(x)
8.       halfadder(F, F) -> mkpair(F, F)
9.       halfadder(F, T) -> mkpair(T, F)
10.      halfadder(T, F) -> mkpair(T, F)
11.      halfadder(T, T) -> mkpair(F, T)
12.      fulladder(F, F, F) -> mkpair(F, F)
13.      fulladder(F, F, T) -> mkpair(T, F)
14.      fulladder(F, T, F) -> mkpair(T, F)
15.      fulladder(F, T, T) -> mkpair(F, T)
16.      fulladder(T, F, F) -> mkpair(T, F)
17.      fulladder(T, F, T) -> mkpair(F, T)
18.      fulladder(T, T, F) -> mkpair(F, T)
19.      fulladder(T, T, T) -> mkpair(T, T)
20.      adder(F, x, nil) -> x
21.      adder(F, nil, x) -> x
22.      bit(F) -> 0
23.      bit(T) -> succ(0)
24.      adder(T, x, nil) -> inc(x)
25.      adder(T, nil, x) -> inc(x)
26.      succ(y) + x -> succ(x + y)
27.      bin-to-nat(x . y) -> bin-to-nat(y) + bin-to-nat(y) + bit(x)
28.      adder(z, x . xva, y . yvb) ->
                 sum(fulladder(x, y, z)) .
```

```
                       adder(carry(fulladder(x, y, z)), xva, yvb)
29.     bin-to-nat(adder(x, y, z)) ->
                       bin-to-nat(y) + bin-to-nat(z) + bit(x)
30.     bin-to-nat(inc(y)) -> succ(bin-to-nat(y))
31.     bit(carry(fulladder(x, y, x1))) +
        bit(carry(fulladder(x, y, x1))) +
        bit(sum(fulladder(x, y, x1))) -> bit(x) + bit(x1) + bit(y)
```

Note, that REVE has discovered two lemmas required for this proof. These are shown as rules 30 and 31. Interestingly, the critical pairs generated during completion are frequently the kind of lemmata a mathematician would come up with [DJ89].

Interpreting the Knuth–Bendix procedure as a set of inference rules not only makes proof possible in some circumstances but it also allows a degree of user interaction in a theorem prover which is otherwise totally automatic.

4.4.4 Equivalent term rewriting systems

Although manual application of the inference rules, as discussed above, facilitates proofs which cannot be obtained automatically within realistic time limits, it does nonetheless introduce a potential source of errors in the proving process. These rules can be applied incorrectly as well as correctly. The problem can be solved by formally showing that the succession of equation sets generated by the application of the inference rules (a P–derivation) have *equivalent* (isomorphic) initial models. For sets of equations $\mathcal{E}_1, \mathcal{E}_2$ we write $\mathcal{E}_1 \cong \mathcal{E}_2$.

Given two sets of equations $\mathcal{E}_1$ and $\mathcal{E}_2$, then in order to prove that $\mathcal{E}_1 \cong \mathcal{E}_2$, we must show that:

$$(\forall e_2 \in \mathcal{E}_2). \quad \mathcal{E}_1 \models e_2 \quad \text{and} \quad (\forall e_1 \in \mathcal{E}_1). \quad \mathcal{E}_2 \models e_1$$

Practically, this means that both sets must be completed and then each equation in one system must be shown to be a consequence of the other. Since equivalence is transitive, if we prove each transformation during the refinement, then the most complex system is equivalent to the simplest one, and thus the theorem is valid in the original system.

In general, if $\mathcal{E}_1$ is simpler than $\mathcal{E}_2$, then to prove that $\mathcal{E}_2 \Rightarrow \mathcal{E}_1$ standard equational reasoning suffices, whereas proving that $\mathcal{E}_1 \Rightarrow \mathcal{E}_2$ would normally require an inductive argument. Both these proofs have been done for the three systems of the previous section using REVE itself.

4.4.5 Traditional vs inductionless induction

Let us now return to the subject of inductionless induction which we mentioned earlier on. Musser [Mus80] has shown that under the condition that the set of equations considered contains the axiomatisation of an equality predicate, the validity problem in the initial algebra reduces to checking the consistency of the set of equations (in the sense that $TRUE = FALSE$ is not derivable) after the equation in question has been added to it. This method, therefore, permits proof or disproof of equations without explicit induction. Musser's results were further simplified by Goguen [Gog80] and Huet and Oppen [HO80]. Huet and Hullot [HH82] have subsequently shown that in the case of inductive definitions over free algebras, and when the Knuth–Bendix algorithm converges, these proofs can be carried out by a simple extension of the completion algorithm and without the need for equality axiomatisation.

In practice, a proof by consistency proceeds by adding the equation to the theory and running the completion procedure. If that procedure terminates without generating an inconsistency, the equation is an inductive consequence of the theory; if it terminates with an inconsistency the equation is not valid in the theory; if it does not terminate, the equation may or may not be an inductive consequence.

The inductionless induction method is simple to implement and when it applies the proofs obtained are surprisingly compact. Experimental evidence [HH82, GG88] suggests that it is powerful enough to apply to the usual proofs of correctness of algebraic data type implementations, proofs of simple primitive recursive programs computing on data types such as integers, lists and trees and proofs about algebraic varieties. The method is not, however, applicable to properties such as the transitivity of the subset relation on sets which require conditional rules (or an if-then-else operator) and permutative equations except for the associative–commutative laws.

Even worse, various experimental studies [GG87, GG88] as well as our work have found that, in practical terms, inductionless induction is inferior to traditional (structural) induction for the following reasons:

1. Traditional induction has a *simpler theoretical basis*, where the soundness of different rules is generally clear. Furthermore, if two rules are sound, it is sound to use them together. In inductionless induction soundness must be established by less transparent algebraic techniques and it is not clear how to use different formulations in conjunction with one another.

2. *No notion of completeness is required* to ensure the soundness of traditional induction. In contrast, the soundness of inductionless induction depends upon a rather strong notion of completeness.

3. When using induction one needs to order the original set of equations into a term rewriting system; but it is *not necessary that the system is convergent*. This contrasts with inductionless induction where convergence is absolutely necessary. As we have seen, proving convergence is not trivial even when it is possible.

4. The *soundness of inductionless induction depends upon the noetherian property* whereas the soundness of induction does not.

5. In traditional induction, all proof steps are deductive and contribute to the proof in an obvious fashion. *Inductionless induction proofs are not deductive.*

6. A proof with traditional induction either succeeds or halts with a finite number of irreducible equations. *These equations frequently suggest lemmas that allow the proof to succeed.* With diverging inductionless induction proofs all one can do is look at an apparently random set of critical pairs which themselves depend on the details of the completion process used.

7. *In traditional induction user interaction points are well defined* with a finite choice of possible actions. Experience suggests that it is easier to supply information about inductive hypotheses than to order critical pairs. Inductionless induction is entirely

automatic. Starting proofs requires no user interaction but getting them to succeed often involves considerable user interaction.

These are serious drawbacks which render inductionless induction unsuitable for the kinds of proofs required in hardware (as well as in software) verification. While the set of theorems provable by traditional induction is not necessarily larger, the proofs are often easier to find. Inductionless induction is of considerable theoretical interest; but traditional induction is of considerable practical utility.

4.5   Relevant work

Here we mention briefly other work involving applications of equational specifications and term rewriting techniques to the specification and verification of hardware.

The first attempt at linking OBJ specifications with hardware is reported in [SPG81], where the original OBJ-T version of the language [GT79] was used to specify and test hardware building blocks. OBJ-T is similar to UMIST OBJ; the only difference between them is the provision of error operators and equations in OBJ-T. [SPG81] used OBJ-T to model functional properties of the Am25LS157, a simple multiplexor (15 gates).

The RAP system [GH86a] is intended for rapid prototyping of algebraic specifications. It also includes narrowing, an algorithm for solving equations in conditional and unconditional equational theories [Hus85]. Narrowing is similar to the resolution algorithms used in logic programming languages. The largest reported specification processed by RAP is a specification of the INTEL 8085 microprocessor which contains about 250 axioms [Ges86].

[CPC87] addresses verification of functional correctness of combinational devices. Their design verification system is based on term rewriting techniques and supports a combination of procedures including the Kapur and Narendran version of the Knuth–Bendix algorithm [KN84]. Their normaliser implements a decision procedure for Hsiang's axiomatisation of Boolean algebra [Hsi81] where normal forms consist of AND and XOR. The proofs are refutational. The system compares well with simulators; an 8-bit ALU slice with 200 gates was completely verified in 25 minutes compared with 270 minutes of estimated simulation time. However, the modularity of designs is not exploited, and the system cannot handle sequential circuits.

Narendran and Stillman [NS86] have used the AFFIRM-85 verification system [MC85] and later the RRL theorem prover [KSZ86] for hardware verification work as part of the Interactive VHDL Workstation project. Behavioural descriptions are first-order predicate calculus sentences. Such descriptions include initialisation assumptions, operational assumptions as well as the behavioural statement. The structural specification of a circuit is then obtained by instantiating these descriptions with actual names of wires. This approach can handle combinational as well as sequential systems. However, using an automatic theorem prover such as RRL does not allow user interaction which is nearly always necessary for complicated proofs.

[MNP87] contains an elaborate model of hardware devices tackling issues such as bidirectionality, gate capacitance and charge sharing. All these concepts are modelled as abstract data types. This approach has been used with the AFFIRM-85 and RRL systems.

	REVE	UMIST OBJ
Expressive power	low	fair
Verification	automatic	N/A
Simulation	yes	yes
CAD interface	no	no
Reasoning framework	term rewriting and inductionless induction	N/A
Reasoning overheads	fair	N/A
User friendliness	fair	good
Performance	good for small examples	fair
Required expertise	high	low

Table 4.1: Summary evaluation of the term rewriting approach

The verification approach used by Garland, Guttag and Staunstrup [GGS88, SGG92] is the closest to our work here. In the place of UMIST OBJ, they use the techniques of synchronised transitions [SG90] for specification purposes. In their notation, state components are denoted by variables and combinatorial functions by transitions. The underlying computational model views a circuit as a collection of asynchronously computing automata, i.e. as a parallel program. Verification consists of proving functional properties of circuits based on invariant assertions on transitions [LS84] and is carried out using LP [GG89], a successor of REVE, developed to verify properties of LARCH specifications [GH86b]. LP has a variety of inference rules such as reduction to normal form, induction, inductionless induction, proof by cases and contradiction, instantiation, transformation and critical pairs. The approach has been used to verify properties of arbiter trees and a ring oscillator. Interestingly, the LP team has built a compiler which extracts axioms and proof obligations from the circuit specification which are then used as input to the theorem prover [SGG92]. Deciding exactly what to prove about a design is a significant issue which we also address later on in this book in our CHDL, FUNNEL.

Kapur and Musser have recently developed Tecton, an algebraic framework for specifying and verifying generic components [KMN92, KM92]. The Tecton language is related to both OBJ and LARCH and is implemented on top of RRL. The language has relatively simple denotational semantics and the corresponding proof theory requires only first order and inductive proof methods as do LARCH and OBJ.

4.6 Discussion

We summarise our findings on UMIST OBJ and REVE in table 4.1. Specifying hardware components as abstract data types in a language such as UMIST OBJ seems to provide an interesting alternative to traditional hardware description languages. It combines executability with hierarchically structured and readable component specifications. In contrast with traditional CHDLs, it has formal semantics which allows verification. These conclusions must, however, be conditioned by the ability to satisfactorily model sequential as well as combinational devices. UMIST OBJ is strictly first order and therefore it is not possible to specify behaviour in time through second order functions. The concept of Lucid histories does not seem to be suitable for this purpose either. In this respect, the absence of parameterisation is the most serious obstacle. Furthermore, the efficiency of the implementation of the language is of vital importance when animating specifications. Even for this small adder example, the performance of UMIST OBJ was far removed from what would be considered acceptable simulation speeds.

Verifying behaviour using REVE is problematic. In common with other automatic theorem provers REVE suffers from three fundamental drawbacks:

1. The proof of many theorems requires some degree of user interaction. Such interactive facilities can make the difference between a proof being successful or not. REVE does not allow any user interaction apart from asking user guidance in performing function symbol orderings. However, the proof optimisation techniques presented in Section 4.3.3 effectively provide an implicit interactive facility.

2. It is unlikely that the first description of a circuit will be correct. It is therefore very important that the theorem prover provides diagnostic information when it fails. When a REVE proof fails there is no indication as to what might have gone wrong.

3. We have seen that inductionless induction is not a viable technique for most of the problems that must be dealt with in hardware verification. REVE therefore offers a severely limited proof environment. This has been recognised in its successor, LP, where traditional induction has effectively replaced inductionless induction.

In summary, we have found UMIST OBJ a suitable notation for specifying combinational devices but a poor candidate for dealing with sequential systems. Although REVE proofs can be surprisingly succinct, they are rare for the set of problems that is of interest of us. RRL and LP rectify this problem to a large extent; but they offer limited scope for specification purposes. The next three chapters address and solve both these deficiencies of the term rewriting approach.

Chapter 5

OBJ3 as a Hardware Specification Language

5.1 Introduction

In the previous chapter we identified the shortcomings of UMIST OBJ as a specification language and of term rewriting as a generalised theorem proving technique. The work which we will describe in this and the next two chapters was motivated by our desire to combine specification, simulation and verification within a single formalism whilst retaining the advantages of term rewriting and equational logic. The essential ingredients of the OBJ3 paradigm on which we expand here, are algebraic semantics and controlled term rewriting. The expressive power of OBJ3 is fully explored allowing the definition and manipulation of second order functions without leaving the domain of first order equational logic.

   Although, as we have seen, this is not the first attempt to use the OBJ family of languages in the design of digital systems it is the most accomplished one. The work described here is related to [Gog88] where Goguen develops the theoretical basis of the theorem proving approach and uses OBJ3 for specifying hardware in a limited context. In comparison, our approach has a practical bias in that we are primarily interested in the methodological aspects of using OBJ3 to specify, simulate and verify a wide range of synchronous digital systems.

   This chapter begins with an introduction to OBJ3. We then formulate and use the methodological principles of specification with OBJ3 which are illustrated on a wide variety of device classes ranging from switch level circuits to synchronous concurrent algorithms.

5.2 Aspects of OBJ3

5.2.1 Overview

OBJ3 [GW88] is the latest in a series of incremental implementations of OBJ. Although the original language was intended as an attempt to extend algebraic data type theory to handle errors and partial functions, in the years hence, OBJ has come to be viewed and used, first as an executable algebraic specification language [GM82, GCS89] (Goguen notes that the original motivation for implementing OBJ was the observation that published equational ADT specifications were very often wrong!), then as a programming language [GKMW87] and finally as a theorem proving tool [Gog88]. In what follows, we will use the term **OBJ** to refer to the family of languages and **OBJ3** to refer to the latest implementation. A brief history of OBJ and its applications is shown in [GW88].

There are two major syntactic entities in OBJ3; *objects* which contain executable code and *theories* which contain non executable assertions. The denotational semantics of OBJ3 is given by order sorted algebras (OSAs) [GM89] and its operational semantics is given by order sorted term rewriting. The denotation of an OBJ3 text P is a standard (initial) model of P if P is an object and the variety of all models of P if P is a theory. The operational semantics of objects is defined by (conditional) equations which are interpreted as *left $\rightarrow$ right* rewrite rules. The latest versions of OBJ3 support (limited) rewriting on theories which corresponds to reasoning about the variety in theorem proving terms.

Objects and theories support two fundamental features of OBJ3, namely *subsorts* and *parameterisation*. In the following section we will present those features of OBJ3 which are particularly relevant for hardware specification. For a detailed exposition of the language the reader is referred to [GW88, Win89].

5.2.2   Semantics

The initial algebra approach [MG85] takes the unique (up to isomorphism) initial algebra as the standard or most representative model of a set of equations, that is as the representation independent standard of comparison for correctness. [BG82] shows that an algebra is initial iff it satisfies the following properties:

No junk Every element can be named using the given constant and operation symbols.

No confusion All ground equations true of the algebra can be proved from the given
     equations.

For canonical systems, the rewrite rule operational semantics agrees with initial algebra semantics in the sense that the reduced forms constitute an initial algebra [Gog80]. Since OBJ3 is based on OSAs, it is important to note that this result easily extends to this case [SNGM89]. OSAs, and thus OBJ3, provide a completely general programming formalism, in the sense that any partially computable functions can be defined (unpublished theorem of J. Meseguer).

5.2.3   Subsorting

Single sorted logic offers the dubious advantage that anything can be applied to anything. We have seen in the previous chapter that a serious drawback of REVE is the lack of sorting which leads to a massive search space during proofs. The obvious alternative, many sorted logic is too restrictive since it does not support overloaded function symbols and has no satisfactory way of handling errors such as division by zero or popping an empty stack.

OSA overcomes these obstacles by allowing functions that would otherwise have to be partial to be total by restricting them to a subsort. The essence of OSA is to provide a preorder, $<$, on sorts. The standard interpretation of $<$ is the subset relation. For any two sorts s, s' of a signature Σ, $s < s'$ holds in a Σ–algebra A if $A_s \subseteq A_{s'}$. OSA specifications support inheritance (a sort may have more than one distinct supersort) and sort polymorphism (operator overloading).

5.2.4 Hierarchical structure

A digital system specification is likely to contain a multiplicity of modules. It is therefore desirable to make the hierarchical structure of module dependency explicit, so that whenever one module uses sorts or operations declared in another, the other must be explicitly imported to the first, and must also be defined earlier in the text. A specification developed in this way has the abstract structure of an *acyclic graph* of modules. In this sense, lower level (less abstract) modules do not implement higher level (more abstract) modules, but rather, higher level modules include lower level ones. Module hierarchies do not only represent system structure; they can also be used for maintaining multiple, mutually inconsistent structures as subhierarchies, for example, a family of partially overlapping system designs. The module hierarchy may, therefore, be used for experimenting with different design decisions.

OBJ3 has four import modes, the meaning of which is related to the initial algebra semantics of objects. An importation of module M' by module M is

protecting iff M' adds no new data items of sorts from M and also identifies no old data items of sorts from M (no junk and no confusion).

using if none of the initiality properties are guaranteed.

extending iff the no confusion property is preserved.

including which is similar to using but operationally is treated as protecting.

To reuse specifications or other components, they and their contexts must be available. Files provide a convenient way to store and retrieve modules and their contexts. OBJ3 files may contain modules as well as top level commands which can be used to fetch the context of the file. Any persistent file system, such as Unix for example, can then be used to organise files into libraries. Thus, OBJ3 easily accommodates the need to maintain component libraries which is standard practice in digital design.

5.2.5 Parameterisation

Parameterised programming is a general and powerful technique for software design, production, reuse and maintenance. All these issues are also relevant to digital design and generality of hardware specifications and proofs is desirable. OBJ3 contains substantial parameterisation facilities. Specifications are broken into highly parameterised, mind sized, internally coherent modules and new designs are constructed by instantiating, transforming and combining these modules. Maintenance is facilitated by editing and re-executing such designs. Reusability is enhanced by the flexibility of the parameterisation, composition and transformation mechanisms.

Moreover, a language with sufficiently powerful parameterised modules can achieve highly structured designs *without* higher order functions. We have seen that the lack of higher order functions is a severe handicap in the specification of sequential circuits with UMIST OBJ. OBJ3 rectifies this deficiency. This is fortunate and useful because it means that correctness proofs can be done entirely within first order logic without the reasoning overheads of higher order logics. Moreover, it is possible to impose and assert semantic requirements on modules and hence on functions. Later on in this chapter we expand on the associated specification methodology and the next chapter will state the theoretical basis of reasoning about higher order functions within the domain of first order equational logic. The case against the use of higher order functions in programming is eloquently made in [Gog89].

The basic building blocks of parameterised specifications in OBJ3 (which are considered as free extensions of the parameter requirement specifications) are theories, views and module expressions, each of which can be parameterised.

Theories express semantic properties of modules and module interfaces. In general, OBJ3 theories have the same structure as objects; in particular theories have sorts, subsorts, operations, variables and equations, can import other theories and objects, can be parameterised and can have views. The difference is that objects are executable, while theories just define properties. The ability to express semantic properties such as the associativity of an operation as part of the interface of a module is unique in OBJ3 specifications.

Views show how a module satisfies a theory; that is they describe a binding of an actual parameter to a requirement theory. More precisely, a view v from a theory T to a module M, denoted by $v : T \Rightarrow M$, consists of a mapping from the sorts of T to the sorts of M preserving the subsort relation, and a mapping from the operations of T to the operations of M preserving arity, value sort and the meaning of attributes, such that every equation in T is true in every model of M. Default views are allowed when they are obvious.

Parameterised modules (objects or theories) are *instantiated* by supplying actual modules to formal parameters. This requires a view from each formal parameter requirement theory to the corresponding actual module. The result of such an instantiation is to replace each requirement theory by its corresponding actual module, using the views to bind actual names to formal names, without producing multiple copies of shared submodules.

Module expressions describe complex interconnections of modules. They also permit modifying modules in various ways, thus making it possible to use a given module in a variety of contexts and to improve the efficiency of existing designs. The major combination modes are instantiation and summation. A module can be modified by:

extending a module by adding to its functionality,

renaming some of its external interface,

restricting by eliminating some of its functionality,

encapsulating existing specifications, and by

modifying its contents.

This approach allows design transformations right inside the specification.

5.2.6 Controlled modulo rewriting

It is natural and convenient to consider certain properties of an operation as attributes that are declared at the same time as its syntax. These properties include axioms such as associativity, commutativity and identity which have both syntactic and semantic consequences. OBJ3's operational semantics are supported by a powerful, order sorted, modulo attributes, term rewriting engine. An important variant of term rewriting, called rewriting modulo, involves rewriting *equivalent classes* of terms rather than individual terms. For example, in rewriting modulo the associativity of +, terms that differ only in the association of subterms that are the arguments of + are considered equivalent (e.g. a + (b + c) and (a + b) + c). Rewriting modulo associativity and the other attributes allows rewrites that would be impossible if these properties were regarded as rewrite rules (consider what happens when a rule such as a + b = b + a is introduced in the rewrite system). Rewriting modulo attributes, eliminates many tedious manipulations required in systems with less sophisticated term rewriting capabilities such as LCF or HOL where manual instantiations are required.

In OBJ3 terms can be rewritten to canonical form by exhaustive application of the appropriate rules. Although this is a very convenient feature, once more eliminating tedious manipulations, in some circumstances it is desirable to have the ability to control the rewriting process. OBJ3 supports controlled rewriting by labelling rules and allowing selective application to terms and subterms. Rules may be reversed and may contain let clauses for readability purposes. Allowing the controlled application of conditional rules requires shifting the focus of reduction to the instantiated condition of a rule, thus allowing controlled application of rules to this condition.

5.3 Specifying with OBJ3

In the previous section we have shown that OBJ3 has features, in particular parameterisation, which render it very convenient for expressing and manipulating digital designs specifications. Here we show how various aspects of synchronous digital systems can be modelled in OBJ3.

5.3.1 Combinational devices

Combinational devices exhibit behaviour which is merely dependent on input values and therefore do not require modelling of time dependency. Since their behaviour is causal, it can be modelled directly with functions. Wires are constants and are represented by the values which they carry. *Power* and *ground* are represented by TRUE and FALSE respectively. Components are considered as breaking lines. The circuit of figure 5.1 is then modelled by the following object:

```
obj CIRCUIT is extending BOOL.
  ops x y z w o : -> Bool.
  eq w = y and z.
  eq o = x or w.
endo
```

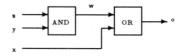

Figure 5.1: A simple combinational circuit

The circuit is modelled by a set of linear equations. The simplest combinational circuits (not involving feedback) have what Goguen calls a *triangular form* [Gog88]. Given a set of input variables $i_1, \ldots, i_n$ and an ordering of internal variables $p_1, \ldots, p_m$ such that each p_k is a boolean function of input and smaller internal variables, a circuit has the following form:

$$p_1 \;=\; f_1(i_1, \ldots, i_n)$$
$$\vdots$$
$$p_k \;=\; f_k(i_1, \ldots, i_n, p_1, \ldots, p_{k-1})$$

A circuit is *consistent* [Gog88] with respect to a given set of inputs, iff for each choice of input values there is at least one possible value for each internal variable that satisfies its system of equations. A consistent circuit is *underdetermined* [Gog88] with respect to a given set of inputs, iff for some choice of input values, there is more than one possible value for some internal variable, satisfying its system of equations.

5.3.2   Synchronous sequential devices

As we have seen, modelling sequential devices requires dealing with time dependency since such devices "remember" their past, that is their behaviour depends on past (through current state) as well as current inputs. Such behaviour can be naturally modelled by viewing wires as functions from times to values rather than as simple constants. Components, therefore, need to accept functions as values thus taking the specification into the second order domain.

OBJ3 is a first order notation and therefore its use in a higher order context needs to be semantically justified. The theoretical underpinnings are discussed in [Gog88], where ordinary equational logic which only permits quantification over constants, is generalised to an extended case which permits quantification over arbitrary function symbols. Equations containing variable function symbols consist of a signature Φ of variables disjoint from Σ, where Σ is an indexed family of sets, plus two $(\Sigma \cup \Phi)$ terms. Equations are written abstractly as $(\forall \Phi)\, t = t'$ or concretely $(\forall x, y, f, g)\, t = t'$ when $\Phi = \{x, y, f, g\}$. In the ordinary case Φ contains no function symbols and equations are written abstractly as $(\forall X)\, t = t'$ or concretely $(\forall x, y)\, t = t'$ when $X = \{x, y\}$. The result is a powerful first order calculus for reasoning about first order functions.

In fact, the verification of combinational circuits can also be carried out by viewing the circuit as potentially sequential. This can be done easily by replacing each wire variable, whether an input i_k or a non input p_k, by a function of type `Time -> Prop` (that is from a copy of the natural numbers to truth values represented by propositions) evaluated at an arbitrary time t, e.g. by $f_k(t)$.

The treatment of time dependency in OBJ3 is similar to the one in Boyer–Moore logic since both notations are based on first order logics without existential quantification. Components in OBJ3 are modelled by observing the behaviour of their input/output ports. One important difference is however, whereas the overall structure of a system is obscure in Boyer–Moore (because components cannot be *named*), OBJ3 allows *explicit* modelling of components through its parameterisation facilities and thus enhances structure. For instance the D type flip flop of chapter 3 is defined as follows:

```
obj DTYPE[D :: D-th , RESET :: RESET-th ] is
  ops q q-bar : Time -> Prop .
  var T : Time .
  ceq  q(s T) = false if reset(T) .
  ceq  q(s T) = d(T) if not reset(T) .
  eq  q-bar(T) = not q(T) .
endo
```

Time is modelled by natural numbers (with the usual successor operator s_) and **Prop** denotes propositions in the propositional calculus (as encoded in section 6.3.1.6) which we use for reasoning in the next chapter. From now on wires will be modelled as functions from times to propositions. The *parameters* of the object are the *input ports* and the *operations* defined by the object are the *output ports*. We adopt this convention which, although not necessary, does lead to more readable specifications. The input theories shown below define the requirements that the actual parameters should meet when instantiating the object.

```
obj PRIMS is protecting TIME + PROPC . endo

th RESET-th is protecting PRIMS .
  op reset : Time -> Prop . endth

th D-th is protecting PRIMS .
  op d : Time -> Prop . endth
```

This notion of modular component construction allows the development of a library of primitives which can be instantiated whenever required thus enhancing component reuse. In the case of the twisted ring counter for instance, 3 D type flip flops are needed which are obtained by simply *renaming* the standard D type:

```
obj DTYPE1[D :: D-th , RESET :: RESET-th]
  is protecting DTYPE[D, RESET] *
     (op q to q1, op q-bar to q1-bar) . endo

obj DTYPE2[D :: D-th , RESET :: RESET-th]
  is protecting DTYPE[D, RESET] *
     (op q to q2, op q-bar to q2-bar) . endo

obj DTYPE3[D :: D-th , RESET :: RESET-th]
  is protecting DTYPE[D, RESET] *
     (op q to q3, op q-bar to q3-bar) . endo
```

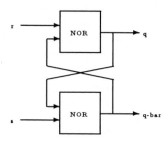

Figure 5.2: An RS flip flop

Primitive components are composed using module expressions in a way similar to that used for binding names to ports in structured VHDL descriptions [VHD87]. The twisted ring counter specification is shown below:

```
obj TRC'[D3 :: D3-th, RESET :: RESET-th ] is
   protecting DTYPE2[view from D2-th to DTYPE3[D3,RESET] is
                     op : d2 to : q3 .
                  endv, RESET] . endo

obj TRC[D3 :: D3-th , RESET :: RESET-th ] is
   protecting DTYPE1[view from D1-th to TRC'[D3,RESET] is
                     op : d1 to : q2 .
                  endv, RESET] .
   var T : Time .
   eq  d3(T) = (q1-bar(T)) and ((q2-bar(T)) or (q3(T))) . endo
```

5.3.3   Circuits with feedback

Circuits often involve feedback. This is naturally modelled with mutually recursive equations. Whereas these are problematic in Boyer–Moore logic, they can be trivially used in OBJ3 specifications. The RS flip flop of figure 5.2 is specified by the following object:

```
th R-th is protecting PRIMS .
op r : Time -> Prop . endth

th S-th is pr R-th * (op r to s) . endth

obj RSFF[R :: R-th, S :: S-th] is
   ops q q-bar : Time -> Prop .
   var T : Time .
   eq q(s T) = not (r(T) or q-bar(T)) .
   eq q-bar(s T) = not (q(T) or s(T)) .
endo
```

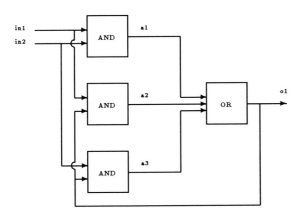

Figure 5.3: A Müller C-element

5.3.4   Generic devices and composition

The parameterisation features of OBJ3 allow the specification of generic components which can be instantiated as required in designs. Moreover, this generality is available without any extra effort on the designer's part as for example is the case when generic HOL specifications are required [Joy91]. This fact applies to all specifiable types of devices. In addition, the ability to combine components using bindings provided by views allows specifications with explicit structure. Below we illustrate these aspects using a Müller C-element.

The circuit of figure 5.3 implements a consensus mechanism. The gates have unit delay values. The intended behaviour is that the output of the circuit remains constant as long as the input values are different and changes to the value of the inputs when these are in agreement.

A non generic, non compositional specification which expresses the connectivity of the circuit is given by the following object:

```
obj MULLER is protecting PRIMS .
  ops in1 in2 a1 a2 a3 o1 : Time -> Prop .
  var T : Time .
  eq a1(s T) = in1(T) and in2(T) .
  eq a2(s T) = in1(T) and o1(T) .
  eq a3(s T) = in2(T) and o1(T) .
  eq o1(s T) = a1(T) or a2(T) or a3(T) .
endo
```

The specification is compact and, for a circuit of this complexity, adequate. But it is not general enough and when specifications grow larger, the intended structure is obscured. Furthermore, this type of specification does not lend itself to reuse through libraries. The specification is typical of first order notations such as Boyer–Moore logic and equational logic as implemented, amongst others, by the RRL and LP theorem proving tools.

Using the parameterisation facilities in OBJ3, a general specification can be written where structure is explicit and component reuse is enhanced. The first step involves the construction of the input requirement theories:

```
th INPUT is protecting PRIMS . op in_ : Time -> Prop . endth
th INPUT1 is protecting PRIMS . op in1_ : Time -> Prop . endth
th INPUT2 is protecting PRIMS . op in2_ : Time -> Prop . endth
th INPUT3 is protecting PRIMS . op in3_ : Time -> Prop . endth
```

The same result can also be obtained by using module expressions to effect the required renamings. We now proceed to define the behaviour of parameterised AND and OR gates which are taken as primitives and are, therefore, purely defined by behaviour:

```
obj AND[IN1 :: INPUT1, IN2 :: INPUT2] is
  op out : Time -> Prop .
  var T : Time .
  eq out(0) = false .
  eq out(s T) = (in1 T) and (in2 T) .
endo

obj OR[IN1 :: INPUT1, IN2 :: INPUT2, IN3 :: INPUT3] is
  op out : Time -> Prop .
  var T : Time .
  eq out(0) = false .
  eq out(s T) = (in1 T) or (in2 T) or (in3 T) .
endo
```

We now need to make instances of these components for use in our specification. We use module importations and module expressions.

```
obj AND1[IN1 :: INPUT1, IN2 :: INPUT2] is
  pr AND[IN1,IN2] * (op out to a1) . endo

obj AND2[IN1 :: INPUT1, IN2 :: INPUT2] is
  pr AND[IN1,IN2] * (op out to a2) . endo

obj AND3[IN1 :: INPUT1, IN2 :: INPUT2] is
  pr AND[IN1,IN2] * (op out to a3) . endo

obj OR1[IN1 :: INPUT1, IN2 :: INPUT2, IN3 :: INPUT3] is
  pr OR[IN1,IN2,IN3] * (op out to o1) . endo
```

We are now ready to compose these instances in order to obtain the Müller C-element.

```
obj MULLER[IN1 :: INPUT1, IN2 :: INPUT2] is
  op med : Time -> Prop .
  pr OR1[(a1).(AND1[IN1,IN2]),
         (a2).(AND2[IN1,op med]),
         (a3).(AND3[op med,IN2])] .
  var T : Time .
  eq med(T) = o1(T) .
endo
```

Figure 5.4: CMOS n-transistor

Figure 5.5: CMOS p-transistor

The specification uses default views, for instance AND1[IN1, IN2] and the composition is achieved by using *qualifiers* (selectors) as in (a1).AND1[IN1, IN2] to select port bindings. A further feature of this specification concerns the treatment of feedback. The operator med and the equation binding it to the output of the OR gate, show how mutually recursive module instantiations are constructed.

We believe that the second specification is better because it is more general, has explicit structure and encourages reuse. OBJ3 uniquely allows such specifications, in contrast with other first order notations.

5.3.5 Switch level devices

CMOS devices are modelled using conditional equations. The n-transistor of figure 5.4 conducts when its gate is high and is modelled as a switch:

$$a = b \text{ if } g$$

Similarly, the p-transistor of figure 5.5 is modelled by the equation:

$$a = b \text{ if } not(g)$$

Using these two models, the CMOS exclusive OR gate of figure 5.6 can be specified as follows:

```
obj XOR is extending PROP.
  ops i1 i2 p1 p2 p3 o : -> Prop.
  ceq p3 = p2 if i1.
  ceq i2 = o if not(i1).
  ceq i2 = o if p3.
  ceq i1 = o if not(i2).
  ceq o = p3 if i2.
endo
```

As we have seen previously, these models are logically correct but not physically accurate because real transistors do not behave as switches. In this respect, although OBJ3 is not

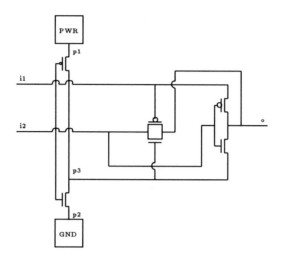

Figure 5.6: A CMOS XOR gate

superior to other notations, it is as good as much more expressive notations such as the typed λ-calculus of HOL.

In fact, in cases of unidirectional devices, OBJ3 provides more accurate models than HOL because functions are unidirectional whereas relations are not. As Musser points out [MNP87] the predicate $inv(i, o) = (o = \neg i)$ can be shown to be true of the circuit in figure 5.7. This however implies that the *reverse* is also true, that is $inv(i, o) = (i = \neg o)$ which manifestly is not the case. The same circuit can be specified in OBJ as follows:

```
obj INV is extending PROP.
  ops i o p1 p2 : -> Prop.
  eq p1 = true.
  eq p2 = false.
  ceq o = p1 if not(i).
  ceq o = p2 if i.
endo
```

It is easily deduced from these equations that o = not(i). It is, however, impossible to deduce that i = not(o) because equations are interpreted as *left → right* rewrite rules.

5.3.6   Synchronous concurrent algorithms

A synchronous concurrent algorithm (SCA) consists of a network of modules and channels which are synchronised by a global clock and compute and communicate data in parallel. SCAs are a powerful paradigm with applications ranging from clocked hardware and systolic arrays to neural networks and cellular automata. The mathematical theory of SCAs is based on several, computationally equivalent models of deterministic parallel computing devised for the theory of computable functions on many sorted algebras. The theory of SCAs is studied thoroughly in [Tho87]. [Har89] contains a treatment of hardware specifications using SCAs. It is with this guise of SCAs that we are concerned here.

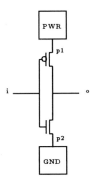

Figure 5.7: A CMOS inverter

These parallel algorithms are complex and extensive simulation is required in order to understand their behaviour. Our aim here is to provide standard ways of encoding SCA specifications into OBJ3 in order to facilitate simulation and verification of their properties. Below, we present a systematic method applicable to a wide variety of SCAs which formulates algorithms and specifications algebraically and maps them onto OBJ3 specifications in a routine way, thus allowing experimentation. Although here we present a simple example, these techniques are fully expanded upon and used on the linear expression evaluator of Fuch's pixel planes architecture [Fuc88] of a graphics engine later on in this book. The treatment of a line drawing architecture is shown in [Eke91].

We consider an SCA as a network of *sources* and *channels* computing and communicating data as shown in figure 5.8. For simplicity, we assume that all the data is drawn from a single set A. The network has a global discrete clock $T = \{0, 1, 2, \ldots\}$ to synchronise computations and the flow of data between modules. There are c sources labelled $s_1, \ldots, s_c$ and k modules labelled $m_1, \ldots, m_k$. The sources perform no computation; they are simply input ports where fresh data arrives at each clock cycle. The action of a module m_i is specified by a function $f_i : A^{p(i)} \to A$ where $p(i)$ is the number of inputs to the module. Results are read out from a subset of the modules $m_{a(1)}, \ldots, m_{a(d)}$ which are called *sinks*. New data are available at each source, and new results at each sink, at every tick of the global clock T. Thus, the algorithm processes infinite sequences or data streams. A data stream from A is represented by a map $\underline{a} : T \to A$ and the set of data streams is represented by the set $[T \to A]$ of all such maps. Thus the I/O behaviour of an architecture initialised by b, is specified by a mapping V_b (stream transformer) from source streams to sink streams:

$$V_b : [T \to A]^c \to [T \to A]^d$$

Each module m_i is represented by a *value function*

$$v_i : T \times [T \to A]^c \times A^k \to A$$

In the formulation of SCAs, the functions f_i that specify the actions of the modules together with the constant 0 and operations $t + 1$ and *eval*, form a stream algebra with carriers T, A and $T \to A$. We call this the *component algebra*. The value functions v_i that

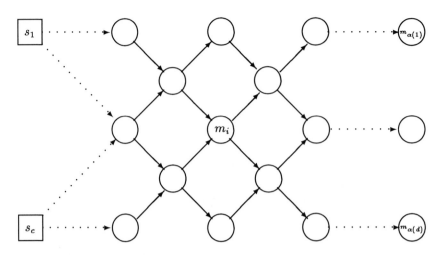

Figure 5.8: Synchronous concurrent algorithm as a network

define the SCA, similarly give rise to a stream algebra which we call the *program algebra*. Finally, if we just consider the value functions $v_{a(i)}$ of the output modules, we get a third stream algebra which we call the *task algebra*.

The sort A and its operations in the component algebra may be defined abstractly by a set of equations in which case we have a class of component algebras which are *standard* in that time T has its standard interpretation. In this case the algorithm determines classes of program and task algebras which are also standard.

The equational logic of OBJ3 is very simple but is powerful enough to allow the encoding and verification of many SCA correctness problems. This is because any set of recursive functions can be mapped into algebraic specifications [TT91]. Thus the essence of our method for expressing SCA hardware algorithms into OBJ3 specifications consists of the following steps:

1. Formulate the hardware in terms of SCAs.

2. Formalise the data and component modules of each SCA as a class of stream algebras and find an appropriate axiomatisation of this class.

3. Formalise each SCA by means of value functions over the class of its component algebras.

4. Translate the axiomatisation of the component algebras and the primitive recursive equations that define the value functions into appropriate OBJ3 theories.

We show below the application of these techniques to a very simple example of delay modules composed to form a shift register as shown in figure 5.9. The value functions are $q_i : T \times [T \rightarrow R]^2 \rightarrow R$ where R is the algebra $\langle R|0, +\rangle$. The functions are defined as follows:

$$q_i(0, \underline{v}) = 0$$

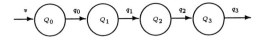

Figure 5.9: SCA network for a shift register

$$q_0(t + 1, \underline{v}) = \underline{v}(t)$$
$$q_{i+1}(t + 1, \underline{v}) = q_i(t, \underline{v})$$

Time T is defined by the following OBJ3 object:

```
obj TIME is sort Time.
  op 0 : -> Time.
  op s_ : Time -> Time.
endo
```

R is defined by the following theory:

```
theory ABS is sort Abs.
  op 0 : -> Abs.
  op _+_ : Abs Abs -> Abs.
  vars A B C : Abs.
  eq A + (B + C) = (A + B) + C.
  eq A + 0 = A.
endth
```

Now, for a shift register of length 4, we have the following definition:

```
theory SHIFT is protecting TIME + ABS.
  ops q0 q1 q2 q3 : Time -> Abs.
  var T : Time.
  eq q0(0) = 0.
  eq q0(s T) = v(T).
  eq q1(0) = 0.
  eq q1(s T) = q0(T).
  eq q2(0) = 0.
  eq q2(s T) = q1(T).
  eq q3(0) = 0.
  eq q3(s T) = q2(T).
endth
```

Once this encoding is complete, the algorithm can be simulated or verified using the term rewriting engine of OBJ3. The type of stream transformers that SCAs give rise to, while second order objects, can be reasoned about using first order methods. Moreover, the SCA simultaneous primitive recursive definitions of the value functions are expressed in OBJ3 in a very natural way which eliminates the need for counter intuitive encodings which are required for example by the Boyer–Moore logic[PS89]. OBJ3 offers, therefore, a very convenient framework for expressing a wide variety of computational paradigms which are encompassed by SCAs.

This specification concludes the specification case studies. In the next chapter we discuss ways of reasoning about such specifications using OBJ3.

Chapter 6

Theorem Proving with OBJ3

6.1 Introduction

The use of OBJ3 as a theorem proving tool, which is discussed in this chapter, completes the OBJ3 paradigm and allows the use of the language for specifying, simulating and reasoning about synchronous digital designs.

We begin by presenting a straightforward simulation technique which we then extend to general theorem proving. The theoretical underpinnings of the theorem proving approach have been established by Goguen [Gog88, Gog90, Gog91] and are summarised here. We then discuss our proof methodology and illustrate the techniques with a number of examples.

6.2 Simulating with OBJ3

As we have seen, it is desirable to perform specification, simulation and verification within a single formalism in order to avoid overheads and transcription errors. Uniquely amongst the formalisms we have discussed, OBJ3 allows the use of the specification text for simulation *without* changes, thus essentially offering a *gratis* simulator. This is of course because OBJ was designed as a (partially) executable specification language.

A parameterised specification can be used for simulation by merely defining instantiating objects. In the case of simulation these objects define the input test patterns; we shall see later that for verification purposes they simply assert that the inputs exist. Here is the text of the instantiating objects for the Müller C-element:

```
obj INST is pr PRIMS .
  ops in1 in2 : Time -> Prop . endo

obj TEST is extending MULLER[(in1).INST, (in2).INST] .
  var T : Time .
  eq in1(0) = false .
  eq in1(s 0) = false .
  eq in1(s s T) = not in1(T) .
  eq in2(0) = false .
  eq in2(s T) = not in2(T) .
endo
```

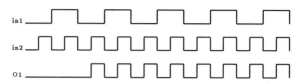

Figure 6.1: Müller C-element I/O waveforms

Figure 6.1 shows the input test patterns and the expected outputs after 2 time cycles. Since the specification is built from unit delay components, the outputs will settle to the predicted values after two clock ticks.

The simulation runs are conducted by running reductions in the test object as follows:

```
reduce in TEST : o1(0) .
reduce in TEST : o1(1) .
reduce in TEST : o1(2) .
reduce in TEST : o1(3) .
reduce in TEST : o1(4) .
reduce in TEST : o1(5) .
reduce in TEST : o1(6) .
reduce in TEST : o1(7) .
```

Sample simulation results are shown below:

```
reduce in TEST : o1(3)
rewrites: 50
result Bool: false
==========================================
reduce in TEST : o1(4)
rewrites: 80
result Bool: false
==========================================
reduce in TEST : o1(5)
rewrites: 136
result Bool: true
```

Even though this kind of simulation is straightforward in the context of OBJ3, it has to be noted that the efficiency of term rewriting implementations, although acceptable for simple cases, is not appropriate for medium or large scale simulation. Therefore, alternative simulation techniques need to be developed if OBJ3 is to be used for such a task. Ways of achieving this, although beyond the scope of this book, are briefly discussed in the next chapter. The need for some initial experimentation with specifications is evident when one considers the investment required by verification. We have found the ability to experiment with designs before attempting verification very useful throughout this work. Despite the inherent inefficiency of term rewriting, direct, *investigative* simulation with OBJ3 has proved to be necessary for design time testing of specifications.

6.3 Verifying with OBJ3

At first glance, it may appear odd that a specification language can be used for theorem proving. But OBJ3 *has* formal semantics. Moreover, its semantics *is* the semantics of equational logic and therefore it can be used as a theorem prover for equational logic. It is in fact surprising how much theorem proving can be done with a language that was not intended as a theorem prover.

This third aspect of OBJ3 completes the picture; we now have a notation and tool where we can construct flexible specifications, perform exploratory simulation and conduct formal proof without ever leaving the notation and thus avoiding the need for manual, tedious and error prone transformations or transcriptions. We will discuss the theorem proving environment of OBJ3 by first summarising the theoretical foundations of the approach and then by deliberating on methodological issues of theorem proving.

6.3.1 The logical framework

In general, a logical system consists of a language for stating goals and assumptions plus a set of inference rules together with notions of models and satisfaction. In this approach the language is OBJ3, the inference rules are those of the propositional calculus and we are concerned with initial models and the associated notions of satisfaction. Theoretical work by Goguen [Gog88, Gog90, Gog91] provides justification for various proof methods such as structural induction and deduction.

6.3.1.1 Satisfaction

A *presentation* is a pair $\langle \Sigma, \mathcal{E} \rangle$ consisting of a signature Σ and a set $\mathcal{E}$ of Σ-equations. A Σ-algebra A satisfies $\mathcal{E}$ iff it satisfies every $e \in \mathcal{E}$, denoted by $A \models_\Sigma \mathcal{E}$. In this case, we call A a *P-algebra* where $P = \langle \Sigma, \mathcal{E} \rangle$. If P is ordinary (that is only contains equations without function variables), it is known [MG85] that there exists an initial *P-algebra*, denoted T_P. *Initial satisfaction* is then defined as follows:

Definition 1 $P \overset{\sim}{\models} e \Longleftrightarrow T_P \models e$

6.3.1.2 Variables as constants

In equational logic, variables are defined to be unconstrained constants. This can be exploited to prove equations with variables by regarding the variables as constants and using ground term reduction only. The theorem of constants is well known for first order logic and can be stated in equational logic as follows:

Theorem 1 *Let* Σ, X *be disjoint signatures, let* $\mathcal{E}$ *be a set of of* Σ*-equations and let* A *be a ground* $(\Sigma \cup X)$*-equation. We can consider* A *as a* Σ*-equation,* $(\forall X).A(X)$ *by universally quantifying all constant and function symbols drawn from* X*. Then* $\forall X.A(X)$ *is true in every* $\langle \Sigma, \mathcal{E} \rangle$ *model iff* A *is true in every* $\langle \Sigma \cup X, \mathcal{E} \rangle$ *model.*

Proof See e.g. [Gog88].

6.3.1.3   Reduction as deduction

The theorem of constants together with the term rewriting engine of OBJ3 allow the use of ground term reduction as deduction, that is as a way of calculating what is true. We need a syntactically defined (semi) decidable relation $\vdash_\Sigma$ such that $\mathcal{E} \models_\Sigma e \iff \mathcal{E} \vdash_\Sigma e$ for any finite set of axioms $\mathcal{E}$ and any single sentence e[1]. Although deduction relations with this completeness property cannot be found for all notions of satisfaction, there are many ways to define such a relation for the equational case [Bar77], including the following (due to Goguen [Gog90]):

Definition 2 *Given a signature Σ and a set $\mathcal{E}$ of Σ–equations the following rules of deduction define the Σ–equations that are deducible from $\mathcal{E}$:*

1. **Reflexivity**. *Each equation of the form $(\forall X)\, t = t$ is deducible.*

2. **Transitivity**. *If the equations $(\forall X)\, t = t'$ and $(\forall X)\, t' = t''$ are deducible, then so is $(\forall X)\, t = t''$.*

3. **Bidirectional One Occurrence Subterm Replacement**. *Given $t_0 \in T_\Sigma(\{z\} \cup Y)$ with exactly one occurrence of z and with $z \notin Y$, and given a substitution $\sigma : X \to T_\Sigma(Y)$, if $(\forall Y)\, t_1 = t_2$ or $(\forall Y)t_2 = t_1$ is in $\mathcal{E}$, then $(\forall Y)\, t_0(z \leftarrow \sigma(t_1)) = t_0(z \leftarrow \sigma(t_2))$ is deducible.*

Rewriting is the restriction of (3) above to ground terms in the forward direction.

Theorem 2 (Completeness) *Given a signature Σ, a set of Σ–equations $\mathcal{E}$ and a Σ–equation e, then $\mathcal{E} \models e \iff \mathcal{E} \vdash e$.*

Proof See for example [Bar77].

A limitation of the current OBJ3 implementation is that it provides no way of checking whether a representation is canonical. Although the Knuth–Bendix algorithm can often check the Church–Rosser property, OBJ would need order sorted Knuth–Bendix and unification algorithms for conditional equations and these are not yet sufficiently developed. It seems doubtful in any case, that it would be appropriate to incorporate such nondeterministic procedures in what is after all a specification language. A further complication is of course the need to check termination and as we have seen in the previous chapter this is undecidable.

However, it is *not necessary* that the presentations used in OBJ3 are canonical. If a presentation is not canonical, then some valid formulae may not reduce to true; but because reduction is always sound, we certainly do have a proof whenever the given reductions evaluate to true. On the other hand, it is necessary for the presentation to be canonical if we want a *decision procedure* for which failure of an expression to reduce to true implies that the theorem is really false.

6.3.1.4   Induction

In general, pure equational reduction is inadequate for proving hard properties of standard models and it is necessary to use induction or other techniques. There are some very useful

---

[1]Recall the definition of the equational theory in section 4.2.3; the relation $\vdash_\Sigma$ is equivalent to $=_\mathcal{E}$.

structural induction principles for initial models which let us prove that some predicate holds for all values by proving that it holds for each constructor whenever it holds for the arguments to that constructor.

Given a signature Σ and a Σ–algebra A, a *signature of constructors* for A is a subsignature $\Pi \subseteq \Sigma$ such that the unique Π–homomorphism $T_P \to A$ is surjective. A signature of constructors for a presentation P is a signature of constructors for $A = T_P$. The usual formulation of structural induction is given as follows:

Theorem 3 (Structural induction) *Given a presentation $P = \langle \Sigma, \mathcal{E} \rangle$ and a signature Π of constructors for P, let $Q(x)$ be a $(\Sigma \cup \{x\})$–sentence. Then $\mathcal{E} \overset{\sim}{\models}_\Sigma (\forall x).Q(x)$ if:*

$c \in \Pi_0 \Rightarrow \mathcal{E} \overset{\sim}{\models}_\Sigma Q(c)$ *and* $f \in \Pi_n$ *for* $n > 0 \wedge t_i \in T(\Sigma)$ *for* $i = 1, \ldots, n \Rightarrow$
$\mathcal{E} \overset{\sim}{\models}_\Sigma Q(t_1) \wedge \ldots \wedge Q(t_n) \Rightarrow Q(f(t_1, \ldots, t_n))$.

These results are due to Goguen and are deliberated in [Gog88, Gog90] for the unsorted and the many sorted cases. Examples of inductive proofs are shown later on in this book and elsewhere [Gog88, Gog90, EST91, Eke91] etc.

6.3.1.5   Parameterised modules

[Gog88] contains results which justify techniques for verifying the correctness of OBJ3 parameterised modules. This is important because it extends reuse from components to proofs about components. Once a property of a parameterised module has been verified, we know that it is true of any instantiation of the module, which saves having to prove it separately for each instantiation. This differs from other theorem provers in the sense that properties need *not* be explicitly instantiated for different instances (as in HOL) and component inheritance and polymorphism carry over to proofs.

6.3.1.6   Propositional calculus

Although OBJ3 can be used as a generalised theorem proving tool in the sense that more than one logical system may be built on it, here we will concentrate on the propositional calculus which we use as a decision procedure. This is the reason for treating signal values as *propositions* rather than as booleans. The decision procedure used here is due to Hsiang [Hsi81] and was first coded in OBJ by David Plaisted. Note that the decision procedure *is* canonical for the reasons explained earlier.

```
obj PROPC is sort Prop .
  protecting TRUTH + QID .
  subsorts Id Bool < Prop .

  op _and_ : Prop Prop -> Prop [assoc comm prec 2] .
  op _xor_ : Prop Prop -> Prop [assoc comm prec 3] .
  vars p q r : Prop .
  eq p and false = false .
  eq p and true = p .
  eq p and p = p .
  eq p xor false = p .
  eq p xor p = false .
```

```
   eq p and (q xor r) = (p and q) xor (p and r) .

   op _or_ : Prop Prop -> Prop [assoc comm prec 7] .
   op not_ : Prop -> Prop [prec 1] .
   op _implies_ : Prop Prop -> Prop [prec 9] .
   op _iff_ : Prop Prop -> Prop [assoc prec 11] .
   eq p or q = (p and q) xor p xor q .
   eq not p = p xor true .
   eq p implies q = (p and q) xor p xor true .
   eq p iff q = p xor q xor true .
endo
```

where the object TRUTH contains the truth values *true* and *false* and the operations `_==_`,
`_=/=_` and `if_then_else_fi` and the object QID provides identifiers beginning with the
apostrophe symbol. Both TRUTH and QID are built-ins of OBJ3.

6.3.2   Theorem proving aspects

Let us now return to the twisted ring counter for our first verification example. The
specification is complete and exploratory simulation has been carried out. We need to
define the instantiating object which simply states that the inputs to the circuit exist:

```
obj SIGNALS is
   extending TIME .
   extending PROPC .
   ops t reset d1 d2 d3 : -> Time .
endo
```

The operator t : Time -> Prop is an introduced constant which is perceived as a variable
using the constants theorem. By convention, uppercase names denote variables, whereas
lowercase names denote constants used as variables. Here is the instantiation of our
parameterised twisted ring counter.

```
obj CASE0 is protecting TRC[SIGNALS, SIGNALS]. endo
```

We now make some assumptions about initial conditions which will enable us to show
that the circuit recovers from illegal states within the specified time limits.

```
obj CASE1 is
   protecting CASE0 .
   var T : Time .
   eq  reset(T) = false .
   eq  q1(t) = false .
   eq  q2(t) = true .
   eq  q3(t) = false .
endo

obj CASE2 is
   protecting CASE0 .
   var T : Time .
```

```
  eq  reset(T) = false .
  eq  q1(t) = true .
  eq  q2(t) = false .
  eq  q3(t) = true .
endo
```

The first case corresponds to the circuit being in illegal state 010 at time t while the second one deals with illegal state 101 at time t. The following reductions evaluate as indicated and complete the proofs about the illegal states.

```
reduce in CASE1  : q1(s t) .
---> Should be true
reduce in CASE1  : q2(s t) .
---> Should be false
reduce in CASE1  : q3(s t) .
---> Should be false

reduce in CASE2  : q1(s s t) .
---> Should be true
reduce in CASE2  : q2(s s t) .
---> Should be false
reduce in CASE2  : q3(s s t) .
---> Should be false
```

Similar reductions can be used to show that the circuit cycles through the legal states in the desired sequence.

6.3.2.1 Theorem proving methodology

In terms of methodology, the basic theorem proving principle within the OBJ3 framework is the transformation of problems into *proof scores*. A proof score for a sentence s, is a program P such that if P executes correctly then s is proved. Such OBJ programs consist of modules with sorts, subsorts, functions and equations as well as some reductions such that if all reductions evaluate correctly, then s is true. Proof scores are therefore analogous to LCF or HOL tactics. This approach uses OBJ3 in two distinct ways: as a *reduction engine* for performing the calculations and as a *metalanguage* for expressing the structure and contents of proofs. The basic structure of a proof is summarised by the acyclic graph of its proof score.

We will illustrate the construction of proof scores and inductive arguments through an example. The following proof score is used to prove that if a list is reversed twice the result is the original list.

```
obj LIST is sorts List Elt .
  op nil : -> List .
  op _cons_ : Elt List -> List .
  op _#_ : List Elt -> List .
  op reverse : List -> List .
  vars E E' : Elt .
  var L : List .
  eq nil # E = (E cons nil) .
```

```
  eq (E cons L) # E' = E cons (L # E') .
  eq reverse(nil) = nil .
  eq reverse(E cons L) = reverse(L) # E .
endo

obj VARS is extending LIST .
  ops e e' : -> Elt .
  op l : -> List .
endo

reduce in VARS : reverse(nil # e) == e cons reverse(nil) .

obj HYP-LEMMA is using VARS .
eq reverse(l # e) = e cons reverse(l) .
endo

reduce in HYP-LEMMA :
    reverse((e' cons l) # e) == e cons reverse(e' cons l) .

obj LEMMA is protecting LIST .
  var E : Elt .
  var L : List .
  eq reverse(L # E) = E cons reverse(L) .
endo

reduce in VARS : reverse(reverse(nil)) == nil .

obj HYP is using VARS .
  eq reverse(reverse(l)) = l .
endo

reduce in HYP + LEMMA : reverse(reverse(e cons l)) == e cons l .
```

The object LIST introduces the list of elements data type with nil and _ cons _ as the constructors and the state updating operators _ # _ (right append) and reverse. The object VARS introduces three unconstrained constants to act as variables. We need the following lemma:

```
reverse(L # E) = E cons reverse(L)
```

The first reduction evaluates to **true** thereby proving the lemma base case. The object HYP-LEMMA asserts the induction hypothesis and the second reduction proves the induction step. Once a lemma such as this has been proved, it can be used for the proof of the main theorem by asserting it in a fresh object with real variables. This is done in object LEMMA. The proof of the main theorem is also inductive and proceeds along similar lines as shown in object HYP and the two final reductions. The following object asserts the theorem ready for use in further proofs.

```
obj REV-REV-LIST is protecting LIST .
  var L : List .
```

```
  eq reverse(reverse(L)) = L .
endo
```

Although this facility is not currently available in OBJ3, inductive proof scores can be automatically generated from knowing what the constructors are, what the proposed theorem is and what variable to do induction over.

This approach to theorem proving is a compromise between fully automatic provers and proof checkers; the proof strategy is constructed by the user while the calculations are performed automatically. Proof strategies are high level user decisions about the problem, such as stating the goals and deciding on the use of appropriate techniques such as substitution, reduction, induction and so on; they must therefore be distinguished from proof scores which are concrete implementations of proof strategies. While it is possible to automate some aspects of proof score generation and the techniques of [Gog88] indicate a method for doing this, it is of course much harder to generate working proof strategies; therein lies the true challenge of current theorem proving technology. The consolation must be, especially to those aversed to machine proofs [Fet88], that the general methods of correctness proofs are studied by humans within the realm of mathematics and are thus amenable to the so called "social processes" of discussion, criticism, refinement and generalisation.

A usable theorem prover should, however, help the user to discover a proof rather than simply to check a fully constructed proof or to generate a fully automatic proof because the former is tedious and the latter often not viable. When OBJ3 proof scores fail, the results often directly suggest what to try next. This is very important as it allows *incremental* proof construction. As an example, consider the proof about the reverse of the reverse of a list that we have already seen. The base case of the theorem is easily proved but if we remove the lemma, the induction step fails with the result:

$$\texttt{reverse(reverse(l) \# e) == e cons l}$$

This suggests that we need to prove a lemma about the definition of **reverse** on lists consisting of right append terms. This is precisely what our lemma does. In the next chapter we will see an example of a failed proof which actually suggests ways of reformulating the goal so that the proof succeeds.

To summarise, reasoning in OBJ3 is a form of semi automatic theorem proving where the user builds up proofs incrementally, possibly using feedback from failed proof attempts, without ever leaving the specification language or manually transforming the specifications.

6.3.2.2 A comparison with other theorem proving approaches

We have already seen the drawbacks of simple, single or many sorted variants of equational logic as embodied in the LP, RRL, REVE and RAP systems. We have chosen not to use bare term rewriting as a theorem proving paradigm in spite of the term rewriting operational semantics of OBJ3. Experience shows that inductionless induction is a weak proof method compared with structural induction for many hardware verification problems. Unification in order sorted equational theories with conditional rules is an open problem and the termination of arbitrary term rewriting systems is undecidable. It is furthermore the case that the uncontrollable search space of completion algorithms results in an explosion of less and less relevant rules (particularly in the case of AC completion) which can be very counter intuitive when a proof fails. As we have seen, however, OBJ3 proofs are controllable, do not require termination proofs for new rule sets and failed proofs often provide intuition into the cause of the failure.

As pointed out earlier, specifying sequential devices in OBJ3 is related to the Boyer–Moore approach, since they are both based on first order logics without existential quantification. However, the powerful parameterisation facilities of OBJ3 allow *explicit naming* of components which is comparable with second order notations. Thus, together with the benefits of reuse through libraries of primitives, OBJ3 offers modularity, abstraction and hierarchical structure which are not attainable in Boyer–Moore logic. The OBJ3 theorem proving paradigm is also more flexible than the automatic approach of Boyer–Moore in that it allows finding user-guided proofs when the built-in heuristics of Boyer–Moore do not apply.

Higher order notations such as HOL offer superior expressive power. Although this is useful for some applications, it appears unnecessary in the case of many hardware specifications. Because reasoning overheads are proportional to the expressive power of a notation, it is wise to use the simplest logic possible for a given problem. Order sorted equational logic seems sufficient for a large class of hardware devices. HOL in particular, is a manual proof checker and the user has to manage many tedious, detailed proof aspects. To the uninitiated eye, HOL proof scripts can be impenetrable. On the other hand, OBJ3 proof scores have the structure of programs and using module hierarchies and generic modules are much easier to manage.

Temporal logics and model checking are particularly well suited for reasoning about reactive systems expressed as state machines for verification purposes. They have sufficient expressive power and model checkers have become efficient enough to deal with a large number of states. In the sense, however, of proofs being automatic, we maintain that OBJ3 offers more flexibility by means of user interaction and guidance.

A further advantage of our approach is its generality. The logic system in which proofs are conducted is not hardwired into the system. In this work we use extended first order equational logic and the propositional calculus. It is, however, possible to encode other logical systems with varying inference rules in OBJ3. For instance, current work includes the encoding of a logic of authentication [BAN89] in OBJ3 to allow the analysis of authentication protocols. In addition, [Sam90] uses OBJ3 to prove compiler correctness where proof obligations are discharged through algebraic transformations. In [Sam90], OBJ3 has been studied in comparison with the B-Tool, Veritas and the Occam Transformation System and has been found to be a better option for that particular application as a result of features such as parameterisation, subsorts, attributes and term rewriting facilities.

6.3.2.3   Theorem proving principles

We will now summarise some principles that motivate our theorem proving approach. It is worth noting that these observations are the result of extensive practical experimentation rather than theoretical deliberations.

1. **Use the simplest logic possible for a given application** because reasoning overheads are proportional to the expressive power of the logic.

2. **A usable theorem prover should help the user discover a proof** rather than simply check a fully constructed proof or generate a fully automatic proof, because the former is tedious and the latter often not viable.

3. **Strong typing is very useful** because it drastically reduces proof search space and thus theorem proving becomes much more efficient.

4. **Proof strategies must be readable** as this makes third party scrutiny easier. The structure of strategies and proofs must be explicit as otherwise it is difficult to have faith in either. It seems that software engineering considerations such as structure, encapsulation, generality, locality and so on are equally applicable to proof scripts.

5. **Proofs should be incremental** both in the sense of upwards extensions (proving further theorems) and constructive backtracking (revising strategies and scores with information from failed proof attempts). If we take a parallel in software development, proof construction should be incremental just as software construction is. If not many programs work the first time, it is hardly surprising that most proof scores do not either, since their construction is at least as complex as that of software. In fact, this analogy reveals the severe constraints upon proof construction brought about because of the lack of support tools such as proof editors and proof debuggers.

6. **Proofs are programs** in the sense they aim to solve a well defined problem in a finite number of steps. Automatic proof generation is as hard as automatic program generation and proof checking is as tedious as machine language programming.

Although the OBJ3 approach we have presented here does not solve all these problems, it is, we believe, a step in the right direction. Proof is at least as intellectually demanding as programming and therefore cannot be seriously contemplated in full scale use without adequate supporting mechanisms.

Chapter 7

OBJ3 Case Studies

The objective of this chapter is to present the OBJ3 approach in an integrated way and to show that it is applicable to non trivial synchronous systems. By way of an introduction, we present two simple but complete examples of sequential systems; a synchronous radar controller and an asynchronous pump controller. We then describe two substantial experiments, the Pixel Planes linear expression evaluator and Gordon's computer, which demonstrate that the OBJ3 approach is applicable to non trivial systems.

7.1   A radar controller

A radar system operates in four modes: wide angle scan, narrow angle scan, penetration mode and lock-to-target mode. In the last two modes the position of the beam is specified by the navigation computer as shown in figure 7.1. Each time the push button is activated and released the controller switches from one mode to the next in a fixed sequence. The signals defining the four modes of operation are:

  w = 1   for wide angle scan
  n = 1   for narrow angle scan
  p = 1   for penetration mode
  t = 1   for lock-to-target mode
   The system is designed to cycle through wide angle scan, narrow angle scan, penetration mode and lock-to-target mode. The state diagram is shown in figure 7.2. The controller can be implemented as shown in figure 7.3, from two level triggered JK flip flops and a multiplexor.
   In this example we take the state diagram of the system as the specification. The objective of verification will be, therefore, to show that the implementation behaves as the abstract state machine of figure 7.2. We begin by defining the multiplexor and its input theory:

```
th LTH is protecting PRIMS .
  ops l1 l2 : Time -> Prop .
endth

obj MUX[IN :: LTH] is
  ops pp n t w : Time -> Prop .
```

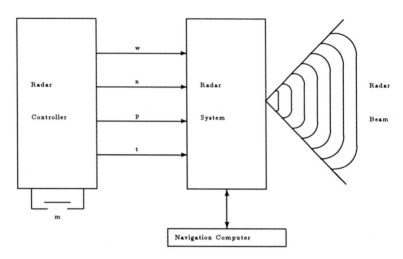

Figure 7.1: A radar system

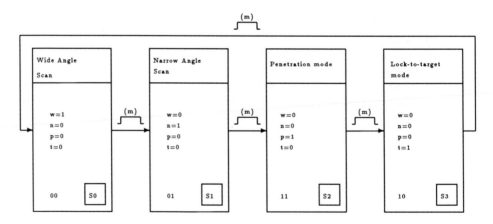

Figure 7.2: State diagram of the radar controller

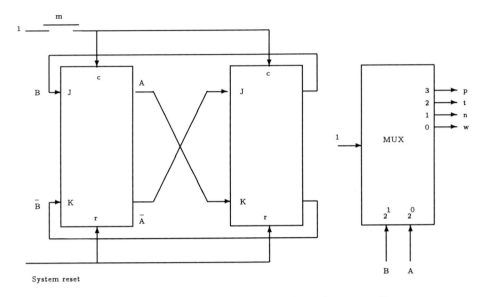

Figure 7.3: The implementation of the radar controller

```
  var T : Time .
  eq  pp(T) = l1(T) and l2(T) .
  eq  t(T) = l1(T)  and not(l2(T)) .
  eq  n(T) = not(l1(T)) and l2(T) .
  eq  w(T) = not(l1(T)) and not(l2(T)) .
endo
```

We define a generic JK flip flop in a similar way, in this case by renaming LTH.

```
th JKTH is extending LTH * (op l1 to J, op l2 to K) .
  ops cl rs : Time -> Prop . endth

obj JKFF[JK :: JKTH] is
  ops q q-bar : Time -> Prop .
  var T : Time .
  eq  q-bar(T) = not(q(T)) .
  ceq q(s T) = q(T) if
                  (not(J(T)) and not(K(T)) and not(rs(T)) and cl(T)) .
  ceq q(s T) = false if rs(T) .
  ceq q(s T) = q(T) if not(cl(T)) and not(rs(T)) .
  ceq q(s T) = false if
                  (not(J(T)) and K(T) and not(rs(T)) and cl(T)) .
  ceq q(s T) = true if
                  (J(T) and not(K(T)) and not(rs(T)) and cl(T)) .
  ceq q(s T) = not(q(T)) if
                  (J(T) and K(T) and not(rs(T)) and cl(T)) .
endo
```

We now instantiate the generic JK flip flop to produce two copies which we need here.

```
obj JKFF-A[JK :: JKTH] is
  protecting JKFF[JK] * (op q to A, op q-bar to A-bar) . endo

th JKBTH is protecting JKTH * (op J to Jb, op K to Kb) . endth

obj JKFF-B[JKB :: JKBTH] is
  protecting JKFF[view to JKB is
                      op : J to : Jb .
                      op : K to : Kb .
                  endv] * (op q to B, op q-bar to B-bar) .
endo
```

We proceed by combining the two JKs

```
obj JKs[JK :: JKTH] is
  protecting JKFF-B[view from JKBTH to JKFF-A[JK] is
                      op : Jb to : A-bar .
                      op : Kb to : A .
                  endv] .
  var T : Time .
  eq  J(T) = B(T) .
  eq  K(T) = B-bar(T) .
endo
```

Finally, we join the JKs to the multiplexor:

```
obj CONTROLLER[INP :: JKTH] is
  protecting MUX[view from LTH to JKs[INP] is
                      op : l1 to : A .
                      op : l2 to : B .
                  endv] .
endo
```

Having completed the specification, the first step is to proceed with investigative simulation. The object INST provides some test values for the clock and the system reset and object TEST initialises the simulation with state S_3.

```
obj INST is protecting PRIMS .
  ops J K cl rs : Time -> Prop .
  var T : Time .
  eq  cl(0) = false .
  eq  cl(s T) = not(cl(T)) .
  eq  rs(T) = false .
endo

obj TEST is extending CONTROLLER[INST] .
  op m : -> Time .
  ops S0 S1 S2 S3 : Time -> Prop .
  var T : Time .
```

```
  eq  S0(T) = not(A(T)) and not(B(T)) .
  eq  S1(T) = not(A(T)) and B(T) .
  eq  S2(T) = A(T) and B(T) .
  eq  S3(T) = A(T) and not(B(T)) .
  eq  A(0) = true .
  eq  B(0) = false .
endo
```

Simulation is now carried out using reductions in the test object.

```
reduce in TEST  : cl(6) .
reduce in TEST  : rs(2) .
reduce in TEST  : A(7) .
reduce in TEST  : B(6) .
reduce in TEST  : w(5) .
reduce in TEST  : n(4) .
reduce in TEST  : pp(8) .
reduce in TEST  : t(2) .
```

Once the design passes these tests we start the verification. We first want to show that the implementation produces correct outputs for each state. For each proof we assume that we are in the desired state and show that the outputs comply with the specification, for instance, at state S_0 wide angle scan mode is on and all the other modes are turned off:

```
obj PROOF is protecting PRIMS .
ops J K cl rs : Time -> Prop . endo

obj STATE0 is extending CONTROLLER[PROOF] .
  op m : -> Time .
  eq A(m) = false .
  eq B(m) = false .
  eq cl(m) = true .
  eq rs(m) = false .
endo
```

```
reduce in STATE0 : w(m) and not(n(m)) and not(pp(m)) and not(t(m)) .
```

When these proof obligations have been discharged we move on to the next set of goals which show that the circuit cycles through the states correctly. For instance, if the circuit is in state S_0, the clock has been switched on and no reset signal has arrived, the circuit will move to state S_1 when the B input is turned on:

```
obj S0toS1 is extending CONTROLLER[PROOF] .
  op m : -> Time .
  eq A(m) = false .
  eq B(m) = false .
  eq cl(m) = true .
  eq rs(m) = false .
  ops S0 S1 S2 S3 : Time -> Prop .
  var T : Time .
```

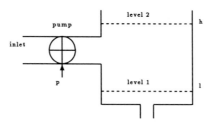

Figure 7.4: A water pump

Figure 7.5: The pump controller

```
  eq S0(T) = not(A(T)) and not(B(T)) .
  eq S1(T) = not(A(T)) and B(T) .
  eq S2(T) = A(T) and B(T) .
  eq S3(T) = A(T) and not(B(T)) .
endo

reduce in S0toS1 :  S1(s m) and not(S2(s m)) and
                    not(S3(s m)) and not(S0(s m)) .
```

The rest of the properties are proved in a similar way.

7.2   A pump controller

We will now present our second example, a controller for the water pump of figure 7.4. The intended pump operation is as follows. The pump is to turn on when the water drops below level 1 and is to remain on until it reaches level 2, at which point it turns off. The pump is to remain turned off until the water goes below level 1 again. Two level sensor inputs, h and l are provided. When the water is at or above level 1 $l = 1$, otherwise $l = 0$. Similarly, $h = 1$ when the water is at or above level 2, otherwise $h = 0$. It is impossible for the water not to be at level 1 if it is at level 2 so an input combination of 10 indicates sensor malfunction and therefore the alarm should be raised.

  The system is shown in figure 7.5 and its state diagram is shown in figure 7.6.   This circuit is interesting because it has *unstable* as well as stable states. The state table is shown in figure 7.7. The stable states are:

S_0 – hl = 01 or hl = 11, pump = 0, alarm = 0
S_1 – hl = 00 or hl = 01, pump = 1, alarm = 0

The unstable states are:

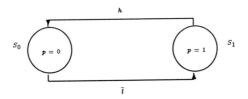

Figure 7.6: State diagram for the pump controller

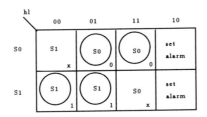

Figure 7.7: State table for the pump controller

S_0 - hl = 11, pump = X (don't care), alarm = 0
S_1 - hl = 00, pump = X, alarm = 0

The alarm will be raised when 10 appears at the sensor inputs.

A NAND implementation of the circuit is shown in figure 7.8. We assume that the average delay of a NAND gate to be one unit of time. The circuit will function correctly if the minimum hold time of the inputs is greater than or equal to the cumulative delay through the gate network. We are now ready to define the primitive NAND gate and its input theories.

```
th INPUT1 is protecting PRIMS .
   op in1_ : Time -> Prop . endth

th INPUT2 is protecting PRIMS .
   op in2_ : Time -> Prop . endth

obj NAND[IN1 :: INPUT1, IN2 :: INPUT2] is
```

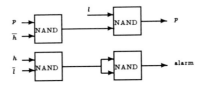

Figure 7.8: Pump controller implementation

```
    op out : Time -> Prop .
    var T : Time .
    eq  out(0) = false .
    eq  out(s T) = not((in1 T) and (in2 T)) .
endo
```

For this design we need four gates which are obtained by the following instantiations:

```
obj NAND1[IN1 :: INPUT1, IN2 :: INPUT2] is
  pr NAND[IN1,IN2] * (op out to n1) . endo

obj NAND2[IN1 :: INPUT1, IN2 :: INPUT2] is
  pr NAND[IN1,IN2] * (op out to n2) . endo

obj NAND3[IN1 :: INPUT1, IN2 :: INPUT2] is
  pr NAND[IN1,IN2] * (op out to n3) . endo

obj NAND4[IN1 :: INPUT1, IN2 :: INPUT2] is
  pr NAND[IN1,IN2] * (op out to n4) . endo
```

The circuit is now obtained by the following composition:

```
th LTH is pr PRIMS . op l_ : Time -> Prop . endth
th HTH is pr PRIMS . op h_ : Time -> Prop . endth
th L-BARTH is pr PRIMS . op l-bar_ : Time -> Prop . endth
th H-BARTH is pr PRIMS . op h-bar_ : Time -> Prop . endth
th TEMPTH is pr PRIMS . op temp_ : Time -> Prop . endth

obj CONTROLLER[L :: LTH, H :: HTH, L-BAR :: L-BARTH,
               H-BAR :: H-BARTH, TEMP :: TEMPTH] is
   protecting
     NAND2[(n1).(NAND1[(l-bar_).L-BAR, (h_).H]) ,
           (n1).(NAND1[(l-bar_).L-BAR, (h_).H])] *
                (op n2 to (alarm_))
             +
     NAND4[(n3).(NAND3[(h-bar_).H-BAR, (temp_). TEMP]),
           (l_).L] *
                (op n4 to (pump_)) .
   var T : Time .
   eq  temp T = pump T .
   eq  l-bar T = not(l T) .
   eq  h-bar T = not(h T) .
endo
```

As we have argued earlier on, we believe that this style of generic specification is better than specifications that simply treat components as "breaking" wires. This is not obvious for simple examples such as this, but it is certainly the case with substantial designs. The pump controller can easily be specified with four equations if we dispense with generality:

```
obj PUMP-CONTROLLER is pr PRIMS .
   ops (h_) (l_) (n1_) (n2_) (pump_) (alarm_) : Time -> Prop .
```

h(t)	l(t)	pump(t+2)	alarm(t+2)
0	0	1	0
0	1	1	0
1	0	X	1
1	1	0	0

Table 7.1: Pump controller simulation pattern

```
var T : Time .
eq n1 (s T) = not((pump T) and not(h T)) .
eq n2 (s T) = not((h T) and not(l T)) .
eq pump (s T) = not((n1 T) and (l T)) .
eq alarm (s T) = not((n2 T) and (n2 T)) .
endo
```

Investigative simulation requires results according to table 7.1 and is carried out with the following test data:

```
obj INST is extending PRIMS .
  ops (l_) (h_) (l-bar_) (h-bar_) (temp_) : Time -> Prop .
  var T : Time .
  eq  l 0  = false .
  eq  l (s 0) = false .
  eq  l (s s T) = not(l T) .
  eq  h 0  = false .
  eq  h (s 0) = false .
  eq  h (s s 0) = false .
  eq  h (s s s 0) = false .
  eq  h (s s s s T) = not(h T) .
  eq  temp 0 = true .
endo
```

```
obj TEST is pr CONTROLLER[(l_).(INST),(h_).(INST),(l-bar_).(INST),
                          (h-bar_).(INST),(temp_).(INST)] . endo
```

A sample test run is shown below:

```
reduce in TEST : h 6 .
reduce in TEST : l 6 .
reduce in TEST : pump 6 .
reduce in TEST : alarm 6 .
```

Verification aims to establish that the outputs are correct for each stable state, for instance:

```
obj PROOF is protecting PRIMS .
  ops (l_) (h_) (l-bar_) (h-bar_) (temp_) : Time -> Prop .
  var T : Time .
  eq  h-bar T = not(h T) .
```

```
    eq  1-bar T = not(1 T) .
endo


obj STATE0a is
   extending CONTROLLER[(1_).(PROOF),(h_).(PROOF),(1-bar_).(PROOF),
                       (h-bar_).(PROOF),(temp_).(PROOF)] .
   op t : -> Time .
   eq  h t = false .
   eq  l t = true .
   eq  h (s t) = false .
   eq  l (s t) = true .
   eq pump t = false .
   eq pump (s t) = false .
endo


reduce in STATE0a : (not(pump (s s t))) and (not(alarm (s s t))) .
```

We also want to show that the alarm will go off if the sensors malfunction:

```
obj ALARM-CHECK is
   extending CONTROLLER[(1_).(PROOF),(h_).(PROOF),(1-bar_).(PROOF),
                       (h-bar_).(PROOF),(temp_).(PROOF)] .
   op t : -> Time .
   eq  h t = true .
   eq  l t = false .
   eq  h (s t) = true .
   eq  l (s t) = false .
endo


reduce in ALARM-CHECK : alarm (s s t) .
```

The proofs conclude by showing that the circuit cycles correctly through its stable states. The unstable states must be taken into account for timing purposes as it may take the device more than one time cycle before it settles into a stable state.

```
obj STATES is
   ex CONTROLLER[(1_).(PROOF),(h_).(PROOF),(1-bar_).(PROOF),
                (h-bar_).(PROOF),(temp_).(PROOF)] .
   ops S0a S0b S0x S1a S1b S1x : Time -> Prop .
   op t : -> Time .
   var T : Time .
   eq S0a(T) = ((not (h T)) and (l T) and (not (pump T))) .
   eq S0b(T) = (h T) and (l T) and (not (pump T)) .
   eq S0x(T) = (h T) and (l T) .
   eq S1a(T) = ((not (h T)) and (not (l T)) and (pump T)) .
   eq S1b(T) = ((not (h T)) and (l T) and (pump T)) .
   eq S1x(T) = (not (h T)) and (not (l T)) .
endo


obj S0btoS0a is ex STATES .
   eq  h t = true .
```

```
    eq  h (s t) = true .
    eq  h (s s t) = false .
    eq  h (s s s t) = false .
    eq  h (s s s s t) = false .
    eq  l t = true .
    eq  l (s t) = true .
    eq  l (s s t) = true .
    eq  l (s s s t) = true .
    eq  l (s s s s t) = true .
    eq  pump t = false .
    eq  pump (s t) = false .
endo
```

```
reduce in S0btoS0a : S0a(s s s s t) .
```

The verification of the pump controller offers another example of proofs benefiting from feedback from failed proof attempts. When this work was done, the state cycle proofs failed in the sense that they did not evaluate to **true**. The result of the reductions was always some term involving the subterm pump(t). This indicated that the proofs were somehow dependent on this irreducible term. Sure enough, upon a closer examination of the equations defining the various states in object STATES revealed that the equations were in fact incomplete as they consistently omitted the pump(t) term. For instance, the equation for state S_{0_a} was S0a(T) = not(h T) and (l T) whereas it should have been S0a(T) = not(h T) and (l T) and not(pump T). With hindsight, this should have been obvious since the states depend on the current pump output as well as the sensor inputs. In this case, OBJ3 actually helped reveal the specification error which caused the proof to fail.

7.3 Pixel Planes

The Pixel Planes architecture [FP81, FPPB82] is a high performance graphics system that contains a novel tree structured computation unit called a *Linear Expression Evaluator* (LEE). This LEE was formalised as a synchronous concurrent algorithm (SCA) and manually verified in [ET89]. In [EST91] the equations defining a LEE tree of fixed height were translated into OBJ3 and a correctness proof obtained by term rewriting. In this section we extend this work to the case where the height of the LEE tree is a parameter n and we verify it for all n by using induction over tree paths[1].

7.3.1 Informal description of Pixel Planes' LEE

The *Linear Expression Evaluator* (LEE) is a section of the Pixel Planes architecture [FP81, FPPB82]. Further extensions are described in [FGH+85] and implementation details are given in [PFA+85]. A review of current experimental and commercial VLSI graphics systems, including Pixel Planes, is given by Fuchs [Fuc88]. We examine the

---

[1]This section was contributed by Steven M. Eker, INRIA-LORRAINE, Campus Scientifique, 615 rue du Jardin Botanique - BP 101, F-54602 VILLERS-LES-NANCY Cedex, France. The work described was done whilst the author was an ERCIM Research Fellow at CWI, Amsterdam.

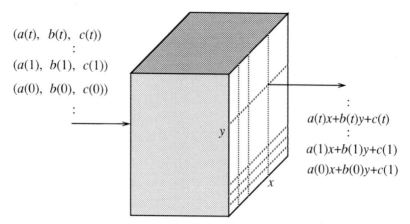

Figure 7.9: The LEE section of Pixel Planes.

algorithm in its pure form without the modifications (such as super trees) required to implement it in current VLSI technology.

The Pixel Planes LEE has the task of taking an input stream

$$(a(0), b(0), c(0)), (a(1), b(1), c(1)), \ldots$$

of triples of numbers, and generating in parallel for each point (x, y) on a discrete $n \times m$ grid, the stream

$$a(0)x + b(0)y + c(0), a(1)x + b(1)y + c(1), \ldots$$

of values of the linear expression $ax + by + c$. This is shown diagramatically in figure 7.9. At this top level of description it suffices to assume that input and output data are numbers (such as integers or reals); in more specific accounts the input and output data are bit representations.

The architecture that implements this specification consists of 1-dimensional LEE modules which evaluate $w + vz$ on an input (v, w) for each value of z. Note that the 2-dimensional expression $ax + by + c$ is evaluated as $(c + ax) + by$. The way the 1-dimensional LEE modules are connected together to perform this is shown in figure 7.10 with the 1-dimensional LEE modules represented by triangles. Each output of the first 1-dimensional LEE module, which computes the $ax + c$ terms in parallel for each value of x, is connected to a 1-dimensional LEE module, which adds the by term in parallel for each value of y. It is with these 1-dimensional LEEs that we concern ourselves here.

The internal structure of the 1-dimensional LEE module is shown in figure 7.11. It is composed of a tree of smaller modules. The structure of the tree nodes is shown in figure 7.12. The left output is simply the top input delayed by one clock cycle. The right output is formed by adding the two inputs, together with the carry bit saved from the previous addition.

7.3.2   Specification of the 1-dimensional LEE

Rather than specify and verify the Pixel Planes 1D LEE at the bit level where numbers are represented by a finite sequence of bits and are processed bit serially, we choose a

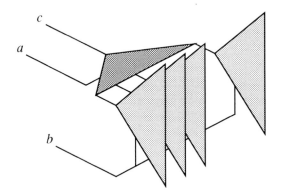

Figure 7.10: Inside the LEE section.

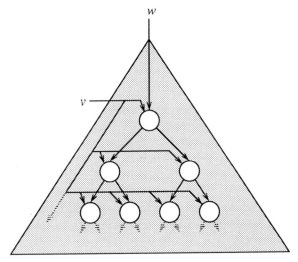

Figure 7.11: Inside a 1-dimensional LEE module.

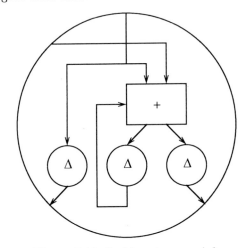

Figure 7.12: Inside a tree module.

higher level model where each number is considered to be an element of an abstract data type, whose equational axioms are chosen to be just strong enough for the design to be verified. This approach considerably simplifies the verification process but there is a price to be paid.

In the real bit level Pixel Planes 1D LEE numbers are represented by sequences of bits, the least significant bit first (earliest). Thus multiplication by two can be done cheaply by a one cycle delay. Similarly division by two can be done by letting the bit sequence representing the number to be divided 'get ahead' by one cycle of the bit sequences representing the other numbers being pumped around the architecture. In the real Pixel Planes 1D LEE each number fed in to the v input is multiplied by 2^{n-1} by preceding it with $n-1$ zeros and is effectively divided by two at each level in the tree as it gets progressively 'out of step' with the numbers generated by each tree processor.

In our abstract model of the Pixel Planes 1D LEE each clock cycle represents a whole new element being fed into each input, not just the current bit of a number and therefore streams of elements cannot be allowed to 'get out of step'. Thus we have to add explicit one cycle delays and multipliers to keep the elements 'in step' and to handle the implicit computations on the elements sent to the v input.

7.3.2.1   Abstract data types

The data type we choose to specify the Pixel Planes 1D LEE is built from three smaller data types. Time is represented by a copy $\mathbf{T} = \langle \mathbf{T} \mid 0, t{+}1 \rangle$ of the natural numbers without the addition and multiplication operations. The natural numbers $\mathbf{N} = \langle \mathbf{N} \mid 0, n{+}1, +, \times \rangle$ are used to generate particular abstract numbers via a mapping which we define below. In order to generate abstract numbers to play the rôle of powers of two in the multiplier modules, it is convenient to add the operation 2^n to the natural numbers. We also need the abstract numbers on which we actually do the computations. We need two operations to represent addition and multiplication and a constant to represent the zero element. We thus have an algebra $\langle R \mid 0, +, \times \rangle$. It was shown in [EST91] that this algebra needs to satisfy just four equational axioms.

$$(a + b) + c \;=\; a + (b + c) \tag{7.1}$$
$$a + 0 \;=\; a \tag{7.2}$$
$$0 \times a \;=\; 0 \tag{7.3}$$
$$(a + b) \times c \;=\; (a \times c) + (b \times c) \tag{7.4}$$

We can thus consider the abstract data type R to be the class of all algebras which satisfy these axioms.

In order to generate abstract numbers to represent particular natural numbers we define the following function. Let α be any element of R. Then we define the function $r_\alpha : \mathbf{N} \to R$ inductively.

$$r_\alpha(0) = 0$$
$$r_\alpha(n + 1) = r_\alpha(n) + \alpha$$

Thus $r_\alpha(0) = 0$, $r_\alpha(1) = 0 + \alpha$, $r_\alpha(2) = 0 + \alpha + \alpha$ and so on.

Lemma 1 *The mapping r_α is a homomorphism w.r.t. the '+' operations in $\mathbf{N}$ and R; that is $r_\alpha(a + b) = r_\alpha(a) + r_\alpha(b)$.*

This fact is easily proved by induction and we shall prove it in section 7.3.3.2 as an illustration of how to do inductive proofs with OBJ3. We note that every ring satisfies these axioms. Particularly important is the case where $R = \mathbf{Z}$ and $\alpha = 1$.

7.3.2.2 Implementation specification

This specification is for a generic 1D LEE of height n with 2^n outputs. Since the number of modules (and hence functions and equations defining them) is dependent on n we cannot write a fixed list of equations. Instead, we subscript the module and function names and write *equation templates*.

The ease of the specification and verification of a family of SCAs defined by equation templates is very sensitive to the subscripting scheme used. For linear columns of modules the obvious subscripts to use are the natural numbers. For trees of modules the choice of subscripts is not so clear. One possibility is to subscript each module on a tree of modules by a pair of natural numbers where the first denotes the module's level in the tree and the second denotes the module's position among the modules at that level. This scheme was used in [ET89, EST91]. This has the disadvantage that is is possible to refer to modules that do not exist and thus each equation template which refers to a tree of modules in this way will need to have conditions on the subscripts to explicitly exclude this possibility.

An alternative subscripting scheme which we use here is to subscript each module in a (binary) tree by its *tree path*. A module's tree path is the list of elements from $\{l, r\}$ which describe the path to the module as a sequence of left and right branches, starting at the root module. Under this scheme the root module of the tree is subscripted by the empty list *nil* and its left and right sons are subscripted by l and r respectively. Going one level down the tree left and right sons of the root module's left son get the subscripts $l.r$ and $r.r$ respectively[2].

The disadvantage of using tree paths is the need to convert them to and from pairs of natural numbers in order to specify input/output connections to the tree. For this purpose we define the following operations on tree paths inductively[3]:

$$| \ | : \{l, r\}^* \to \mathbf{N}$$

$$|nil| = 0$$

$$|l.\phi| = 1 + |\phi|$$

$$|r.\phi| = 1 + |\phi|$$

$$\# : \{l, r\}^* \to \mathbf{N}$$

$$\#(nil) = 0$$

$$\#(l.\phi) = 2 * \#(\phi)$$

$$\#(r.\phi) = 2 * \#(\phi) + 1$$

---

[2]Note that our lists should be read right to left—this somewhat counter intuitive order is chosen to correspond to the right to left order in which lists are traditionally constructed in functional languages.

[3]Note that we consider '.' to be the list concatenation operation and *nil* to be the left and right identity of this operation.

Intuitively, for a module subscripted by ϕ, $|\phi|$ is its level in the tree and $\#(\phi)$ is its position within that level where both levels and positions start at 0. We also need the following partial operation

$$@ : \mathbf{N} \times \mathbf{N} \to \{l, r\}^*$$

$$@(0, 0) = nil$$

$$@(i + 1, j) = \begin{cases} l.@(i, j/2) & \text{if } j \text{ is even} \\ r.@(i, (j - 1)/2) & \text{if } j \text{ is odd} \end{cases}$$

where $@(i, j)$ is only defined for $j \in \{0, \ldots, 2^i - 1\}$. Intuitively $@(i, j)$ is the tree path for the jth module at level i.

In writing down our equation templates we use natural numbers and tree paths as subscripts to the modules and function symbols and make use of various operations on them. It must be stressed that this notation is simply a mechanism for writing down a specification of a parameterised family of SCAs. The extra copy of the natural numbers and the set of tree paths together with their operations are not part of the SCA formalism, do not affect the actual computations performed by the architecture and can be eliminated whenever the parameter n is instantiated to a particular natural number. However as we shall see later on this mechanism can be formalised and used to prove theorems about a parameterised family of SCAs. The abstract version of the Pixel Planes 1D LEE which we specify is shown in figure 7.13 (compare it with figure 7.11).

The process of writing down the implementation specification is straightforward—for each module shown in figure 7.13 we assign a value function. Note that we use the following convention; modules which have more than one distinct output are split and each output gives rise to a value function. All modules are initialised to $0 \in R$ at time 0.

We start with the one cycle delays, $Q_0, \ldots, Q_{n-2}$. Module Q_0 takes its input from the $\underline{v}$ input stream; the others each take their input from their immediate predecessor. The value functions for the delay modules are q_i for $i \in \{0, \ldots, n - 2\}$:

$$q_i : \mathbf{T} \times [\mathbf{T} \to R]^2 \to R$$

$$q_i(0, \underline{v}, \underline{w}) = 0$$

$$q_0(t + 1, \underline{v}, \underline{w}) = \underline{v}(t)$$

$$q_{i+1}(t + 1, \underline{v}, \underline{w}) = q_i(t, \underline{v}, \underline{w})$$

Next we have the multiplication processors $M_0, \ldots, M_{n-1}$. Module M_0 takes its input directly from the $\underline{v}$ input stream; the others take their inputs from the preceding delay module. Each multiplication processor M_i multiplies its input by the element $r_\alpha(2^{n-1-i})$. The value functions for the multiplication processors are m_i for $i \in \{0, \ldots, n - 1\}$:

$$m_i : \mathbf{T} \times [\mathbf{T} \to R]^2 \to R$$

$$m_i(0, \underline{v}, \underline{w}) = 0$$

$$m_0(t + 1, \underline{v}, \underline{w}) = r_\alpha(2^{n-1}) \times \underline{v}(t)$$

$$m_{i+1}(t + 1, \underline{v}, \underline{w}) = r_\alpha(2^{n-(i+2)}) \times q_{i-1}(t, \underline{v}, \underline{w})$$

Finally we have the tree processors. The topmost tree processor P is simply a one cycle delay with a single value function f_{nil}. The processors P_ϕ for $\phi \in \{l, r\}^*$, $|\phi| < n$ have

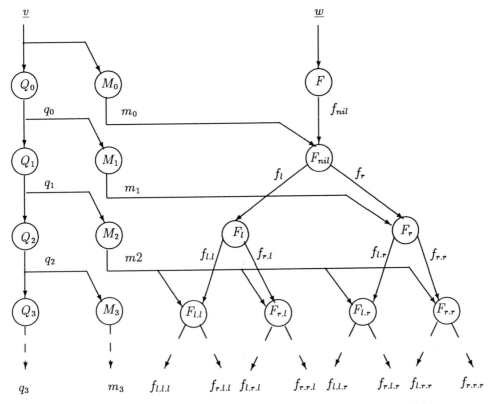

Figure 7.13: The abstract version of the Pixel Planes 1-dimensional LEE.

two outputs; a left one with value function $f_{l.\phi}$ and a right one with value function $f_{r.\phi}$. We define these value functions as follows, for $\phi \in \{l, r\}^*$, $|\phi| \leq n$:

$$f_\phi : \mathbf{T} \times [\mathbf{T} \to R]^2 \to R$$

$$f_\phi(0, \underline{v}, \underline{w}) = 0$$

For $\phi \in \{l, r\}^*$, $|\phi| < n$:

$$f_{l.\phi}(t + 1, \underline{v}, \underline{w}) = f_\phi(t, \underline{v}, \underline{w})$$

$$f_{r.\phi}(t + 1, \underline{v}, \underline{w}) = f_\phi(t, \underline{v}, \underline{w}) + m_{|\phi|}(t, \underline{v}, \underline{w})$$

The stream transformer defined by this implementation specification is

$$LEE^n : [\mathbf{T} \to R]^2 \to [\mathbf{T} \to R]^{2^n}$$

$$LEE^n(\underline{v}, \underline{w})(t) = (f_{@(n,0)}(t, \underline{v}, \underline{w}), \ldots, f_{@(n,2^n-1)}(t, \underline{v}, \underline{w}))$$

7.3.2.3   User specification

Let R be any structure satisfying equations (7.1)–(7.4). Our user specification is

$$U^n : [\mathbf{T} \to R]^2 \to [\mathbf{T} \to R \cup \{u\}]^{2^n}$$

defined by its coordinate functions. For $j \in \{0, \ldots, 2^{n-1}\}$:

$$U^n_j(\underline{v}, \underline{w})(t) = \begin{cases} u & \text{if } t < n+1 \\ \underline{w}(t - (n+1)) + r_\alpha(j) \times \underline{v}(t - (n+1)) & \text{otherwise} \end{cases}$$

Here $(n+1)$ is the time delay between the data arriving at the sources and valid results being available at the sinks.

For verification purposes we want the I/O specification to satisfy the user specification. We derive the following equivalent condition on value functions; for $j \in \{0, \ldots, 2^n - 1\}$:

$$\forall t \in \mathbf{T}.[t \geq n+1 \Rightarrow f_{@(n,j)}(t, \underline{v}, \underline{w}) = \underline{w}(t - (n+1)) + r_\alpha(j) \times \underline{v}(t - (n+1)))]$$

For automatic verification it is convenient to eliminate the subtraction operations and replace the partial operation @ with the fully defined operations # and $||$. An equivalent condition is given in the following theorem.

Theorem 1 *If R satisfies equations (7.1)–(7.4) then for $\phi \in \{l, r\}^*$ and $\in \mathbf{T}$,*

$$|\phi| = n \Rightarrow (f_\phi(t + n + 1, \underline{v}, \underline{w}) = \underline{w}(t) + r_\alpha(\#(\phi)) \times \underline{v}(t))$$

It is this condition which expresses the correctness of the algorithm for any structure R that satisfies our abstract arithmetic axioms.

7.3.3   Verification

7.3.3.1   Data types

Since the statement of correctness requires expressions that combine module indices and time we use a single copy of the natural numbers for both purposes. Notice that we also need subtraction on the natural numbers. Since subtraction is only partially defined on the natural numbers we have two options. First we can alter the semantics of subtraction so that $i - j = 0$ for $i < j$. This is called cut-off arithmetic. The second approach is to use the integers with natural numbers as a subsort. Although this latter approach is conceptually cleaner it leads to difficulties when we need to use an expression which syntactically denotes an integer (but which is known to always evaluate to a natural number because of conditions on some of its subexpressions) as an argument to an operation which is only defined on natural numbers. Thus we take the first option. We specify the natural numbers with cut-off subtraction by the following OBJ3 module:

```
obj NAT is sort Nat .
  ops 0 1 2 : -> Nat .
  op _+_ : Nat Nat -> Nat [assoc comm prec 3] .
  op _*_ : Nat Nat -> Nat [assoc comm prec 2] .
  op _-_ : Nat Nat -> Nat [prec 3] .
```

```
op 2^_ : Nat -> Nat [prec 1] .
op _>_ : Nat Nat -> Bool .

vars I J K : Nat .
eq I + 0 = I .
eq I - 0 = I .
eq 0 - I = 0 .
eq (I + K) - (J + K) = I - J .
eq I * 0 = 0 .
eq I * 1 = I .
eq I * (J + K) = I * J + I * K .
eq 2^ 0 = 1 .
eq 2^ (I + 1) = 2^ I * 2 .
eq 0 > I = false .
eq I + 1 > 0 = true .
eq I + K > J + K = I > J .
eq 2 = 1 + 1 .
*** Cut off arithmetic lemmas:
cq (I - J) + K = (I + K) - J if I + 1 > J .
eq (2^ I) * J + (2^ I) * J = 2^ (I + 1) * J .
cq I + K > J = true if I > J .
endo
```

We also include three trivial lemmas that hold in the initial model of this module. Notice that the + and * operations are associative and commutative and we specify this in OBJ3 by means of the **assoc** and **comm** attributes. The **prec** attribute is used to specify the precedences of the operations for the OBJ3 mixfix parser.

We next define the abstract arithmetic data type R. Recall that this has one constant, '0' and two operations, '+' and '×' and satisfies four equational axioms. Since operationally these are considered as rewrite rules directionality is important. For instance if the associativity axiom is written as (A+B)+C=A+(B+C) some of our proofs would fail. The initial model of this signature and set of equations is in fact the unit algebra. Our intention is to verify the LEE over the class of all algebras which satisfy these equations and thus we want variety semantics and so we use an OBJ3 theory.

```
th ABS is sort Abs .
op 0 : -> Abs .
op _+_ : Abs Abs -> Abs [prec 3] .
op _*_ : Abs Abs -> Abs [prec 2] .

vars A B C : Abs .
eq A + (B + C) = (A + B) + C .
eq A + 0 = A .
eq 0 * A = 0 .
eq (A + B) * C = (A * C) + (B * C) .
endth
```

We also need to formalise tree paths and their operations. This is done using two sorts. The sort **Branch** has two constants **l** and **r**. The sort **Path** is intended to be a list of elements from **Branch** and has a constant **nil**. These lists are constructed by an invisible operation (_ _) which takes an element from **Branch** and a list and returns a new list. The operations | | and # which map tree paths into natural numbers are defined as before.

```
obj TREE is protecting NAT .
  sorts Branch Path .
  ops l r : -> Branch .
  op nil : -> Path .
  op __ : Branch Path -> Path .
  op |_| : Path -> Nat .
  op # : Path -> Nat .

  var B : Branch .
  var P : Path .
  eq | nil | = 0 .
  eq | B P | = 1 + | P | .
  eq #(nil) = 0 .
  eq #(l P) = 2 * #(P) .
  eq #(r P) = 1 + 2 * #(P) .
endo
```

We now need the r_α operation to map natural numbers into our abstract numbers. We introduce this as another module defined in terms of the NAT and ABS modules above.

```
th RMAP is protecting NAT + ABS .
  op alpha : -> Abs .
  op r_ : Nat -> Abs [prec 1] .

  var N : Nat .
  eq r(0) = 0 .
  eq r(s N) = r(N) + alpha .
endth
```

7.3.3.2   Proving the homomorphism property of r_α

Earlier on we stated that Lemma 1 could be easily proved by induction. We now do this proof as another example of how to do inductive proofs with OBJ3. We induct on the second argument of r_α.

We start with the base case: $r_\alpha(a, 0) = r_\alpha(a) + r_\alpha(0)$. To prove this in OBJ3 we first create a new module that includes an 'unconstrained' constant to represent the variable a:

```
th BASE is protecting RMAP .
  op a : -> Nat .
endth
```

The proof is done by rewriting the terms on either side of the equality symbol to a normal form and then checking for syntactic equivalence.

```
reduce in BASE : r(a + 0) == r(a) + r(0) .
```

We then do the induction step; assume that $r_\alpha(a + b) = r_\alpha(a) + r_\alpha(b)$ and prove $r_\alpha(a + b + 1) = r_\alpha(a) + r_\alpha(b + 1)$. We write the induction hypothesis as another OBJ3 module:

```
th HYP is protecting BASE .
  op b : -> Nat .
  eq r(a + b) = r(a) + r(b) .
endth
```

The proof is done by rewriting as before:

```
reduce in HYP : r(a + s b) == r(a) + r(s b) .
```

Now that the lemma is proven we create a new module **LEMMA1** containing it so we can use it later.

```
th LEMMA1 is protecting RMAP .
  vars A B : Nat .
  eq r(A + B) = r(A) + r(B) .
endth
```

7.3.3.3 Converting the implementation specification to OBJ3

Recall that our original specification consisted of equation templates which we considered to be a specification of an infinite family of SCAs for $n = 2, 3, \ldots$. Thus each subscripted value function in our specification actually refers to an infinite family of value functions. In order to formalise the equation templates in OBJ3 we use the convention that the subscript on a value function becomes a new argument to the function.

Since OBJ3 does not support higher order functions we must remove the stream arguments $\underline{v}, \underline{w}$ from the value functions in the original specification. We simply declare $\underline{v}$ and $\underline{w}$ to be functions from the naturals to our abstract arithmetic data type without giving any equations to define them.

Using these conventions our implementation specification may be written as the following OBJ3 module.

```
obj LEE is protecting LEMMA1 + TREE .
  op n : -> Nat .
  op v : Nat -> Pix .
  op w : Nat -> Pix .
  op q : Nat Nat -> Pix .
  op m : Nat Nat -> Pix .
  op f : Path Nat -> Pix .

  var I T : Nat .
  var P : Path .
  cq q(I, 0) = 0                    if n > I + 1 .
  eq q(0, T + 1) = v(T) .
  cq q(I + 1, T + 1) = q(I, T)      if n > I + 2 .

  cq m(I, 0) = 0                                    if n > I .
  eq m(0, T + 1) = r(2^ (n - 1)) * v(T) .
  cq m(I + 1, T + 1) = r(2^ (n - (I + 2))) * q(I, T)     if n > I + 1 .

  cq f(P, 0) = 0                              if n + 1 > | P | .
```

```
  eq f(nil, T + 1) = w(T) .
  cq f((l P), T + 1) = f(P, T)                    if n + 1 > | l P | .
  cq f((r P), T + 1) = f(P, T) + m(| P |, T)      if n + 1 > | r P | .
endo
```

7.3.3.4   Verification of the LEE

The general idea is to prove a closed form for each of the (parameterised) value functions using induction on natural numbers, induction on tree paths and case analysis.

   We start with the delay modules.

Theorem 2 *For each $i \in \mathbf{N}$, if $i + 1 < n$ then*

$$q(i, t + i + 1) = \underline{v}(t)$$

We prove this by induction on i. First we create a module to assert that $i + 1 < n$ for the base case where $i = 0$. We then reduce the equation $q(0, t + 0 + 1) = \underline{v}(t)$ in it.

```
obj T2-BASE is protecting LEE .
  op t : -> Nat .
  eq n > 1 = true .
endo
```

```
reduce q(0, t + 0 + 1) == v(t) .
```

Notice that in the module T2-BASE we included the equation $n > 1 = tt$ instead of the equation $n > 0 + 1 = tt$. This simplification by hand is necessary since the left hand side of the latter equation is reducible and any term that might match it could be reduced before a match takes place. In order to prove the induction step we create a module to assert the induction hypothesis together with the condition $(i + 1) + 1 < n$ and reduce the equation $q((i + 1), t + (i + 1) + 1) = \underline{v}(t)$.

```
obj T2-HYP is protecting T2-BASE .
  op i : -> Nat .

  cq q(i, t + i + 1) = v(t) if n > i + 1 .
  eq n > (i + 1)  + 1 = true .
  eq n > i + 1 = true .                    *** extra property
endo
```

```
reduce q(i + 1, t + (i + 1) + 1) == v(t) .
```

Notice that we had to add the extra property that $n > i+1$. Although this follows trivially from $n > (i + 1) + 1$ it cannot easily be proved by rewriting. Handling inequalities is awkward in a pure term rewriting system—ideally we would like a lemma of the form $i > j + 1 \Rightarrow i > j$ but if this were proved and added as a conditional equation we would get nontermination. We create a new module asserting the theorem so that it can be used in later proofs.

```
obj THEOREM2 is protecting LEE .
  var I T : Nat .
  cq q(I, T + I + 1) = v(T) if n > I + 1 .
endo
```

Next we consider the multiplier modules.

Theorem 3 *For each $i \in \mathbf{N}$, if $n > i$ then*

$$m(i, t + i + 1) = r(2^{n-(i+1)}) \times v(t)$$

We prove this by case analysis on i. To prove the case $i = 0$ we create a module to assert that $n > 0$ and reduce $m(0, t + 0 + 1) = r(2^{n-(0+1)}) \times \underline{v}(t)$ in it.

```
obj T3-CASE1 is protecting THEOREM2 .
    op t : -> Nat .
    eq n > 0 = true .
endo
```

```
reduce m(0, t + 0 + 1) == r(2^ (n - (0 + 1))) * v(t) .
```

The other case where $i > 0$ is done by proving the theorem for $i + 1$ where i ranges over all natural numbers. In fact this technique is really induction on natural numbers except we do not use the induction hypothesis.

```
obj T3-CASE2 is protecting THEOREM2 .
    ops i t : -> Nat .
    eq n > i + 1 = true .
endo
```

```
reduce m(i + 1, t + (i + 1) + 1) == r(2^ (n - ((i + 1) + 1))) * v(t) .
```

Again we create a new module to assert the theorem for use later.

```
obj THEOREM3 is protecting THEOREM2 .
    var I T : Nat .
    cq m(I, T + I + 1) = r(2^ (n - (I + 1))) * v(T) if n > I .
endo
```

Finally we consider the tree processors.

Theorem 4 *For each $p \in \{l, r\}^*$, if $|p| < n + 1$ then*

$$f(p, t + |p| + 1) = w(t) + r(2^{n-|p|} \times \#(p)) \times \underline{v}(t)$$

Note that the correctness theorem is just a special case of this theorem when $|p| = n$. We prove this theorem by induction on the tree path p. The basis case where $p = nil$ is straightforward.

```
obj T4-BASE is protecting THEOREM3 .
    op t : -> Nat .
endo
```

```
reduce f(nil, t + | nil | + 1) == w(t) + r(2^ (n - | nil |) * #(nil)) * v(t) .
```

In the induction step we need to consider both left and right branches so we need to reduce two equations in the module containing the induction hypothesis.

```
obj T4-HYP is protecting T4-BASE .
  op p : -> Path .
  vars I J K : Nat .

  cq f(p, t + | p | + 1) =
    w(t) + r(2^ (n - | p |) * #(p)) * v(t) if n + 1 > | p | .
  eq n > | p | = true .
endo
```

```
reduce f((l p), t + | l p | + 1) ==
            w(t) + r(2^ (n - | l p |) * #(l p)) * v(t) .
```

```
reduce f((r p), t + | r p | + 1) ==
            w(t) + r(2^ (n - | r p |) * #(r p)) * v(t) .
```

This completes the verification. We have demonstrated how to represent a SCA by primitive recursive equations over algebras and how to map them into OBJ3. Further, the proof of correctness is performed using equational reasoning in OBJ3. This process is systematic and in principle applies to any SCA. Thus it can be automated using an appropriate compiler. Such a compiler has been built using the theoretical results in [TT91]. However, many theoretical and practical problems arise by such mechanisation. The correctness of a SCA may involve scheduling of input and output streams which complicates the logical structure of the formulae to be proved (see [HTT88b] for example). The SCA may not have unit delay and involve complex timing conditions in the network (see [Hob91]). Research on this problem is ongoing.

This verification experiment with OBJ3 illustrates the potential of the approach on complex but regular structures. Equational logic is powerful enough to allow straight forward encoding of SCA specifications, and simple enough to afford relatively painless proofs. The style of proof used here, which is a compromise between automatic proof construction and proof checking is, we believe, desirable.

In the course of this proof we have also felt the need for a number of theorem proving facilities such as controlled rewriting and automatic construction of inductive proof templates which are, at present, missing from OBJ3. The lack of documentation about the operational semantics of some features of the language, such as module combinators was a source of irritation. Those issues are partly addressed in the next chapter.

7.4 Gordon's computer

We now come to our final case study. We will specify and prove the partial correctness of a microprocessor due to Gordon, who has verified it using LCF–LSM [Gor83a, Gor83b]. The machine, which is generally known as "Gordon's computer", is similar in complexity to a PDP-8 and has also been proved correct by Joyce in a slightly different form under the name Tamarack [Joy87].

According to Gordon, the specification and verification effort took several months and it is certainly the case that this is the largest hardware case study undertaken with OBJ3. We have done this work in order to check the viability of OBJ3 as a specification language and theorem proving tool for non trivial hardware systems. We will present the material

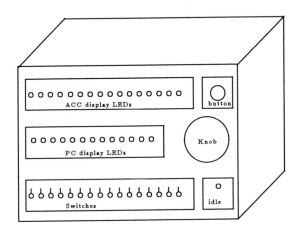

Figure 7.14: The front panel of Gordon's computer

in a way similar to [Gor83b] by starting with the specification of the **target** machine (specification), proceeding with the specification of the **host** machine (implementation) and we will conclude with a partial proof that the host implements the target.

7.4.1 The target

The front panel of the computer is shown in figure 7.14. The target machine has two registers and a RAM. The program counter PC is 13 bits wide and the accumulator ACC is 16 bits wide. The random access memory has 13-bit addresses each of which points to a 16-bit word (thus the RAM holds 8192 words).

On the front panel there are 16 two position switches and two arrays of 13 and 16 display lights which show the contents of the program counter and the accumulator respectively. The four position knob determines what happens when the button at the upper right corner is pushed. There is a further display light at the bottom right corner which is illuminated when the machine is idling. The target has 8 16-bit instructions. Each instruction has a 3–bit opcode part and a 13-bit address part. The address format and instructions are shown in table 7.2.

The effect of pressing the button while the idle light is on depends on the position of the knob. We follow Gordon's convention and refer to the four positions as 0, 1, 2 and 3.

knob = 0 The word determined by the state of the 13 rightmost switches is loaded in the program counter.

knob = 1 The word determined by the state of the 16 switches is loaded in the accumulator.

knob = 2 The contents of the accumulator are stored in the memory at the location held in the program counter.

knob = 3 The program stored in memory is executed starting at the location held in the program counter. The idle light will go off and stay off until execution stops. This

opcode	address	mnemonic	semantics
000	...*addr*...	HALT	Stop execution
001	...*addr*...	JMP L	Jump to *addr*
010	...*addr*...	JZR L	Jump to *addr* if ACC = 0
011	...*addr*...	ADD L	Add *addr* contents to ACC
100	...*addr*...	SUB L	Subtract *addr* contents from ACC
101	...*addr*...	LD L	Load *addr* contents to ACC
110	...*addr*...	ST L	Store ACC contents in *addr*
111	...*addr*...	SKIP	Skip to next instruction

Table 7.2: The instruction set

happens either when a halt instruction is reached or when an interrupt is generated by pushing the button.

The first three options, that is the idling cycle in Gordon's terminology, describe the bootstrapping procedure of the computer and it is the correctness of this that we prove later on in this section.

7.4.1.1   The target data types

Before presenting the specification of the target machine, we need to concentrate briefly on the required data types. Gordon uses the LCF–LSM built-ins *wordn* and *bool list* whereas our primary data type is a user-defined unbounded list. The parameterised LIST object of appendix A.2 is instantiated with boolean values in the object BLIST below:

```
obj BLIST is ex LIST[BOOL] .
  op bitn : Nat List -> Bool .
  op bnot_ : List -> List .
  op adder : Bool List List -> List .
  ops cut pad : Nat List -> List .
  op  inc_ : List -> List .
  op  val_ : List -> Nat .
  op valrev_ : List -> Nat .
  op wordn : Nat Nat -> List [memo] .
  ops opcode address : List -> List .
  ops (add_ _) (sub_ _) : List List -> List .

  vars M N : Nat .
  var L L' : List .
  var E E' C : Bool .
  var Nz : NzNat .

  eq bitn(s 0, E L) = E .
  eq bitn(s Nz, E L) = bitn(Nz, L) .

  eq bnot nil = nil .
```

```
  eq bnot (E L) = (not E) (bnot L) .

  eq adder(C,nil,nil) = C .
  let carry = (E and E') or ((E and C) or (E' and C)) .
  eq adder(C,E L, E' L') = (C xor E xor E') adder(carry,L,L') .

  eq cut(0, E L) = E L .
  eq cut(s N, E L) = cut(N, L) .

  eq pad(N,L) = if N <= length(L) then L else pad(N, false L) fi .

  cq cut(M, (pad(N, L))) = L if M == length(L) .
  cq cut(M, (inc (pad(N, L)))) = inc L if M == length(L) .

  eq val L = valrev (rev L) .
  eq valrev nil = 0 .
  eq valrev (E L) = if E then s(2 * (valrev L))
else 2 * (valrev L) fi .

  eq wordn(0,N) = nil .
  eq wordn(s M, N) = wordn(M, N /2) (N %2 =/= 0) .

  eq inc nil = true .
  eq inc true = false true .
  eq inc false = true .
  eq inc (true L) = false (inc L) .
  eq inc (false L) = true L .

  eq opcode(L) = bitn(16,L) (bitn(15,L) bitn(14,L)) .
  eq address(L) = bitn(13,L) bitn(12,L) bitn(11,L) bitn(10,L)
bitn(9,L) bitn(8,L) bitn(7,L) bitn(6,L) bitn(5,L)
bitn(4,L) bitn(3,L) bitn(2,L) bitn(1,L) .

  eq add L L' = cut(length(L), adder(false,L,L')) .
  eq sub L L' = add L (add (pad(length(L'),true)) (bnot L')) .
endo
```

BLIST enriches lists of booleans with the necessary extra operators such as bitn : Nat List -> Bool which returns the *nth* bit of a list, val_ : List -> Nat which maps boolean vectors onto natural numbers and bnot : List -> List which performs a bitwise complement. The operator cut : Nat List -> List cuts off the n leftmost bits of a list while the operator pad : Nat List -> List pads a list with left 0s until its length reaches n. These two operators are related via two axioms as shown by the conditional equations in BLIST. The operators opcode address : List -> List extract the appropriate bit segments from the instruction. The rest of the operators define the components of the host ALU which are included here for the sake of completeness although we, as Gordon before us, will not prove its correctness.

It is worth pointing out that our specification and proof is *generic* in the sense that correctness does not depend on the width of words or memory locations. Although here

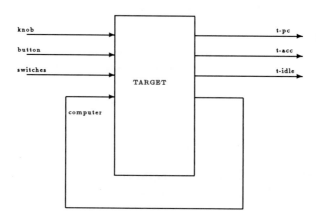

Figure 7.15: The target machine

we will stick to Gordon's conventions regarding word sizes, the proofs for lists of undefined but fixed length are trivial. This is one of the obvious advantages of using OBJ3 in this context.

Further to lists and booleans, we need natural numbers with the usual operations as shown in appendix A.1 and parameterised finite maps which are shown in appendix A.3. The **FINITE-MAP** object is instantiated with **WORD**s to yield the memory data structure which we use to model the RAM of the target machine and the ROM of the host machine. We show this instantiation below:

```
view WORD from TRIV to BLIST is sort Elt to List . endv

obj MEMORY is ex FINITE-MAP[WORD, WORD]  * (sort Map to Memory) . endo
```

7.4.1.2   Target machine specification

We are now ready to specify the target machine of figure 7.15. The operation **next : Memory List List -> State** defines a single step of the machine and, therefore, specifies the semantics of the instruction set. The sort **State** is constructed by the operator **[_ _ _ _] :   Memory List List Bool -> State**. The term **next(M,W1,W2)** gives the state of the machine after executing the instruction at address **W1** in **M** when the accumulator holds **W2**. The boolean value in the result indicates whether the computer is idling or not.

```
obj NEXT-STATE is pr MEMORY .
  sort State .
  op [_ _ _ _] : Memory List List Bool -> State .
  op next : Memory List List -> State .

  var M : Memory .
  vars W1 W2 : List .
  var B : Bool .

  let opr = (val (opcode(M [ W1 ]))) .
```

```
  let addrs = address(M [ W1 ]) .

  cq next(M,W1,W2) = [M W1 W2 true] if opr == 0 .
  cq next(M,W1,W2) = [M addrs W2 false] if opr == 1 .
  eq next(M,W1,W2) = if ((val W2) == 0) and (opr == 2)
     then [M addrs W2 false]
     else [M (inc W1) W2 false] fi .
  cq next(M,W1,W2) = [M (inc W1) (add W2 (M [ addrs ])) false]
     if opr == 3 .
  cq next(M,W1,W2) = [M (inc W1) (sub W2 (M [ addrs ])) false]
     if opr == 4 .
  cq next(M,W1,W2) = [M (inc W1) (M [ addrs ]) false]
     if opr == 5 .
  cq next(M,W1,W2) = [(M [ addrs ] := W2) (inc W1) W2 false]
     if opr == 6 .
  cq next(M,W1,W2) = [M (inc W1) W2 false] if opr == 7 .
endo
```

The term **M [W1]** yields the contents of the memory **M** at location **W1** and thus models the memory read operation. The memory write operation is modelled by the term **M [W1] := W2** which stores **W2** at location **W1**. Note that the mixfix syntax of OBJ3 allows intuitive operator templates such as the array-like _ [_] : **Memory List -> List** for the lookup operation above.

The target machine can now be specified as shown below.

```
th TARGET-INTERFACE is protecting NEXT-STATE .
  ops switches knob t-pc t-acc : Nat -> List .
  ops button t-idle : Nat -> Bool .
endth

obj TARGET-WIRES[including I/O :: TARGET-INTERFACE] is
  op ram : Nat -> Memory .
  ops wa wb : Nat -> List .
  op t : Nat -> Bool .
  op computer : Nat -> State .
  op 1st : State -> Memory .
  ops 2nd 3rd : State -> List .
  op 4th : State -> Bool .

  var M : Memory .
  vars W1 W2 : List .
  var B : Bool .

  eq 1st([M W1 W2 B]) = M .
  eq 2nd([M W1 W2 B]) = W1 .
  eq 3rd([M W1 W2 B]) = W2 .
  eq 4th([M W1 W2 B]) = B .
endo

obj TARGET[including I/O :: TARGET-INTERFACE] is
```

```
                            including TARGET-WIRES[I/O] .
  var T : Nat .
  eq ram(T) = 1st(computer(T)) .
  eq wa(T) = 2nd(computer(T)) .
  eq wb(T) = 3rd(computer(T)) .
  eq t(T) = 4th(computer(T)) .
  eq t-pc(T) = wa(T) .
  eq t-acc(T) = wb(T) .
  eq t-idle(T) = t(T) .

  eq computer(s T) =
  if t(T) then
    (if button(T) then
      (if val(knob(T)) == 0 then [ram(T) cut(3,switches(T)) wb(T) true]
      else
        (if val(knob(T)) == 1 then [ram(T) wa(T) switches(T) true]
        else
          (if val(knob(T)) == 2
          then [(ram(T) [wa(T)] := wb(T)) wa(T) wb(T) true]
          else
             [ram(T) wa(T) wb(T) false]
          fi)
        fi)
      fi)
    else
       [ram(T) wa(T) wb(T) true]
    fi)
  else
    (if button(T) then [ram(T) wa(T) wb(T) true]
    else
      next(ram(T), wa(T), wb(T))
    fi)
  fi .
endo
```

The operators 1st through to 4th extract the respective components of the machine state. The theory TARGET-INTERFACE defines the external target signals whereas the object TARGET-WIRES specifies the internal signals, that is the state preserving elements. The convention of using a theory XXXX-INTERFACE for externals and an object XXXX-WIRES for internals will be used throughout our specification. In LCF–LSM terms, external wires are universally quantified and internal ones are existentially quantified.

Let us now briefly turn to the question of timing. The target specification above updates the state and produces the outputs in one time cycle. Timing decisions are, therefore, obvious from the specifications since we use time explicitly in our axioms. This is one of the fundamental differences between our approach and LCF–LSM.

Since the target specification is parameterised over its external wires, we need to instantiate the TARGET object. This is done using the **make** command below.

```
obj SPEC-WIRES is protecting NEXT-STATE .
```

```
  ops switches knob t-pc t-acc : Nat -> List .
  ops button t-idle : Nat -> Bool .
endo
```

```
make SPEC-MOD is TARGET[SPEC-WIRES] endm
```

The object **SPEC-WIRES** contains the operator definitions which are required in order to satisfy the **TARGET-INTERFACE** theory.

This completes the specification of the target machine. Note that the definition is as concise as the LCF–LSM equivalent. We want to stress this point since OBJ3 can achieve similarly concise descriptions with much less expressive power than LCF–LSM affords.

7.4.2 The host

We now turn to Gordon's implementation of the target machine. The host machine has a number of registers in addition to the program counter and accumulator of the target. The instruction currently being executed is held in the instruction register CIR. The addresses being looked up in the memory, are held in the memory address register MAR. Arguments to the arithmetic logic unit (ALU) are held in the ARG register while the results of the ALU are kept in the buffer register BUF. The fetch-decode-execute cycle is driven by a microcoded control unit. The microcode is stored in the ROM which can hold 32 microinstructions each 30 bits wide. The host machine is broadly divided into the **controller** and **data part**. We tackle these in turn.

7.4.2.1 The host controller

The controller is shown in figure 7.16. It consists of the microprogram counter MPC, the read only memory ROM which contains the microcode and the DECODER unit. The microprogram counter is specified below.

```
th MPC-INTERFACE is protecting MEMORY .
  ops inm outm : Nat -> List .
endth
```

```
obj MPC-WIRES[including I/O :: MPC-INTERFACE] is
  op w : Nat -> List .
endo
```

```
obj MPC[including I/O :: MPC-INTERFACE] is including MPC-WIRES[I/O] .
  var T : Nat .
  eq outm(T) = w(T) .
  eq w(s T) = inm(T) .
endo
```

The microprogram counter is modelled with state and this is shown in object **MPC-WIRES** where the operator w : Nat -> List is defined. Note that the counter produces its output after one time cycle. Since the host machine consists of a number of such components, it takes more cycles to produce a result than the target. The host cycles are, therefore, considered as "microcycles" which implement one target "macrocycle". The host has a

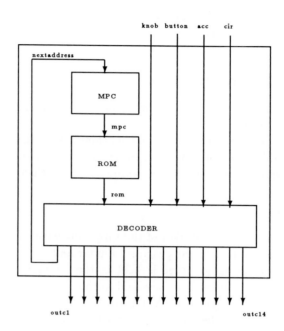

Figure 7.16: The controller of the host machine

done line called **ready** which signals the end of a sequence of microcycles implementing a single target macrocycle. Merging microcycles to produce macrocycles is a problem which we address when presenting the correctness proof later on.

The read only memory is modelled as follows.

```
th ROM-INTERFACE is protecting MEMORY .
  ops inr outr : Nat -> List .
endth
```

```
obj ROM-WIRES[including I/O :: ROM-INTERFACE] is
  including MICROCODE .
  op r : -> Memory  .
  op D : -> List .
  eq r = < D > [ addr 0 ] := microcode(wordn(5, 0))
         [ addr 1 ]  := microcode(wordn(5, 1))
         [ addr 2 ]  := microcode(wordn(5, 2))
         [ addr 3 ]  := microcode(wordn(5, 3))
         [ addr 4 ]  := microcode(wordn(5, 4))
         [ addr 5 ]  := microcode(wordn(5, 5))
         [ addr 6 ]  := microcode(wordn(5, 6))
         [ addr 7 ]  := microcode(wordn(5, 7))
         [ addr 8 ]  := microcode(wordn(5, 8))
         [ addr 9 ]  := microcode(wordn(5, 9))
         [ addr 10 ] := microcode(wordn(5, 10))
         [ addr 11 ] := microcode(wordn(5, 11))
```

```
         [ addr 12 ] := microcode(wordn(5, 12))
         [ addr 13 ] := microcode(wordn(5, 13))
         [ addr 14 ] := microcode(wordn(5, 14))
         [ addr 15 ] := microcode(wordn(5, 15))
         [ addr 16 ] := microcode(wordn(5, 16))
         [ addr 17 ] := microcode(wordn(5, 17))
         [ addr 18 ] := microcode(wordn(5, 18))
         [ addr 19 ] := microcode(wordn(5, 19))
         [ addr 20 ] := microcode(wordn(5, 20))
         [ addr 21 ] := microcode(wordn(5, 21))
         [ addr 22 ] := microcode(wordn(5, 22))
         [ addr 23 ] := microcode(wordn(5, 23))
         [ addr 24 ] := microcode(wordn(5, 24))
         [ addr 25 ] := microcode(wordn(5, 25)) .
endo

obj ROM[including I/O :: ROM-INTERFACE] is including ROM-WIRES[I/O] .
  var T : Nat .
  eq outr(s T) = r [ inr(T)] .
endo
```

The constant r :   -> Memory contains the microcode instructions at the appropriate
addresses. The constant D : -> List is a dummy used for returning a value when a
lookup operation has failed, that is it stands for the contents of an out of range address.
We do not specify the microinstructions with addresses 26 to 31.

The microcode itself is shown in object MICROCODE below. This was derived from Gordon's microcode by straight transliteration. In [Gor83b], Gordon describes a simple microassembler written in ML which is used to generate the microcode for each of the 26
microinstructions. We have chosen not to repeat this exercise with OBJ3 as the work
required is exactly the same as for Gordon's ML microassembler.

```
obj MICROCODE is including BLIST .
  op microcode : List -> List [strat (0)] .
  op addr_ : Nat -> List .
  var N : Nat .
  eq addr N = wordn(5,N) .

  eq microcode(wordn(5,0)) = rev (wordn(17,3) wordn(13,9)) .
  eq microcode(wordn(5,1)) = rev (wordn(22,1) wordn(8,3)) .
  eq microcode(wordn(5,2)) = rev (wordn(2,1) wordn(4,1) wordn(24,0)) .
  eq microcode(wordn(5,3)) = rev (wordn(2,1) wordn(6,1) wordn(22,0)) .
  eq microcode(wordn(5,4)) =
  rev (wordn(3,1) wordn(4,1) wordn(15,7) wordn(8,0)) .
  eq microcode(wordn(5,5)) = rev (wordn(16,1) wordn(5,3) wordn(9,1)) .
  eq microcode(wordn(5,6)) =
  rev (wordn(3,1) wordn(4,1) wordn(12,1) wordn(11,0)) .
  eq microcode(wordn(5,7)) = rev (wordn(4,1) wordn(5,1) wordn(21,0)) .
  eq microcode(wordn(5,8)) =
  rev (wordn(5,1) wordn(5,1) wordn(12,9) wordn(8,0)) .
  eq microcode(wordn(5,9)) = rev (wordn(21,5) wordn(9,4)) .
```

```
eq microcode(wordn(5,10)) = rev (wordn(30,0)) .
eq microcode(wordn(5,11)) =
rev (wordn(6,1) wordn(5,1) wordn(11,5) wordn(8,0)) .
eq microcode(wordn(5,12)) =
rev (wordn(18,1) wordn(6,5) wordn(3,3) wordn(3,2)) .
eq microcode(wordn(5,13)) = rev (wordn(12,9) wordn(10,19) wordn(8,0)) .
eq microcode(wordn(5,14)) = rev (wordn(12,9) wordn(10,22) wordn(8,0)) .
eq microcode(wordn(5,15)) =
rev (wordn(3,1) wordn(8,1) wordn(8,3) wordn(12,0)) .
eq microcode(wordn(5,16)) =
rev (wordn(3,1) wordn(8,1) wordn(11,25) wordn(8,0)) .
eq microcode(wordn(5,17)) =
rev (wordn(7,1) wordn(11,17) wordn(3,1) wordn(9,0)) .
eq microcode(wordn(5,18)) =
rev (wordn(6,1) wordn(9,1) wordn(7,5) wordn(8,0)) .
eq microcode(wordn(5,19)) =
rev (wordn(3,1) wordn(8,1) wordn(9,5) wordn(10,0)) .
eq microcode(wordn(5,20)) =
rev (wordn(5,1) wordn(8,1) wordn(9,21) wordn(8,0)) .
eq microcode(wordn(5,21)) =
rev (wordn(8,1) wordn(10,9) wordn(4,1) wordn(8,0)) .
eq microcode(wordn(5,22)) =
rev (wordn(3,1) wordn(8,1) wordn(11,23) wordn(8,0)) .
eq microcode(wordn(5,23)) =
rev (wordn(5,1) wordn(9,3) wordn(8,21) wordn(8,0)) .
eq microcode(wordn(5,24)) =
rev (wordn(5,1) wordn(3,1) wordn(14,17) wordn(8,0)) .
eq microcode(wordn(5,25)) =
rev (wordn(4,1) wordn(5,1) wordn(13,17) wordn(8,0)) .
endo
```

The term wordn(n,m) yields the binary representation of m in an n-bit wide word. Thus the axiom

```
eq microcode(wordn(5,0)) = rev (wordn(17,3) wordn(13,9)) .
```

stores the appropriate microinstruction at ROM location 00000. The term (wordn(17,3) wordn(13,9)) makes two lists, 00000000000000011 and 0000000001001 and then joins them together to form the word 000000000000000110000000001001. The join is achieved using the _ _ : List List -> List operator defined in object LIST of appendix A.2. Finally, the rev_ : List -> List operator simply reverses the word to match Gordon's convention.

Before defining the microinstruction decoding device we must describe the 30-bit microinstructions. Bits 1 to 3 are a 3-bit opcode called the test field. Bits 9 to 13 hold a 5-bit microinstruction address called the A-address and bits 4 to 8 hold another 5-bit address called the B-address. The remaining bits are all control fields, each field determining the value of a control line during a microcycle. The address of the next microinstruction to be executed is normally given by the contents of the A-address field, unless:

1. The value of the test field is 1 and the button is pressed, or the value of the test field is 2 and the value of the 16-bit word in the accumulator is zero. In either case, the next address is given by the contents of the B-address field.

2. The value of the test field is 3. In this case, the address is obtained by adding the value of the knob incremented by 1 to the value of the A-address field.

3. The value of the test field is 4. The next address is obtained by adding the value of the opcode in the current instruction register to the value of the A-address field.

The object DLIST below defines the auxiliary operators needed for the specification of the decoder.

```
obj DLIST is including BLIST * (op bitn to cntl-bit) .
  op cntl-field : Nat Nat List -> List .
  ops a-addr b-addr : List -> List   .
  op test : List -> Nat .
  vars M N : Nat .
  var W : List .
  eq cntl-field(M,N,W) = cntl-bit(M,W) cntl-bit(N,W) .
  eq a-addr(W) = cntl-bit(13,W) (cntl-bit(12,W) (cntl-bit(11,W)
                 (cntl-bit(10,W) (cntl-bit(9,W))))) .
  eq b-addr(W) = cntl-bit(8,W) (cntl-bit(7,W) (cntl-bit(6,W)
                 (cntl-bit(5,W) (cntl-bit(4,W))))) .
  eq test(W) = val(cntl-bit(3,W) (cntl-bit(2,W) cntl-bit(1,W))) .
endo
```

The decoder specification is shown below.

```
th DECODE-INTERFACE is protecting DLIST .
  ops ind1 ind2 ind4 ind5 outd1 outd4 outd12 : Nat -> List .
  ops ind3 outd2 outd3 outd5 outd6 outd7 outd8 outd9
  outd10 outd11 outd13 outd14 outd15 : Nat -> Bool .
endth
```

```
obj DECODE[including I/O :: DECODE-INTERFACE] is
  var T : Nat .
  eq outd1(s T) =
      if (test(ind1(T)) == 1) and ind3(T) then b-addr(ind1(T))
      else
       (if (test(ind1(T)) == 2) and (val(ind4(T)) == 0)
        then  b-addr(ind1(T))
        else
         (if (test(ind1(T)) == 3) then wordn(5,(val(ind2(T)) + 1) +
                                         val(a-addr(ind1(T))))
         else
          (if (test(ind1(T)) == 4)
           then wordn(5,(val(opcode(ind5(T))) + 1) +
                        val(a-addr(ind1(T))))
           else
             a-addr(ind1(T))
```

```
          fi)
        fi)
      fi)
    fi  .

  eq outd2(s T) = cntl-bit(29,ind1(T)) .
  eq outd3(s T) = cntl-bit(28,ind1(T)) .
  eq outd4(s T) = cntl-field(27,26,ind1(T)) .
  eq outd5(s T) = cntl-bit(25,ind1(T)) .
  eq outd6(s T) = cntl-bit(24,ind1(T)) .
  eq outd7(s T) = cntl-bit(23,ind1(T)) .
  eq outd8(s T) = cntl-bit(22,ind1(T)) .
  eq outd9(s T) = cntl-bit(21,ind1(T)) .
  eq outd10(s T) = cntl-bit(20,ind1(T)) .
  eq outd11(s T) = cntl-bit(19,ind1(T)) .
  eq outd12(s T) = cntl-field(18,17,ind1(T)) .
  eq outd13(s T) = cntl-bit(16,ind1(T)) .
  eq outd14(s T) = cntl-bit(15,ind1(T)) .
  eq outd15(s T) = cntl-bit(14,ind1(T)) .
endo
```

We are now ready for the complete controller specification which consists of the composition of the microprogram counter, the ROM and the decoder. We show this below:

```
th CONTROL-INTERFACE is protecting MEMORY .
  ops inc1 inc3 inc4 outc3 outc11 : Nat -> List .
  ops inc2 outc1 outc2 outc4 outc5 outc6 outc7 outc8
      outc9 outc10 outc12 outc13 outc14 : Nat -> Bool .
endth


obj CONTROL-WIRES[including I/O :: CONTROL-INTERFACE] is
  ops nextaddress mpc rom : Nat -> List .
endo


obj CONTROL[including I/O :: CONTROL-INTERFACE] is
  including MPC[view to CONTROL-WIRES[I/O] is
op inm to nextaddress . op outm to mpc . endv] .
  including ROM[view to CONTROL-WIRES[I/O] is
op inr to mpc . op outr to rom . endv] .
  including DECODE[view to CONTROL-WIRES[I/O] is
      op ind1 to rom . op ind2 to inc1 . op ind3 to inc2 .
      op ind4 to inc3 . op ind5 to inc4 . op outd1 to nextaddress .
      op outd2 to outc1 . op outd3 to outc2 . op outd4 to outc3 .
      op outd5 to outc4 . op outd6 to outc5 . op outd7 to outc6 .
      op outd8 to outc7 . op outd9 to outc8 . op outd10 to outc9 .
      op outd11 to outc10 . op outd12 to outc11 .
      op outd13 to outc12 . op outd14 to outc13 .
      op outd15 to outc14 . endv] .
```

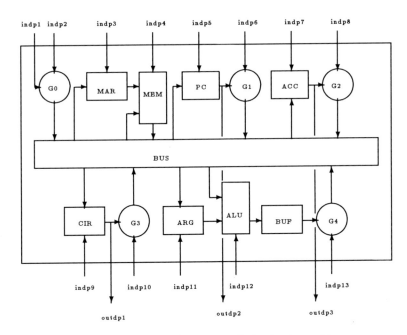

Figure 7.17: The data part of the host machine

endo

7.4.2.2 The host data part

We now proceed to the second major component of the host machine, the data part, which is shown in figure 7.17. The data part consists of the memory and the ALU plus a number of registers which communicate via a bus. Following Gordon's specification, we model the bus using three valued logic with a third constant **x** representing the floating (or high impedance) state. The object **TLIST** below introduces a new sort **Tlist** (tri-list) and declares **List** as a subsort. The operators **mk-tri : List -> Tlist** and **dest-tri : Tlist -> List** make and destroy tri-lists respectively.

```
obj TLIST is including BLIST .
  sort Tlist .
  subsort List < Tlist .
  op x : -> Tlist .
  op mk-tri : List -> Tlist .
  op dest-tri : Tlist -> List .
  op _|_ : Tlist Tlist -> Tlist [assoc comm] .
  vars L L' : List .
  eq dest-tri(mk-tri(L)) = L .
  eq dest-tri(mk-tri(L) | x) = L .
  eq x | L = L .
  eq mk-tri(L) | L' = L' .
  eq x | x = x .
```

```
endo
```

The operator _ | _ : `Tlist Tlist -> Tlist` yields the value which results when several values are simultaneously put on the bus. If only one non floating value L is put on the bus then the resulting value is L. In the definition of BUS below, we output a two state value to avoid having to use **dest-tri** in the specification of all the devices that read from the bus.

```
th BUS-INTERFACE is protecting TLIST .
  ops in1 in2 in3 in4 in5 in6 : Nat -> Tlist .
  op out : Nat -> List .
endth
```

```
obj BUS[including I/O :: BUS-INTERFACE] is
  var T : Nat .
  eq out(s T) = dest-tri( in1(T) | in2(T) | in3(T) | in4(T)
                               | in5(T) | in6(T) ) .
endo
```

We now describe the behaviour of the main memory:

```
th MEM-INTERFACE is protecting MEMORY .
  extending TLIST .
  ops in1 in2 in3 : Nat -> List .
  op out : Nat -> Tlist .
endth
```

```
obj MEM-WIRES[including I/O :: MEM-INTERFACE] is
  op m : Nat -> Memory .
endo
```

```
obj MEM[including I/O :: MEM-INTERFACE] is including MEM-WIRES[I/O] .
  var T : Nat .
  eq out(s T) = if val(in1(T)) == 1 then mk-tri(m(T) [ in2(T) ])
                  else x fi .
  eq m(s T) = if val(in1(T)) == 2 then (m(T) [ in2(T) ] := in3(T))
                  else m(T) fi .
endo
```

Thus, if the value on line **in1** is 1 then the contents of the location on line **in2** are put on the bus, otherwise the output line is floated. The new state of the memory is identical to the old one unless the value on **in1** is 2 in which case the contents of **in3** are stored in the memory at the location given by line **in2**.

The arithmetic logic unit is defined as follows:

```
th ALU-INTERFACE is protecting BLIST .
  ops in1 in2 in3 out : Nat -> List .
endth
```

```
obj ALU[including I/O :: ALU-INTERFACE] is
  var T : Nat .
```

```
  eq out(s T) = if val(in3(T)) == 0 then in2(T)
else
  (if val(in3(T)) == 1 then (inc in2(T))
   else
    (if val(in3(T)) == 2 then (add in1(T) in2(T))
     else
       (sub in1(T) in2(T))
     fi )
   fi )
fi .
endo
```

The host uses three kinds of registers, that is 13 and 16-bit registers with load enable control and a 16-bit register without load enable control. Below, we define the first type which we will then instantiate to yield the required host registers.

```
th REG16-INTERFACE is protecting BLIST .
  ops in out : Nat -> List .
  op ld : Nat -> Bool .
endth

obj REG16-WIRES[including I/O :: REG16-INTERFACE] is
  op w : Nat -> List .
endo

obj REG16[including I/O :: REG16-INTERFACE] is incl REG16-WIRES[I/O] .
  var T : Nat .
  eq out(T) = w(T) .
  eq w(s T) = if ld(T) then in(T) else w(T) fi .
endo
```

We now use the generic REG16 object to specify the accumulator, the current instruction register and the ALU arguments register.

```
obj ACC[including I/O :: REG16-INTERFACE]
       is pr REG16[I/O] * (op w to w2) . endo

obj CIR[including I/O :: REG16-INTERFACE]
       is pr REG16[I/O] * (op w to w3) . endo

obj ARG[including I/O :: REG16-INTERFACE] is
       pr REG16[I/O] * (op w to w4) . endo
```

The 13-bit register definitions of the memory address register and the program counter below are similar. Note that in this instance we can again obtain descriptions similar to LCF–LSM.

```
th REG13-INTERFACE is protecting BLIST .
  ops in out : Nat -> List .
  op ld : Nat -> Bool .
endth
```

```
obj REG13-WIRES[including I/O :: REG13-INTERFACE] is
  op w : Nat -> List .
endo

obj REG13[including I/O :: REG13-INTERFACE] is incl REG13-WIRES[I/O] .
  var T : Nat .
  eq out(T) = w(T) .
  eq w(s T) = if ld(T) then cut(3,in(T)) else w(T) fi .
endo

obj MAR[including I/O :: REG13-INTERFACE]
        is pr REG13[I/O] * (op w to w0) . endo

obj PC[including I/O :: REG13-INTERFACE]
        is pr REG13[I/O] * (op w to w1) . endo
```

The ALU buffer register is the only example of a 16-bit register with no enable control, so we define this directly as follows:

```
th BUF-INTERFACE is protecting BLIST .
  ops in out : Nat -> List .
endth

obj BUF-WIRES[including I/O :: BUF-INTERFACE] is
  op w5 : Nat -> List .
endo

obj BUF[including I/O :: BUF-INTERFACE] is including BUF-WIRES[I/O] .
  var T : Nat .
  eq out(T) = w5(T) .
  eq w5(s T) = in(T) .
endo
```

We conclude the specification of the host components by defining gates G0 through to G4. Of these, G1 is the only gate with a 13-bit input so we define this directly below:

```
th G1-INTERFACE is protecting TLIST .
  op in : Nat -> List .
  op out : Nat -> Tlist .
  op ld : Nat -> Bool .
endth

obj G1[including I/O :: G1-INTERFACE] is
  var T : Nat .
  eq out(s T) = if ld(T) then mk-tri(pad(16,in(T))) else x fi .
endo
```

The remaining four gates all have 16-bit inputs. We define them in terms of a generic device **GATE** as follows:

```
th GATE-INTERFACE is protecting TLIST .
  op in : Nat -> List .
  op out : Nat -> Tlist .
  op ld : Nat -> Bool .
endth

obj GATE[including I/O :: GATE-INTERFACE] is
  var T : Nat .
  eq out(s T) = if ld(T) then mk-tri(in(T)) else x fi .
endo

obj G0[including I/O :: GATE-INTERFACE] is pr GATE[I/O] . endo
obj G2[including I/O :: GATE-INTERFACE] is pr GATE[I/O] . endo
obj G3[including I/O :: GATE-INTERFACE] is pr GATE[I/O] . endo
obj G4[including I/O :: GATE-INTERFACE] is pr GATE[I/O] . endo
```

We are now ready to define the composition of these elements to yield the overall data part specification of figure 7.17.

```
th DATA-INTERFACE is including TLIST .
  including MEMORY .
  ops indp1 indp4 indp12 outdp1 outdp2 outdp3 : Nat -> List .
  ops indp2 indp3 indp5 indp6 indp7 indp8 indp9
      indp10 indp11 indp13 : Nat -> Bool .
endth

obj DATA-WIRES[including I/O :: DATA-INTERFACE] is
  ops mem g0 g1 g2 g3 g4 : Nat -> Tlist .
  ops bus mar arg alu buf : Nat -> List .
endo

obj DATA[including I/O :: DATA-INTERFACE] is
  including G0[view to DATA-WIRES[I/O] is
     op in to indp1 . op ld to indp2 . op out to g0 . endv] .
  including MAR[view to DATA-WIRES[I/O] is
     op in  to bus . op ld to indp3 . op out to mar . endv] .
  including MEM[view to DATA-WIRES[I/O] is
     op in1 to indp4 . op in2 to mar . op in3 to bus .
     op out to mem . endv] .
  including PC[view to DATA-WIRES[I/O] is
     op in to bus . op ld to indp5 . op out to outdp1 . endv] .
  including G1[view to DATA-WIRES[I/O] is
     op in to outdp1 . op ld to indp6 . op out to g1 . endv] .
  including ACC[view to DATA-WIRES[I/O] is
     op in to bus . op ld to indp7 . op out to outdp2 . endv] .
  including G2[view to DATA-WIRES[I/O] is
     op in to outdp2 . op ld to indp8 . op out to g2 . endv] .
  including CIR[view to DATA-WIRES[I/O] is
     op in to bus . op ld to indp9 . op out to outdp3 . endv] .
  including G3[view to DATA-WIRES[I/O] is
```

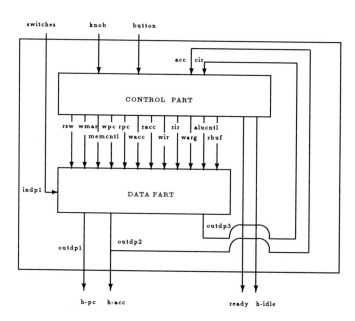

Figure 7.18: The host machine composition

```
      op in to outdp3 . op ld to indp10 . op out to g3 . endv] .
   including ARG[view to DATA-WIRES[I/O] is
      op in to bus . op ld to indp11 . op out to arg . endv] .
   including ALU[view to DATA-WIRES[I/O] is
      op in1 to arg . op in2 to bus . op in3 to indp12 .
      op out to alu . endv] .
   including BUF[view to DATA-WIRES[I/O] is
      op in to alu . op out to buf . endv] .
   including G4[view to DATA-WIRES[I/O] is
      op in to alu . op ld to indp13 . op out to g4 . endv] .
   including BUS[view to DATA-WIRES[I/O] is
      op in1 to mem . op in2 to g0 . op in3 to g1 . op in4 to g2 .
      op in5 to g3 . op in6 to g4 . op out to bus . endv] .
endo
```

7.4.2.3   The host machine specification

The host machine, shown in figure 7.18, is obtained by composing the controller with the data part as shown below.

```
th HOST-INTERFACE is including TLIST + MEMORY .
   ops switches knob h-pc h-acc : Nat -> List .
   ops button ready h-idle : Nat -> Bool .
endth

obj HOST-WIRES[including I/O :: HOST-INTERFACE] is
```

```
    ops memcntl alucntl cir : Nat -> List .
    ops rsw wmar wpc rpc wacc racc wir rir warg rbuf : Nat -> Bool .
endo

obj HOST[including I/O :: HOST-INTERFACE] is
   including CONTROL[view to HOST-WIRES[I/O] is
          op inc1 to knob . op inc2 to button .
          op inc3 to h-acc . op inc4 to cir .
          op outc1 to rsw . op outc2 to wmar .
          op outc3 to memcntl . op outc4 to wpc .
          op outc5 to rpc . op outc6 to wacc .
          op outc7 to racc . op outc8 to wir .
          op outc9 to rir . op outc10 to warg .
          op outc11 to alucntl . op outc12 to rbuf .
          op outc13 to ready . op outc14 to h-idle . endv] .
   including DATA[view to HOST-WIRES[I/O] is
          op indp1 to switches . op indp2 to rsw .
          op indp3 to wmar . op indp4 to memcntl .
          op indp5 to wpc . op indp6 to rpc .
          op indp7 to wacc . op indp8 to racc .
          op indp9 to wir . op indp10 to rir .
          op indp11 to warg . op indp12 to alucntl .
          op indp13 to rbuf . op outdp1 to h-pc .
          op outdp2 to h-acc . op outdp3 to cir . endv] .
endo
```

Finally, we complete the host specification by instantiating the parameterised HOST object using the **make** command.

```
obj IMP-WIRES is protecting TLIST + DLIST + MEMORY + SPEC-WIRES .
   ops h-pc h-acc : Nat -> List .
   ops ready h-idle : Nat -> Bool .
endo
```

```
make IMP-MOD is HOST[IMP-WIRES] endm
```

Before proceeding to the verification work, we want to reflect upon the specification of the computer and draw some conclusions. The OBJ3 specification is generic in more ways than one as it allows:

- Words of undefined but fixed length.

- Components parameterised over their external interface.

- Instantiating parameterised components to produce specific instances.

Despite the fact that timing is explicit in the axioms, clearly OBJ3 has enough expressive power for producing specifications concise enough to be comparable with those in LCF–LSM. Compared with HOL, the complexity of the axioms is very similar since HOL definitions also contain explicit time variables.

We are confident that OBJ3 has enough expressive power to deal with non trivial synchronous digital systems. Nonetheless, we would like to improve the structure and readability of hardware specifications and we will outline a solution in the next chapter.

7.4.3   Proving the correctness of the bootstrapping sequence

The first issue that needs to be addressed is the way in which several host microcycles are merged to produce a single target macrocycle. As we have seen, the host machine implementation has a ready line which goes high when the end of a series of microinstructions implementing a macroinstruction has been reached. In this sense, the target executes "faster" than the host and subsequently "waits" until the host has signalled ready. In [Gor83b] Gordon uses the special LSM term *until l do t* where *l* is a boolean and *t* is a term denoting a device with *l* as an output line. OBJ3 has no such special primitive and, fortunately, one is not needed. Instead we view the ready line going high as an external clocking event which subsumes the internal and target and host clocks. In other words, we observe the outputs of the target and host (holding the inputs constant) only when a "tick" event occurs on the ready line. This solution is sufficient for dealing with devices which have a done line. In other cases, it is necessary to set up an elaborate timing function which relates macrocycles and microcycles for each instruction. This is the solution adopted, for instance, by Hunt in his proof of the FM8501 processor [Hun85]. A similar function can be easily set up in OBJ3.

Let us now proceed to the verification itself. In [Gor83b], Gordon shows that the host is equivalent to the target subject to the *until* rule. The overall proof obligations in OBJ3, assuming that the inputs are held constant, are as follows:

```
ready(N) implies t-pc(N)   == h-pc(N)
ready(N) implies t-acc(N)  == h-acc(N)
ready(N) implies t-idle(N) == h-idle(N)
```

These sentences are universally quantified over the time variable N and the interface wires and existentially quantified over the internal wires. The proof strategy consists of connecting the same set of inputs to the target and host and then showing that the two machines are behaviourally equivalent, that is they produce the same outputs provided that the ready line is high.

Since our primary objective is to test the viability of OBJ3 for non trivial hardware examples rather than to prove the correctness of Gordon's computer, we do not discharge these proof obligations. Instead we prove three instances of the above theorems which verify the bootstrapping sequence of the computer. The fetch-decode-execute cycle can be verified in a similar manner.

We prove the following facts, assuming a start address of 0 which is the start address of the bootstrapping sequence in the microcode. The effect of pressing the button while the idle light is on is:

1. If the value of the knob is 0, the word determined by the state of the 13 rightmost switches is loaded in the program counter:

$$\texttt{ready(n + 10) implies h-pc(n + 10) == t-pc(n + 10)}$$

where n is a time constant used as a variable.

2. If the value of the knob is 1, the word determined by the state of the 16 switches is loaded in the accumulator.

$$\texttt{ready(n + 10) implies h-acc(n + 10) == t-acc(n + 10)}$$

3. If the value of the knob is 2, the contents of the accumulator are stored in the memory at the location given by the contents of the program counter.

$$\texttt{ready(n + 10) implies mem(n + 10) == ram(n + 10)}$$

Let us explain the (n + 10) term. Each of these operations require the execution of 3 microinstructions for each macroinstruction. Each microinstruction is fetched and decoded in three host cycles and is executed in four cycles since data has to be propagated through four components (for example DECODER, GO, BUS and PC for the first theorem) before it reaches the output lines that we observe. Since we assume the first microinstruction (at address 0) the operation requires 6 cycles, three each for the remaining microinstructions, plus 4 cycles for data propagation, which yields the (n + 10) term. Thus, for the bootstrapping sequence, each target cycle is implemented by 10 host cycles.

We now present the proofs themselves. The object PROOF below combines the host and target specification and introduces the constants n :   -> Nat and RAM : -> Memory as well as the input and target assumptions.

```
obj PROOF is including SPEC-MOD + IMP-MOD .
  op n   : -> Nat .
  op RAM : -> Memory .
  var T : Nat .
  eq button(T) = true .
  eq computer(n) = [RAM wordn(13,0) wordn(16,0) true] .
endo
```

The button is held permanently to true and the target is initialised with the appropriate state. Note that the state of the switches at time n is immaterial and is, therefore, left unspecified. The object below introduces the host assumptions.

```
obj HOST-ASSUMPTIONS is including PROOF .
  eq memcntl(n) = wordn(2,1) .
  eq alucntl(n) = wordn(2,0) .
  eq cir(n) = wordn(5,0) .
  eq rsw(n) = false .
  eq wmar(n) = false .
  eq wpc(n) = false .
  eq rpc(n) = false .
  eq wacc(n) = false .
  eq racc(n) = false .
  eq wir(n) = false .
  eq rir(n) = false .
  eq warg(n) = false .
```

```
      eq rbuf(n) = false .
      eq nextaddress(n) = wordn(5,0) .
      eq mpc(n) = wordn(5,0) .
      eq rom(n) = microcode(wordn(5,0)) .
      eq mem(n) = mk-tri(wordn(16,0)) .
      eq g0(n) = mk-tri(wordn(16,0)) .
      eq g1(n) = mk-tri(wordn(16,0)) .
      eq g2(n) = mk-tri(wordn(16,0)) .
      eq g3(n) = mk-tri(wordn(16,0)) .
      eq g4(n) = mk-tri(wordn(16,0)) .
      eq bus(n) = wordn(16,0) .
      eq mar(n) = wordn(13,0) .
      eq arg(n) = wordn(16,0) .
      eq alu(n) = wordn(16,0) .
      eq buf(n) = wordn(16,0) .
      eq m(n) = RAM .
      eq w(n) = wordn(5,0) .
      eq w0(n) = wordn(13,0) .
      eq w1(n) = wordn(13,0) .
      eq w2(n) = wordn(16,0) .
      eq w3(n) = wordn(16,0) .
      eq w4(n) = wordn(16,0) .
      eq ready(n) = true .
      eq h-idle(n) = true .
endo
```

Thus the host is initialised with the microinstruction at location 0. These assumptions
were taken from the relevant theorem of [Gor83b].

We will now concentrate on the proof of our first theorem. For this, we need the extra
assumption that the knob is held at position 0.

```
obj HKNOB0 is including HOST-ASSUMPTIONS .
   var T : Nat .
   eq knob(T) = wordn(2,0) .
endo
```

The theorem is proved with the following series of reductions which all evaluate as indicated and amount to symbolic execution of the target and host machines:

```
red rom(n) .
---> Should be microcode(wordn(5,0))
red nextaddress(n + 1) .
---> Should be 00001
red mpc(n + 2) .
---> Should be 00001
red rom(n + 3) .
---> Should be microcode(wordn(5,1))
red nextaddress(n + 4) .
---> Should be 00010
red mpc(n + 5) .
```

```
---> Should be 00010
red rom(n + 6) .
---> Should be microcode(wordn(5,2))
red rsw(n + 7) .
---> Should be true
red g0(n + 8) .
---> Should be switches(n) .
red bus(n + 9) .
---> Should be switches(n)
red wpc(n + 9) .
---> Should be true
red h-pc(n + 10) .
---> Should be cut(3,switches(n))
red ready(n + 10) .
---> Should be true
red t-pc(n + 10) .
---> Should be cut(3,switches)
```

This proves that ready(n + 10) implies h-pc(n + 10) == t-pc(n + 10).   Note that we do not directly reduce the term in order to avoid the "false implies everything" problem.

For the second theorem we assume that the knob is held at position 1 and perform the following set of reductions:

```
obj HKNOB1 is including HOST-ASSUMPTIONS .
  var T : Nat .
  eq knob(T) = wordn(2,1) .
endo
```

```
red rom(n) .
---> Should be microcode(wordn(5,0))
red nextaddress(n + 1) .
---> Should be 00001
red mpc(n + 2) .
---> Should be 00001
red rom(n + 3) .
---> Should be microcode(wordn(5,1))
red nextaddress(n + 4) .
---> Should be 00011
red mpc(n + 5) .
---> Should be 00011
red rom(n + 6) .
---> Should be microcode(wordn(5,3))
red rsw(n + 7) .
---> Should be true
red g0(n + 8) .
---> Should be switches(n)
red bus(n + 9) .
---> Should be switches(n)
red wacc(n + 9) .
```

```
---> Should be true
red h-acc(n + 10) .
---> Should be switches(n)
red ready(n + 10) .
---> Should be true
red t-acc(n + 10) .
---> Should be switches(n)
```

A similar set of assumptions and reductions prove the third theorem. In this case we also assume that the bus holds the appropriate values at the given times in order to avoid having to load the program counter and the accumulator (which would take 20 microcycles).

```
obj HKNOB2 is including HOST-ASSUMPTIONS .
  var T : Nat .
  eq knob(T) = wordn(2,2) .
  eq bus(n + 9) = h-pc(n) .
  eq bus(n + 10) = h-acc(n) .
endo
```

```
red rom(n) .
---> Should be microcode(wordn(5,0))
red nextaddress(n + 1) .
---> Should be 00001
red mpc(n + 2) .
---> Should be 00001
red rom(n + 3) .
---> Should be microcode(wordn(5,1))
red nextaddress(n + 4) .
---> Should be 00100
red mpc(n + 5) .
---> Should be 00100
red rom(n + 6) .
---> Should be microcode(wordn(5,4))
red wmar(n + 7) .
---> Should be true
red w0(n + 8) .
---> Should be bus(n + 7)
red nextaddress(n + 7) .
---> Should be 00111
red rom(n + 9) .
---> Should be microcode(wordn(5,7))
red memcntl(n + 9) .
---> Should be 10
red mem(n + 10) .
---> Should be mem(n + 9) [h-pc(n) !is h-acc(n)]
red ready(n + 10) .
---> Should be true
red ram(n + 10) .
---> Should be  ram(n + 9) [ t-pc(n) !is t-acc(n) ]
```

	Specification	Simulation	Verification
Expressive power	adequate	n/a	n/a
Executability	incremental construction	direct	prerequisite
CAD interface	none (desirable)	none (desirable)	n/a
Style	n/a	n/a	semi-automatic
Reasoning framework	n/a	n/a	extended equational logic term rewriting induction
Reasoning overheads	n/a	n/a	low
User friendliness	good	good	fair
Performance	n/a	poor	poor
Required expertise	low	low	fair

Table 7.3: Summary evaluation of OBJ3 approach

This concludes the correctness proof of the bootstrapping sequence. As we have seen, all the above proofs have been obtained by straightforward rewriting and involve symbolic execution of the machine. Therefore, OBJ3 encourages simple proof strategies which are supported by an equally simple inference mechanism. We have found that the strong typing of the language is very helpful in non trivial proofs; a similar proof with Boyer–Moore would be cluttered with type checking right inside the axioms and theorems. Furthermore, we are convinced that the simulation capability of OBJ3 is a very useful asset in debugging such large specifications. It seems unlikely that we would have been able to complete this case study in such a short time, had we not been able to animate the specifications. The whole exercise took approximately six weeks which compares well with Gordon's "several months". However, it must be borne in mind, that we followed Gordon's specification very closely and we were in this sense walking a well trodden path, we made no modifications to the OBJ3 software and of course we have only proved partial correctness.

We conclude from this exercise, that OBJ3 can be used for non trivial hardware verification, at least theoretically speaking. It seems to us, that the biggest obstacle to such work is the, currently, inefficient OBJ3 implementation. The reduction engine is slow, performing at approximately 2,500 rewrites/hour for a rule set of about 300 axioms on an 8Mb Sparc2 workstation; comparable languages such as Axis [C$^+$88], achieve 2,500 rewrites/second. Our work was practical only on a 32Mb Sparc2 with 80Mb of local swap space. Even then the 300,000 rewrites required to reduce the term h-pc(n + 10) took 24 CPU hours. The whole proof effort required approximately 10 CPU days.

7.5   Discussion

We summarise our evaluation of the OBJ3 approach in table 7.3. We have found that the

OBJ3 framework is superior to the term rewriting approach both in terms of specification and verification activities. Specifications in OBJ3 are general, simple, structured and readable; in short they reap the benefits of many years of research in the specification and design of software. In terms of verification, the semi automatic approach proposed here offers relief from tedious calculations whilst still allowing substantial user guidance. Investigative simulation can be easily carried out although we do not believe that realistic simulation is possible due to the inherent inefficiency of term rewriting operational semantics.

We now need to note the drawbacks of the approach. We have found that quality of the OBJ3 software wanting for three reasons. First, the implementation we used for this work (version of 3/1/91) contained serious bugs such as an incomplete pattern matcher and a rewrite engine which sometimes "forgets" sets of rules. Secondly, there is no support for incremental compilation; the smallest change in the specification necessitates a full recompilation. This problem is particularly acute when the specification contains a large number of parameterised/instantiated modules. In such circumstances (as was the case with our microprocessor example), both compilation and rewriting become impractical on less than massive machines. Finally, the operational semantics of the module combinators are not clearly defined; again a serious handicap for largely parameterised specifications. This last problem, coupled with the lack of a standard module library can hamper specification reuse.

Throughout this book we have argued for the importance of a designer friendly formalism; it is true to say, however, that OBJ3 is yet another alien formalism to practising designers. Moreover, there are certain aspects of designs such as bus specifications, which can be long and cumbersome, and bidirectionality which is not allowed in specifications. If we manage to shield the engineer from a formal specification notation, he still needs to tell us what properties he expects from his design; he therefore needs a friendly language in which to express his intentions which are, essentially, the proof obligations for the design. All these observations, led us to the conclusion that a further formalism is needed as an OBJ3 front end; we shall discuss current work in this direction in the next and concluding chapter.

We also need ways of improving the simulation capabilities. In this respect, it is desirable to take direct advantage of existing simulators incorporating existing best practice in industry. Again, we outline our intentions for the provision of a CAD interface for OBJ3 in the next chapter.

Finally, OBJ3 was not designed as a theorem prover. In spite of this, we have shown that substantial reasoning efforts are already supported by the tool. We would however prefer a better engineered solution, providing for instance automatically generated proof scores for inductive arguments as well as better proof management facilities. These problems can be addressed by the provision of a theorem proving interface for OBJ3; we sketch this in the following chapter.

In conclusion, we feel that the use of OBJ3 in the hardware domain is a neat and elegant approach. In spite of the current implementation problems, we have been able to demonstrate its utility in three major design activities, namely specification, simulation and verification. Perhaps the most important aspect of this work is its contribution to the maturity of VLSI engineering by directly harnessing the body of knowledge produced over many years by the software engineering community.

Chapter 8

Conclusions

8.1 Summary

In our introductory chapter we presented our view of the system development process. The second chapter identified the requirements on formalisms proposed for use in the design of digital systems, thereby setting out our terms of reference in the form of certain evaluation criteria.

The third chapter presented our case studies with a number of formalisms and discussed our investigation in terms of the defined criteria.

Following on, we presented our first approach which concentrated on UMIST OBJ and term rewriting. Having identified the strengths and weaknesses of the approach we proceeded to improve the techniques via the OBJ3 paradigm in the fifth and sixth chapters. In the seventh chapter we demonstrated the viability of the OBJ3 approach for the specification and verification of non trivial hardware systems.

8.2 Discussion

In this book we have striven both to formulate a hypothesis and test it. We have formulated our requirements and conducted experiments with a number of approaches before proposing our own. The following facts became obvious during this work:

Formal methods and digital design

1. VLSI engineering is in many respects a less mature discipline in terms of methods when compared to software engineering.

2. No formal approach will be industrially acceptable in the long term unless it efficiently addresses at least some aspects of digital design as discussed in our second chapter, thereby resulting in commercial advantage.

3. Formal methods utility must be soberly assessed and presented especially in high integrity applications.

4. The ultimate goal must be that hardware verification is done by hardware designers, not specially "bought in" mathematicians who should rather be viewed as consultants to this process.

157

Specification aspects

1. No formalism and associated approach is perfect when evaluated against our criteria.

2. It makes sense to use the simplest possible logical framework for a given application area. Otherwise, there is a heavy price to pay when formal reasoning is undertaken.

3. Although directly executable notations are not necessary, they do provide an easy way of carrying out investigative simulation and are therefore desirable.

4. Interfaces with state of the art VLSI CAD tools are desirable.

Verification aspects

1. Fully automatic theorem provers are unsatisfactory but automatic verification remains an interesting research problem. Proof checkers are also disappointing. The current state of the art goes as far as semi automatic theorem proving.

2. The task of machine aided reasoning should be seen in the same terms as programming. It is an intellectually demanding task and its execution would benefit from tools analogous to those for software engineering. Using proof checkers is similar to writing assembly language programs whereas automatic theorem provers can be seen as a metaphor for program generators. We argue that semi automatic proving corresponds to imperative programming where the user decides on control flow (proof strategy) and the machine executes predefined functions (proof scores).

3. An interesting research direction would be to apply the notions of refinement (the *improvement* of our first chapter) to proof design and development.

8.3   The FUNNEL CHDL

Our work has led to the recognition that although the OBJ3 paradigm is suitable for the treatment of digital systems, we have but the bare necessities for the task. A number of problems have been identified in the preceding chapter. We will now outline current work and future plans for embedding the approach in a more appropriate framework.

We believe that we need an integrated environment, suitable for industrial use, that supports all three major activities associated with the design of digital systems, namely specification, simulation and formal verification.

We recognise that OBJ3 specifications can be cumbersome for some designs, for instance those involving buses, and we also accept that digital designers will find the notation alien. We have, therefore, decided to provide a CHDL front end to OBJ3 in order to overcome the problem of tedious or weird encodings. To this end we have designed FUNNEL [SGEA91, AGSE92, SGS⁺92], a CHDL with formal semantics and we have implemented a FUNNEL to OBJ3 compiler. FUNNEL specifications can therefore be used for simulation and verification. We have also mentioned that the abilities of OBJ3 as a theorem prover can be enhanced by the provision of a theorem proving front end. This is currently under development, by Goguen *et al*, as the 2OBJ tool [GSHH92] which provides a generic, graphical interface to OBJ3.

FUNNEL-1 is a strongly typed CHDL which aims to provide a basic minimum of features for describing data, device behaviour and interconnections. The data types are restricted to integers and user defined finite sorts. Devices may be described by their behaviour (for primitive components) or by their structure (for devices built out of smaller devices) or by a mixture.

8.3.1 Data types

A FUNNEL-1 specification has exactly one data type declaration, starting with the keyword **datatype** and ending with the keyword **endd**. Each statement in the data type declaration can have one of four forms:

1. A *sort declaration* which declares a new finite sort together with names for each of its elements (constants), for example:

   ```
   Bit is {true, false, unknown};
   ```

2. An *operation declaration*, for example:

   ```
   and : Bit Bit -> Bit;
   ```

3. A *variable declaration* which may declare one or more variables of the same sort, for example:

   ```
   var X, Y : Bit;
   ```

4. An (multiple) *equation* defining an operation, for example:

   ```
   and(false, X) = and(X, false) = false;
   ```

Multiple equations of the form $t_1 = t_2 = \cdots = t_n = t$ are equivalent to a sequence of equations $t_1 = t, t_2 = t, \ldots, t_n = t$. The left hand side of each equation may contain only the name of the operation being defined with constants and variables as arguments. The right hand side may contain references to other operations as well as constants and variables. Such operations must have already been defined on all arguments needed to evaluate the right hand side on any assignment to the variables.

All user defined operations are prefix and have their arguments enclosed in parentheses. No identifier may be used before it is declared, no operation can be defined to have more than one distinct value on any given arguments and all operations must be totally defined by the end of the data type declaration.

There are three built in sorts. The sort *Int* has constants $0, 1, 2, \ldots$, binary operations $+, -$ and $*$ and the unary operation $-$ with their usual interpretations (negative numbers are formed by a unary minus). The sort *Time* has a constant 0 and the prefix successor operation $++$ and is isomorphic to the natural numbers without the plus and times operations. The sort *Bool* has constants *true* and *false* and a polymorphic equality operation '=='. Since *Bool* is a finite sort, connectives such as 'and' and 'or' may be defined by the user.

8.3.2   Modules

A FUNNEL-1 specification has one or more module declarations which follow the data type declaration. A module declaration starts with the keyword **module** and ends with the keyword **endm**. The first item inside the module declaration is the module name, which is followed by a list of I/O connections enclosed in parentheses. Several I/O connections of the same sort can be declared with only one mention of the sort name by separating them by commas. I/O connections with differing sorts are separated by semicolons, for example:

```
module INTMUX(in1, in2, out : Int; select : Bit)
```

No distinction is made between inputs, outputs, and bidirectional connections and therefore at least some aspects of bidirectionality are captured (bidirectionality is further supported by the language semantics). A module has three optional parts; **contents**, **axioms** and **cspec**. We examine these in turn. The complete BNF syntax of FUNNEL and an example of the compiler output are given in [SGEA91].

8.3.3   Contents

The contents part describes an interconnection of instances of previously defined modules (a netlist). It starts with the keyword **contents** and may contain statements of two kinds:

1. A *wire declaration* declares one or more internal (hidden) wires of the same sort:

    ```
    wire load, q, qbar : Bit;
    ```

2. A *module instantiation*, for example:

    ```
    NOTGATE(q, qbar);
    ```

I/O connections are considered to be a special case of wires and a wire of sort s is considered to be a function $Time \rightarrow s$.

8.3.4   Axioms

The axioms part consists of equations that define the behaviour of a module. A module with no contents is considered an atomic or primitive component. The behaviour of a module can include initialisations, assumptions, axioms and theorems. This kind of structure aids abstraction, encapsulation and locality since all relevant information about a component is stored right inside the defining module. When a module uses another module, it automatically knows all there is to know about the import.

The axioms part must follow the contents part (if one exists) and starts with the keyword **axioms**. It may contain three types of statements:

1. A *variable definition* of the same form as that in the data type declaration.

2. An *equation*. The left hand side may not consist of a single variable and the right hand side may not contain variables not mentioned in the left hand side. There are no other restrictions and wires and I/O connections previously declared in the module may be referenced as functions taking an argument of sort *Time*.

3. A *conditional equation*. This has a similar form to an equation but is followed by an if clause containing a *Bool* expression which may only contain variables mentioned in the left hand side of the equation. For example:

```
drain(T) = source(T) if gate(T) == high
```

8.3.5 Correctness specification

Designer intentions which form the proof obligations of the design are defined in the correctness specification part of the module which starts with the keyword **cspec**. The cspec part is optional and is syntactically similar to the axioms part. The difference is that it is used to record properties which have not yet been proved. For example:

```
q(++ T) = f if clear(T) == t;
```

It is our intention to structure the interaction between FUNNEL and 2OBJ so that once the proof obligations have been discharged, they are moved into the axioms part of the module. Operationally, cspec equations are labelled as conjectures by the compiler so that they can be distinguished from axioms during verification.

As an illustration of the descriptive power of FUNNEL, we show below the specification of the twisted ring counter of section 5.3.2. Note the similarity with the equivalent HOL specification of section 3.4.3 despite the fact that HOL is higher order and FUNNEL is not. We start with the data type which is a straightforward definition of two valued logic.

```
datatype
        Bit is {t, f};
        and : Bit Bit -> Bit;
        or : Bit Bit -> Bit;
        not : Bit -> Bit;
var X : Bit;
        and(f, X) = and(X, f) = f;
        and(t, t) = t;
        or(f, f) = f;
        or(X, t) = or(t, X) = t;
        not(f) = t;
        not(t) = f;
endd
```

We then define modules to represent the primitive components.

```
module ANDGATE(i1, i2, out : Bit)
axioms   var T : Time ;
        out(T) = and(i1(T), i2(T)) ;
endm

module ORGATE(i1, i2, out : Bit)
axioms   var T : Time ;
        out(T) = or(i1(T), i2(T)) ;
endm
```

```
module DTYPE(d, reset, q, q-bar : Bit)
axioms   var T : Time ;
         q(s T) = f if reset == t ;
         q(s T) = d(T) if reset == f ;
         q-bar(T) = not(q(T)) ;
endm
```

Finally, we define a module to represent the counter itself together with the associated proof obligations.

```
module TRC(reset, a, b, c : Bit)
contents wire Da, Db, Dc, a-bar, b-bar, c-bar, x : Bit ;
         ORGATE(b-bar, c, x) ;
         ANDGATE(a-bar, x, Dc) ;
         DTYPE(Da, reset, a, a-bar) ;
         DTYPE(Db, reset, b, b-bar) ;
         DTYPE(Dc, reset, c, c-bar) ;
cspec var T : Time;
/* If a reset occurs the next state is 000 */
         a(++ T) = f if reset(T) == t ;
         b(++ T) = f if reset(T) == t ;
         c(++ T) = f if reset(T) == t ;
/* Rest of proof obligations */
endm
```

Even though FUNNEL is designed as a CHDL, we feel that it is important to allow designers to continue using languages such as VHDL and ELLA because these are representative of existing best practice and have, therefore, the commitment of industry. This is feasible in our context by providing translators from these languages to FUNNEL. The example above is expressed in FUNNEL-1, the first version of the language. A much more expressive version of the language, FUNNEL-2, is currently under development. FUNNEL-2 includes records in the data type declaration and supports replicated modules and vectors of wires. Modules can also be parameterised by size thus allowing the specification of arbitrary sized structures.

The context of the design cycle in the enhanced OBJ3 paradigm is shown in figure 8.1. The engineer is free to express his designs either directly in FUNNEL or in another CHDL such as VHDL or ELLA. The resulting FUNNEL code is translated to OBJ3 and the specification together with the proof obligation are then passed on to 2OBJ for theorem proving. In the long term, it would be desirable to have a much more efficient OBJ3 implementation. In order to mitigate some of the efficiency problems of the current version in the short term, we are working towards a generalised version of Bryant's BDD algorithms [Bry84] which could be incorporated in the existing software.

Instead of designing our own CHDL, we could have provided direct translation from, say, ELLA to OBJ3. We have not chosen this option for the following reasons:

1. It can be difficult to provide precise semantics for some obscure features of existing CHDLs (for example the VHDL δ delay). By starting from scratch we overcome this difficulty. This way, we are also at liberty to choose a style of semantics (sheaf theory and initial algebra in the case of FUNNEL [SGEA91]) which is tailored for proving the transformations to OBJ3 correct.

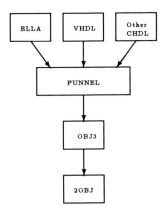

Figure 8.1: Extended OBJ3 design cycle and tools

2. It is desirable to have a generic framework for use with more than one CHDL. FUNNEL is designed as a rational match to both ELLA and VHDL.

3. FUNNEL provides a friendly notation in which the engineer can express his intentions about his designs by writing ELLA-style specifications instead of, say, HOL predicates.

4. It is important to interface with existing CAD tools which are tailored to individual CHDLs. By providing an ELLA to FUNNEL connection for instance, we can take advantage of the ELLA simulator, libraries and the associated CAD tools.

These ideas result in an *integrated digital design support environment* as shown in figure 8.2. We are currently working on building such an architecture which can be extended when required to accommodate tools such as proof editors and debuggers. We are also continuing our experiments in this framework by tackling test cases such as a Sobel image processing chip and further simple microprocessors.

8.4 Postscript

We conclude this ultimate chapter with a subjective account of the state of the art and current issues in the formal specification and verification of hardware.

8.4.1 What we have today

Well developed hardware specification notations and models although there is scope for improvement especially in the areas of asynchronous design and analog circuitry. In the words of Tony Hoare [Hoa90a] models are like seeds scattered in the wind. Most will perish but others will root and flourish. The more seeds the better. A question often asked of us is "which is the best notation/system" to use. It seems to us that the choice of notation for specifying hardware is similar to

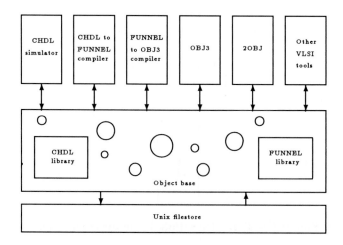

Figure 8.2: Digital design support environment

the choice one has to make on which programming language to use when writing software. Although trends come and go, in the end, the answer must relate to the characteristics of the specific product being developed and the background of the individuals involved.

Well developed theorem proving tools, a selection of which has been described in this book. The differences between the quality of such tools in the mid-80s with their counterparts of today are very marked, particularly through the provision of much improved user interfaces.

Some impressive hardware verification results. Proving the correctness of simple microprocessors is no longer an issue as the representative work at Cambridge and CLInc illustrates. CLInc's work on the FM9001 is particularly interesting as it adds the important dimension of synthesis to hardware verification. However, realistic microprocessors such as the T9000 transputer are still problematic and we can only deal with some of their aspects.

8.4.2   Issues for the future

We must distinguish between the issues relating to technology and those relating to research. By "technology" we mean the transition from research results to methods and tools which are "fit for purpose" with regard to the needs of the VLSI industry. Understanding the difference between technology and research results is crucial and can go some way in explaining the reluctance of industry to pick up formal methods. The fact that, say, on day 1 a highly trained expert proves the correctness of a simple microprocessor in a formal methods laboratory does not imply that on day 2 a multi-billion dollar VLSI manufacturer will have its designers use a theorem prover. Suitable technology must be produced before the process is enabled and as with any other endeavour the user (not the research) community must be the driving force.

8.4.2.1 Technology issues

Industrial quality tools which are well engineered and have suitable user interfaces. As we pointed out earlier, the user interface issue has been the prime beneficiary of theorem proving developments form 1985 onwards. Much remains to be done in improving the efficacy of theorem proving tools by, for instance, incorporating fast decision procedures (such as BDDs) and graph reduction packages where appropriate. Producing industrial quality software of any kind requires levels of funding which are not normally available to research workers. On the other hand, before industry can be convinced to sponsor the development of quality tools they must be persuaded that they have a use for them; but they will not consider such tools useful unless they are well engineered and hence there is a "chicken and egg" situation. The answer must be a level of synergy between the two issues.

Interface to best existing practice. Formal methods are a supplemental *not* a replacement technology. They must therefore work in harmony with existing methods and tools, the purpose of the integration being to strengthen rather than replace existing technology. Happily, there has been a definite trend in this direction by many hardware verification workers. This is happening in two, complementary ways. First, the rôle of formal methods as a supplemental technology is explored by many people (see for example [VVCM92, Ros92, BCF92, BHY92]). Second, efforts to interface to current technology are exemplified by the investigations into the semantics of CHDLs and the subsequent provision of formal reasoning frameworks (e.g. [BGG$^+$92, BGM91, B$^+$91, Goo90, SGS$^+$92, LFMM92, BPS92]).

So, the hardware verification community has, in the past 5 years or so, gone some way in producing results which enable the transformation of research into technology although much remains to be done in terms of technology transfer.

8.4.2.2 Research issues

A concern, separate from ways of transforming research results into technology fit for purpose, is the direction of further research in hardware verification. We believe that much remains to be done in terms of notations and models as we have said earlier. However, a most pressing question is the shape of the future theorem proving activity itself whether it relates to hardware, software or both. We strongly believe that theorem proving methods have a great deal in common with software engineering and future breakthroughs in the area are likely to originate from recognising and exploiting this fact.

In our view *proofs are programs* and the evolution of theorem proving closely resembles the evolution of programming practice. Currently, proofs look and read like machine code programs with all the consequences for the process of producing such proofs. Proof tactics that largely characterise the writing and execution of proofs closely resemble assembler macros. It seems to us that theorem proving will have to make the difficult transition from an activity of the select few to an engineering discipline much the same way as software engineering has evolved from the days of machine/assembly coding of the 50s and the 60s.

The crucial prerequisite of the evolution of software engineering has been the concept of *abstraction*. Abstraction provided by operating systems, high level programming languages and their compilers, specification languages and the associated machinery such as editors, debuggers, configuration managers and so on. We believe that discovering ways of harnessing abstraction in theorem proving will be exciting and empowering.

Liskov and Guttag [LG86] in their excellent textbook on *Abstraction and Specification in Program Development* argue that abstraction is 2-dimensional. First, it can be obtained via *parameterisation*, e.g. the use of procedure parameters so that a piece of code is usable on large, perhaps polymorphic data sets. Second, abstraction by *specification* is used to hide details by concentrating on what needs to be achieved by a piece of code rather than describing ways of achieving what is required. Abstraction by parameterisation is, to some degree, already exploited in theorem proving through the logical framework ideas [HHP87, GSHH92] of having the object logic as a parameter of a theorem prover rather than "hardwiring" it in. Abstraction by specification, however, is a subject largely unresearched. We believe that abstraction by specification is sorely in need of research and holds great promise for the future, if the experience of software engineering is anything to go by. Proof specification languages and proof refinement, automatic or not, are aims well worth striving for. Once these methods have been understood and developed, the theorem provers of today will become the proof compilers of tomorrow.

Appendix A

Data types for Gordon's computer

A.1 Natural numbers for Gordon's computer

```
in propc

obj NAT is protecting PROPC .
  sorts Nat NzNat Int .
  subsorts NzNat < Nat < Int .
  op 0 : -> Nat .
  op s_: Int -> Int [prec 1] .
  op s_: Nat -> NzNat [prec 1] .
  op p_: Int -> Int [prec 1] .
  op p_: NzNat -> Nat [prec 1] .
  op _+_ : Nat Nat -> Nat [memo] .
  op _/2 : Nat -> Nat [memo] .        *** divide by 2
  op _%2 : Nat -> Nat [memo] .        *** remainder of division by 2
  op _/2_ : Nat Int -> Nat [memo] .  *** N /2 T is divide N by 2**T
  op odd_ : Nat -> Prop [prec 1 memo] .
  ops (_<_) (_>=_) (_<=_) : Nat Nat -> Bool .
  op _*_ : Nat Nat -> Nat [memo] .
  ops 1 2 3 4 5 6 7 8 9 10 11 12 13 14 15 16 17 18 19 20
      21 22 23 24 25 26 27 28 29 30 : -> NzNat .
  vars M N : Nat .
  var N' : NzNat .
  var I : Int .
  eq  1 = s 0 .

      :

  eq 30 = s 29 .
  eq 0 * M = 0 .
  eq (s N) * M = M + (N * M) .
  eq M < 0 = false .
  eq s M < s N = M < N .
  eq N' < 0 = false .
  eq N >= M = (M == N) or (M < N) .
  eq N <= M = (M == N) or (N < M) .
```

167

```
  eq s p I = I .
  eq p s M = M .
  eq M + 0 = M .
  eq M + (s N) = s(M + N) .
  eq 0 /2 = 0 .
  eq (s 0) /2 = 0 .
  eq (s s M) /2 = s(M /2) .
  eq M %2 = if (odd M) then (s 0) else 0 fi .
  eq M /2 0 = M .
  eq M /2 p 0 = 0 .
  eq M /2 s N = (M /2) /2 N .
  eq odd 0 = false .
  eq odd s M = not odd M .
endo
```

A.2   Parameterised lists

```
obj LIST[X :: TRIV] is pr NAT .
 sorts List NeList .
 subsorts Elt < NeList < List .
 op nil : -> List .
 op __ : List List -> List [assoc id: nil prec 9] .
 op __ : NeList List -> NeList [assoc prec 9] .
 op head_ : NeList -> Elt .
 op tail_ : NeList -> List .
 op empty?_ : List -> Bool .
 op length : List -> Nat .
 op _#_ : List Elt -> NeList . *** right append
 op rev_ : List -> List .
 vars X X' : Elt .
 var L : List .
 eq head (X L) = X .
 eq tail (X L) = L .
 eq empty? L = L == nil .
 eq length(nil) = 0 .
 eq length(X L) = s (length(L)) .
 eq nil # X = X .
 eq (X L) # X' = X (L # X') .
 eq rev nil = nil .
 eq rev (X L) = (rev L) # X .
endo
```

A.3   Parameterised finite maps

```
obj FINITE-MAP[DOMAIN RANGE :: TRIV] is protecting BOOL .
  sort Map .
  op < _ > : Elt.RANGE -> Map .
  op _ [ _ !is _ ] : Map Elt.DOMAIN Elt.RANGE -> Map . *** store
```

```
op _ without _ : Map Elt.DOMAIN -> Map . *** remove

op _ [ _ ] := _ : Map Elt.DOMAIN Elt.RANGE -> Map . *** assignment
op _ [ _ ] : Map Elt.DOMAIN -> Elt.RANGE . *** fetch
op _ has _ : Map Elt.DOMAIN -> Bool . *** range check

var m : Map .
vars d1 d2 : Elt.DOMAIN .
vars r1 r2 : Elt.RANGE .

eq < r1 > has d1 = false .
eq < r1 > [ d1 ] = r1 .
eq < r1 > without d1 = < r1 > .

cq (m [ d1 !is r1 ]) [ d2 ] = r1 if (d1 == d2) .
cq (m [ d1 !is r1 ]) [ d2 ] = m [ d2 ] if (d1 =/= d2) .

cq (m [ d1 !is r1 ]) without d2 = m if (d1 == d2) .
cq (m [ d1 !is r1 ]) without d2 = (m without d2) [ d1 !is r1 ]
                  if (d1 =/= d2) .

cq (m [ d1 !is r1 ]) has d2 = true if (d1 == d2) .
cq (m [ d1 !is r1 ]) has d2 = m has d2 if (d1 =/= d2) .

eq (m [ d1 ] := r1) = (m without d1) [ d1 !is r1 ] .
endo
```

Bibliography

[A+92]   A. M. Ahi et al. Verification of the HP 9000 Series 700 PA–RISC Worksta-
           tions. *Hewlett–Packard Journal*, pages 34–42, August 1992.

[AGSE92]   S. N. Aloneftis, J. A. Goguen, V. Stavridou, and S. M. Eker. A Sheaf Se-
           mantics for the FUNNEL Hardware Description Language. Draft technical
           note, June 1992.

[AL91]   M. Aargaard and M. E. Leeser. The Implementation and Proof of a Boolean
           Simplification System. In G. Jones and M. Sheeran, editors, *Designing Cor-
           rect Circuits*, pages 171–195. Springer–Verlag, 1991.

[AW77]   E. A. Ashcroft and W. W. Wadge. Lucid - a Non Procedural Language With
           Iteration. *Comms of ACM*, 20(7), July 1977.

[B+89]   D. Bjorner et al. A ProCoS Project Description ESPRIT BRA 3104. *EATCS
           Bulletin*, (39):60–73, October 1989.

[B+91]   H. Barringer et al. Semantics and Verification for Boolean Kernel ELLA. In
           *Proceedings of IFIP TC 10/WG 10.2 Advanced Research Workshop on Cor-
           rect Hardware Design Methodologies*, pages 65–90, Turin, Italy, June 1991.

[Bac78]   J. Backus. Can Programming be Liberated from the von Neumann Style? A
           Functional Style and its Algebra of Programs. *Communications of the ACM*,
           21(8):613–641, August 1978.

[BAN89]   M. Burrows, M. Abadi, and R. Needham. A Logic of Authentication. Tech-
           nical Report 39, DEC Systems Research Center, February 1989.

[Bar77]   K. J. Barwise. *Handbook of Mathematical Logic*, volume 90 of *Studies in Logic
           and the Foundations of Mathematics*. North-Holland, Amsterdam, 1977.

[Bar84]   H. G. Barrow. Proving the Correctness of Digital Hardware Designs. *VLSI
           Design*, pages 64–77, July 1984.

[BC84]   G. Berry and L. Cosserat. The ESTEREL Synchronous Programming Lan-
           guage and its Mathematical Semantics. Technical Report 327, INRIA, Sophia
           Antipolis Research Centre, Domaine de Voluceau, Rocquencourt. B.P. 105,
           78153 Le Chesnay Cedex, France, September 1984.

[BC86]   M. C. Browne and E. M. Clarke. SML: A High Level Language for the
           Design and Verification of Finite State Machines. In *Procs of IFIP WG 10.2
           International Working Conference on From HDL Descriptions to Guaranteed
           Correct Circuit Designs*, Grenoble, France, September 1986. IFIP.

[BCF92]   S. Bainbridge, A. Camilleri, and R. Fleming. Theorem Proving as an In-
           dustrial Tool for System Level Design. In V. Stavridou, T. F. Melham, and
           R. T. Boute, editors, *Theorem Provers in Circuit Design*, volume A-10 of
           IFIP Transactions, pages 253–276. North-Holland, 1992.

[BDH87]   L. Bachmair, N. Dershowitz, and J. Hsiang. Orderings for Equational Proofs.
           In *Procs of Symposium on Logic in Computer Science*, Boulder, Colorado,
           USA, June 1987. IEEE.

[Ber92]   G. Berry. Esterel on Hardware. In C. A. R. Hoare and M. J. C. Gordon,
           editors, *Mechanised Reasoning and Hardware Design*, Prentice Hall Interna-
           tional Series in Computer Science, pages 87–103. Prentice Hall, 1992.

[BG82]   R. Burstall and J. A. Goguen. Algebras, Theories and Freeness: An Intro-
           duction for Computer Scientists. In M. Wirsing and G. Schmidt, editors,
           Theoretical Foundations of Programming Methodology, pages 329–350. Rei-
           del, 1982.

[BGG+92]   R. Boulton, A. Gordon, M. J. C. Gordon, J. Harrison, J. Herbert, and J. Van
           Tassel. Experience with Embedding Hardware Description Languages in
           HOL. In V. Stavridou, T. F. Melham, and R. T. Boute, editors, *Theorem
           Provers in Circuit Design*, volume A-10 of *IFIP Transactions*, pages 129–156.
           North-Holland, 1992.

[BGHT90]   R. Boulton, M. J. C. Gordon, J. Herbert, and J. Van Tassel. The HOL
           Verification of ELLA Designs. preprint, 1990.

[BGM91]   H. Barringer, G. D. Gough, and B. Q. Monahan. Operational Semantics
           for Hardware Design Languages. In *Proceedings of IFIP TC 10/WG 10.2
           Advanced Research Workshop on Correct Hardware Design Methodologies*,
           pages 323–344, Turin, Italy, June 1991.

[BH90]   B. Brock and W. A. Hunt Jr. Report on the Formal Specification and Partial
           Verification of the VIPER Microprocessor. Technical Report 46, Computa-
           tional Logic Inc, 1717 West Sixth Street, Suite 290, Austin, Texas 78703-
           4776, January 1990.

[BHY92]   B. C. Brock, W. A. Hunt Jr., and W. D. Young. Introduction to a Formally
           Defined Hardware Description Language. In V. Stavridou, T. F. Melham,
           and R. T. Boute, editors, *Theorem Provers in Circuit Design*, volume A-10
           of *IFIP Transactions*, pages 3–35. North-Holland, 1992.

[Bir35]   G. Birkhoff. On the Structure of Abstract Algebras. *Procs of the Cambridge
           Philosophical Society*, 31:433–454, 1935.

BIBLIOGRAPHY

[BJ83]   J. C. Barros and B. W. Johnson. Equivalence of the Arbiter, the Synchroniser, the Latch and the Inertial Delay. *IEEE Trans on Computers*, pages 603–614, July 1983.

[BK83]   J. A. Bergstra and J. W. Klop. A Proof Rule for Restoring Logic Circuits. *Integration*, 1:161–178, 1983.

[BM79]   R. S. Boyer and J. S. Moore. *A Computational Logic*. Academic Press, New York, 1979.

[BM88a]   R. S. Boyer and J. S. Moore. *A Computational Logic Handbook*. Academic Press, New York, 1988.

[BM88b]   S. M. Burns and A. J. Martin. Synthesis of Self-Timed Circuits by Program Transformation. In G. J. Milne, editor, *Procs of IFIP WG 10.2 Working Conference on the Fusion of Hardware Design and Verification*, pages 99–116. North-Holland, 1988.

[Boc82]   G. V. Bochman. Hardware Specification with Temporal Logic: an Example. *IEEE Trans on Computers*, 31(3):223–231, March 1982.

[Bou86]   R. T. Boute. Current Work on the Semantics of Digital Systems. In G. J. Milne and P. A. Subrahmanyam, editors, *Formal Aspects of VLSI Design*, pages 99–112. North-Holland, 1986.

[BPS92]   D. Borrione, L. Pierre, and A. Salem. PREVAIL: a Proof Environment for VHDL Descriptions. In P. Prinetto and P. Camurati, editors, *Correct Hardware Design Methodologies*, pages 163–186. Elsevier Science Publishers B.V., 1992.

[Bro84]   S. D. Brookes. Reasoning About Asynchronous Systems. Technical Report CMU-CS-84-145, Department of Computer Science, Carnegie–Mellon University, Pittsburgh, Pennsylvania, USA, 1984.

[Bro86]   M. C. Browne. An Improved Algorithm for the Automatic Verification of Finite State Systems Using Temporal Logic. In *Procs of 1986 Conference of Logic in Computer Science*, pages 260–267, Cambridge, MA, June 1986.

[Bro91]   G. M. Brown. Towards Truly Delay-Insensitive Circuit Realisations of Process Algebras. In G. Jones and M. Sheeran, editors, *Designing Correct Circuits*, pages 120–131. Springer–Verlag, 1991.

[Bry81]   R. E. Bryant. A Switch Level Model of MOS Logic Circuits. In J. P. Gray, editor, *Proceedings of VLSI 81*, London, 1981. Academic Press.

[Bry84]   R. E. Bryant. A Switch Level Model and Simulator for MOS Digital Systems. *IEEE Transactions on Computers*, 33:160–177, 1984.

[Bry86]   R. E. Bryant. Graph–based Algorithms for Boolean Function Manipulation. *IEEE Transactions on Computers*, 35(8), 1986.

[BS92a]   M. Bickford and M. Srivas. Verification of a Fault-Tolerant Property of a
           Multiprocessor System: A Case Study in Theorem Prover-Based Verification.
           In V. Stavridou, T. F. Melham, and R. T. Boute, editors, *Theorem Provers
           in Circuit Design*, volume A-10 of *IFIP Transactions*, pages 225–252. North-
           Holland, 1992.

[BS92b]   J. P. Bowen and V. Stavridou. Safety-Critical Systems, Formal Methods and
           Standards. Technical Report PRG-TR-5-92, Programming Research Group,
           Oxford University Computing Laboratory, 11 Keble Road, Oxford OX1 3QD,
           UK, May 1992. to appear in the Software Engineering Journal.

[BT80]   J. A. Bergstra and J. V. Tucker. A Characterisation of Computable Data
           Types by Means of a Finite Equational Specification Method. In J. W.
           de Bakker and J. van Leeuwen, editors, *Procs of 7th International Confer-
           ence on Automata, Languages and Programming, LNCS No 81*, pages 76–90.
           Springer–Verlag, 1980.

[Bus91]   H. Busch. Proof Based Transformation of Formal Hardware Models. In
           G. Jones and M. Sheeran, editors, *Designing Correct Circuits*, pages 271–
           298. Springer–Verlag, 1991.

[Bus92]   H. Busch. Transformational Design in a Theorem Prover. In V. Stavridou,
           T. F. Melham, and R. T. Boute, editors, *Theorem Provers in Circuit Design*,
           volume A-10 of *IFIP Transactions*, pages 175–196. North-Holland, 1992.

[C+86]   R. L. Constable et al. *Implementing Mathematics with the Nuprl Proof De-
           velopment System*. Prentice Hall, 1986.

[C+88]   D. Coleman et al. An Introduction to the Axis Specification Language. Tech-
           nical Report HPL-ISC-TR-88-031, Hewlett–Packard Laboratories, Filton Rd,
           Stoke Gifford, Bristol BS12 6QZ, UK, September 1988.

[Cam88]   A. J. Camilleri. *Executing Behavioural Definitions in Higher Order Logic*.
           PhD thesis, Cambridge University Computer Laboratory, Corn Exchange
           Street, Cambridge CB2 3QG, UK, February 1988.

[Car82]   L. Cardelli. *An Algebraic Approach to Hardware Description and Verifica-
           tion*. PhD thesis, University of Edinburgh, Mayfield Road, Edinburgh EH9
           3JZ, UK, April 1982.

[CBG+92]   E. M. Clarke, J. R. Burch, O. Grumberg, D. E. Long, and K. L. McMillan.
           Automatic Verification of Sequential Circuit Designs. In C. A. R. Hoare and
           M. J. C. Gordon, editors, *Mechanised Reasoning and Hardware Design*, Pren-
           tice Hall International Series in Computer Science, pages 105–120. Prentice
           Hall, 1992.

[CGM86]   A. Camilleri, M. J. C. Gordon, and T. Melham. Hardware Verification Using
           Higher Order Logic. In *Proceedings of IFIP International Working Confer-
           ence*, Grenoble, France, 1986.

[CH88]   T. Coquand and G. Huet. The Calculus of Constructions. *Information and Computation*, (76):95–120, 1988.

[CHP86]   G. Cousineau, G. Huet, and L. Paulson. The ML Handbook. 1986.

[CHPP87]   P. Caspi, N. Halbwachs, D. Pilaud, and J. A. Plaice. LUSTRE: a Declarative Language for Programming Synchronous Systems. In *Procs of 14th POPL*, Munich, Germany, January 1987. ACM.

[Chu40]   A. Church. A Formulation of the Simple Theory of Types. *Journal of Symbolic Logic*, (5), 1940.

[Chu74]   Y. Chu. Introducing CDL. *IEEE Computer*, 7(12):31–33, December 1974.

[Clo85]   W. F. Clocksin. Logic Programming and the Specification of Circuits. Technical Report 72, University of Cambridge Computer Laboratory, Corn Exchange Street, Cambridge CB2 3QG, 1985.

[CMP91]   P. Camurati, T. Margaria, and P. Prinetto. The OTTER Environment for Resolution Based Proof of Hardware Correctness. In G. Jones and M. Sheeran, editors, *Designing Correct Circuits*, pages 253–270. Springer–Verlag, 1991.

[Coh88a]   A. J. Cohn. Correctness Properties of the Viper Block Model: the Second Level. In P. A. Subramanyan, editor, *Procs of 2nd Banff Workshop on Hardware Verification*, Banff, Canada, June 1988. Springer–Verlag.

[Coh88b]   A. J. Cohn. A Proof of Correctness of the Viper Microprocessor: The First Level. In *VLSI Specification, Verification and Synthesis*, Boston, 1988. Kluwer Academic Publishers.

[Coh89]   A. J. Cohn. The Notion of Proof in Hardware Verification. *Journal of Automated Reasoning*, 5:127–139, May 1989.

[CP85]   W. J. Cullyer and C. H. Pygott. Hardware Proofs Using LCF–LSM and ELLA. Technical Report 3832, RSRE, Malvern, Worcestershire, UK, September 1985.

[CP88]   P. Camurati and P. Prinetto. Formal Verification of Hardware Correctness: Introduction and Survey of Current Research. *IEEE Computer*, pages 8–19, July 1988.

[CPC87]   M. S. Chandrasekhar, J. P. Privitera, and K. W. Conradt. Application of Term Rewriting Techniques to Hardware Design Verification. In *Procs, 24th Design Automation Conference*, Miami, Florida, June 1987.

[Cul84]   W. J. Cullyer. Formal Specification of the Viper Microprocessor. Technical Report 3738, RSRE, Malvern, Worcs, UK, 1984.

[Cul85]   W. J. Cullyer. Hardware Integrity. *Aeronautical Journal of the Royal Aeronautical Society*, pages 263–268, September 1985.

[Das81]   S. Dasgupta. s_A^*: A Language for Describing Computer Architectures. In
            M. Breuer and R. Hartenstein, editors, *Procs of CHDL 81*, Kaiserslautern,
            Germany, September 1981. IFIP.

[Das83]   S. Dasgupta. On the Verification of Computer Architectures Using an Ar-
            chitecture Description Language. *Comms of the ACM*, 1983.

[Dav88]   A. L. Davis. What Do Computer Architects Design Anyway? In *Proceed-
            ings of Banff Hardware Verification Workshop*, Boston, June 1988. Kluwer
            Academic Publishers.

[Die74]   D. L. Dietmeyer. Introducing DDL. *IEEE Computer*, 7(12):34–38, December
            1974.

[DJ89]   N. Dershowitz and J-P. Jouannaud. *Handbook of Theoretical Computer Sci-
            ence*, volume B, chapter 15, Rewrite Systems. North-Holland, 1989.

[DJS90]   J. Davies, D. Jackson, and S. Schneider. Making Things Happen in Timed
            CSP. Technical Report PRG-TR-2-90, Oxford University Computing Labo-
            ratory, 11 Keble Road, Oxford OX1 3QD, 1990.

[DW92]   A. J. DeBaets and K. M. Wheeler. Midrange PA–RISC Workstations with
            Price/Performance Leadership. *Hewlett–Packard Journal*, pages 6–11, Au-
            gust 1992.

[EC81]   E. A. Emerson and E. M. Clarke. Characterizing Properties of Parallel Pro-
            grams as Fixpoints. *LNCS*, 85, 1981.

[Eke91]   S. M. Eker. Verification of a Line Drawing Architecture Using OBJ3. In
            Proceedings of Workshop on Formal Methods in Computer Graphics, Marina
            di Carrara, Italy, June 1991.

[EM85]   H. Ehrig and B. Mahr. *Fundamentals of Alebraic Specification 1: Equa-
            tions and Initial Semantics*, volume 6 of *EATCS Monographs on Theoretical
            Computer Science*. Springer–Verlag, 1985.

[EST91]   S. M. Eker, V. Stavridou, and J. V. Tucker. Verification of Synchronous
            Concurrent Algorithms Using OBJ3: a Case Study of the Pixel Planes Ar-
            chitecture. In G. Jones and M. Sheeran, editors, *Designing Correct Circuits*,
            pages 231–252. Springer–Verlag, 1991.

[ET89]   S. M. Eker and J. V. Tucker. Specification and Verification of Synchronous
            Concurrent Algorithms: A Case Study of the Pixel Planes Architecture. In
            P. M. Dew, R. A. Earnshaw, and T. R. Heywood, editors, *Parallel Processing
            for Computer Vision and Display*, pages 16–49, Wokingham, England, 1989.
            Addison Wesley.

[Eve81]   H. Eveking. The Application of CONLAN Assertions to the Correct Descrip-
            tion of Hardware. In M. Breuer and R. Hartenstein, editors, *Procs of CHDL
            81*, Kaiserslautern, Germany, September 1981. IFIP.

[Eve86]   H. Eveking. Verification, Synthesis and Correctness-Preserving Transforma-
          tions – Cooperative Approaches to Correct Hardware Design. In *From HDL
          Descriptions to Guaranteed Correct Circuit Designs*, pages 207–217, Greno-
          ble, France, September 1986. IFIP WG 10.2 Workshop.

[FB86]   M. D. Fisher and H. Barringer. Program Logics - A Short Survey. Techni-
          cal Report UMCS-86-11-1, Department of Computer Science, University of
          Manchester, Manchester M13 9PL, England, November 1986.

[Fet88]   J. H. Fetzer. Program Verification: the Very Idea. *Comms of the ACM*,
          31(9):1048–1063, September 1988.

[FFFH89] S. Finn, M. Fourman, M. Francis, and R. Harris. Formally Based System De-
          sign – Interactive Synthesis Based on Computer Assisted Formal Reasoning.
          In L. Claesen, editor, *Procs of International Workshop on Applied Formal
          Methods for Correct VLSI Design*. IMEC–IFIP, Elsevier Science Publishers
          B.V., 1989.

[FGH+85] H. Fuchs, J. Goldfeather, J. P. Hultquist, S. Spach, F. P. Brooks Jr., J. G.
          Eyles, and J. Poulton. Fast Spheres, Shadows, Textures, Transparencies and
          Image Enhancements in Pixel Planes. *Computer Graphics*, 19(3):169–187,
          July 1985.

[Fle80]   W. I. Fletcher. *An Engineering Approach to Digital Design*. Prentice-Hall,
          Englewood Cliffs, N.J. 07632, 1980.

[FP81]   H. Fuchs and J. Poulton. Pixel Planes: A VLSI-Orientated Design for a
          Raster Graphics Engine. *VLSI Design*, 2(3):20–28, 1981.

[FPPB82] H. Fuchs, J. Poulton, A. Paeth, and A. Bell. Developing Pixel Planes, a
          Smart Memory-Based Raster Graphics System. In *Proceedings of the 1982
          MIT Conference on Advanced Research in VLSI*, pages 137–146, Dedham
          MA, 1982. Artech House.

[FTMo83] M. Fujita, H. Tinker, and T. Moto-oka. Verification with Prolog and Tem-
          poral Logic. In *Procs of CHDL 83*, pages 105–114, Pittsburgh, USA, May
          1983. IFIP.

[FTMo85] M. Fujita, H. Tinker, and T. Moto-oka. Logic Design Assistance with Tem-
          poral Logic. In *Procs of CHDL 85*, pages 129–137. IFIP, August 1985.

[Fuc88]   H. Fuchs. An Introduction to Pixel Planes and Other VLSI Intensive Graph-
          ics Systems. In R. A. Earnshaw, editor, *Theoretical Foundations of Computer
          Graphics and CAD*, pages 675–688. Springer–Verlag, 1988.

[G+92]   C. A. Gleason et al. VLSI Circuits for Low-End and Midrange PA–RISC
          Computers. *Hewlett-Packard Journal*, pages 12–22, August 1992.

[Gab87]   D. Gabbay. Executable Temporal Logic for Interactive Systems. In *Col-
          loquium on Temporal Logic: Circulated Papers*, Department of Computer
          Science, University of Manchester, April 1987.

[GB88]   G. D. Gough and H. Barringer. A Semantics Driven Temporal Verifica-
            tion System. In H. Ganzinger, editor, *Procs of 2nd European Symposium
            on Programming, LNCS No 300*, pages 21–33, Nancy, France, March 1988.
            Springer–Verlag.

[GCS89]   R. M. Gallimore, D. Coleman, and V. Stavridou. UMIST OBJ: A Language
            for Executable Program Specifications. *Computer Journal*, 32(5):413–421,
            October 1989.

[Ges86]   A. Geser. A Specification of the INTEL 8085 Microprocessor: A Case Study.
            Technical Report MIP-8608, Faculty for Mathematics and Informatics, Uni-
            versity of Passau, May 1986.

[GG87]   S. J. Garland and J. V. Guttag. Why Induct Inductionlessly When You
            Could Induct Inductively? Draft paper, April 1987.

[GG88]   S. J. Garland and J. V. Guttag. Inductive Methods for Reasoning About
            Abstract Data Types. In *Procs of 15th POPL*, pages 219–228, San Diego,
            California, USA, January 1988. ACM.

[GG89]   S. J. Garland and J. V. Guttag. An Overview of LP, the Larch Prover. In
            *Procs of 3rd International Conference on Rewriting Techniques and Applica-
            tions, LNCS 355*, pages 137–151, Chapel Hill, N.C., 1989. Springer–Verlag.

[GGS88]   S. J. Garland, J. V. Guttag, and J. Staunstrup. Verification of VLSI Circuits
            Using LP. In *Procs of Workshop on the Fusion of Hardware Design and
            Verification*. IFIP WG 10.2, North-Holland, 1988.

[GH85]   M. J. C. Gordon and J. M. J. Herbert. A Formal Hardware Verification
            Methodology and its Application to a Network Interface Chip. Technical
            Report 66, University of Cambridge Computer Laboratory, 1985.

[GH86a]   A. Geser and H. Hussmann. Experiences with the RAP System – a Speci-
            fication Interpreter Combining Term Rewriting and Resolution. In *Procs of
            ESOP Conference*, 1986.

[GH86b]   J. V. Guttag and J. J. Horning. Report on the Larch Shared Language.
            Science of Computer Programming, 6(2):103–157, March 1986.

[GKK88]   I. Gnaedig, C. Kirchner, and H. Kirchner. Equational Completion in Order
            Sorted Algebras. In *Procs of CAAP 88, LNCS 299*. Springer–Verlag, 1988.

[GKMW87]   J. A. Goguen, C. Kirchner, J. Meseguer, and T. Winkler. OBJ as a Language
            for Concurrent Programming. In S. Kartashev and S. Kartashev, editors,
            Procs of 2nd International Supercomputing Conference, Vol 1, pages 195–
            198, St. Petersburg, Florida, 1987. International Supercomputing Institute
            Inc.

[GM82]   J. A. Goguen and J. Meseguer. Rapid Prototyping in the OBJ Executable
            Specification Language. *Software Engineering Notes*, 7(5):75–84, December
            1982.

[GM89]   J. A. Goguen and J. Meseguer. Order Sorted Algebra I: Equational Deduction for Multiple Inheritance, Overloading, Exceptions and Partial Operations. Technical Report SRI-CSL-89-10, Computer Science Laboratory, SRI International, July 1989.

[GMW79] M. J. C. Gordon, R. Milner, and C. P. Wadsworth. *Edinburgh LCF: A Mechanised Logic of Computation*, volume 78 of *LNCS*. Springer–Verlag, 1979.

[Gog80]   J. A. Goguen. How to Prove Algebraic Inductive Hypotheses Without Induction, with Applications to the Correctness of Data Type Implementation. In W. Bibel and R. Kowalski, editors, *Procs of 5th Conference on Automated Deduction, LNCS 87*, pages 356–373, Les Arc, July 1980. Springer–Verlag.

[Gog88]   J. A. Goguen. OBJ as a Theorem Prover with Applications to Hardware Verification. In *Procs of 2nd Banff Workshop on Hardware Verification*, Banff, Canada, June 1988.

[Gog89]   J. A. Goguen. Higher Order Functions Considered Unnecessary for Higher Order Programming. Preprint, April 1989.

[Gog90]   J. A. Goguen. Proving and Rewriting. Preprint, August 1990.

[Gog91]   J. A. Goguen. Algebraic Proof Techniques. Forthcoming book, 1991.

[Gol88]   M. Goldsmith. The Oxford occam Transformation System (Version 1.0). Draft user documentation, PRG, Oxford University Computing Laboratory, 8–11 Keble Road, Oxford OX1 3QD, UK, January 1988.

[Goo90]   K. G. W. Goossens. Semantics for picoELLA. Technical report, Department of Computer Science, University of Edinburgh, UK, 1990.

[Goo91]   K. G. W. Goossens. Embedding a CHDL in a Proof System. In *Proceedings of IFIP TC 10/WG 10.2 Advanced Research Workshop on Correct Hardware Design Methodologies*, pages 369–386, Turin, Italy, June 1991.

[Gor81]   M. J. C. Gordon. A Very Simple Model of Sequential Behaviour of nMOS. In J. Gray, editor, *Procs of International VLSI Conference*. Academic Press, 1981.

[Gor83a] M. J. C. Gordon. LCF–LSM: A System for Specifying and Verifying Hardware. Technical Report 41, University of Cambridge Computer Laboratory, Corn Exchange Street, Cambridge CB2 3QG, UK, 1983.

[Gor83b] M. J. C. Gordon. Proving a Computer Correct with the LCF–LSM Hardware Verification System. Technical Report 42, University of Cambridge Computer Laboratory, Corn Exchange Street, Cambridge CB2 3QG, UK, 1983.

[Gor85]   M. J. C. Gordon. HOL: A Machine Oriented Formulation of Higher Order
            Logic. Technical Report 68, University of Cambridge Computer Laboratory,
            Corn Exchange Street, Cambridge CB2 3QG, UK, July 1985.

[Gou84]   G. D. Gough. Decision Procedures for Temporal Logic. Master's thesis, De-
            partment of Computer Science, University of Manchester, Manchester M13
            9PL, England, October 1984.

[GSHH92]   J. A. Goguen, A. Stevens, H. Hilberdink, and K. M. Hobley. 2OBJ: a Meta-
            logical Framework Theorem Prover Based on Equational Logic. In C. A. R.
            Hoare and M. J. C. Gordon, editors, *Mechanised Reasoning and Hardware
            Design*, Prentice Hall International Series in Computer Science, pages 69–86.
            Prentice Hall, 1992.

[GT79]   J. A. Goguen and J. Tardo. An Introduction to OBJ: A Language for Writing
            and Testing Software Specifications. In M. Zelkowitz, editor, *Specification of
            Reliable Software*, pages 170–189. IEEE Press, 1979.

[GTW78]   J. A. Goguen, J. W. Thatcher, and E. G. Wagner. An Initial Algebra Ap-
            proach to the Specification, Correctness and Implementation of Abstract
            Data Types. In R. Yeh, editor, *Current Trends in Programming Methodol-
            ogy*, volume 4, pages 80–149. Prentice Hall, 1978.

[GW88]   J. A. Goguen and T. Winkler. Introducing OBJ3. Technical Report SRI-
            CSL-88-9, Computer Science Laboratory, SRI International, Menlo Park, CA
            94025, August 1988.

[Har89]   N. A. Harman. *Formal Specifications for Digital Systems*. PhD thesis, School
            of Computer Studies, The University of Leeds, Leeds, UK, October 1989.

[HB92]   W. A. Hunt Jr. and B. C. Brock. A Formal HDL and its Use in the FM9001
            Verification. In C. A. R. Hoare and M. J. C. Gordon, editors, *Mechanised
            Reasoning and Hardware Design*, Prentice Hall International Series in Com-
            puter Science, pages 35–47. Prentice Hall, 1992.

[HD85]   F. K. Hanna and N. Daeche. Specification and Verification Using Higher
            Order Logic. In *Procs of 7th International Symposium on Computer Hard-
            ware Description Languages and Applications*, pages 418–443, Tokyo, Japan,
            August 1985.

[HD92]   F. K. Hanna and N. Daeche. Dependent Types and Formal Synthesis. In
            C. A. R. Hoare and M. J. C. Gordon, editors, *Mechanised Reasoning and
            Hardware Design*, Prentice Hall International Series in Computer Science,
            pages 121–135. Prentice Hall, 1992.

[Her92]   J. M. J. Herbert. Incremental Design and Formal Verification of Microcoded
            Microprocessors. In V. Stavridou, T. F. Melham, and R. T. Boute, editors,
            Theorem Provers in Circuit Design, volume A-10 of *IFIP Transactions*, pages
            157–174. North-Holland, 1992.

[HH82]   G. Huet and J. M. Hullot. Proof by Induction in Equational Theories with Constructors. *JCCS*, 2(25), 1982.

[HHP87]   R. Harper, F. Honsell, and G. Plotkin. A Framework for Defining Logics. In *Proceedings of 2nd Symposium on Logic in Computer Science*, pages 194–204. IEEE Computer Society, 1987.

[HKC89]   W. S. Humphrey, D. H. Kitson, and T. C. Casse. The State of Software Engineering Practice: A Preliminary Report. In *Proceedings of 11th International Conference on Software Engineering*, pages 277–288, Pittsburgh, May 1989. IEEE.

[HL78]   G. Huet and D. S. Lankford. On the Uniform Halting Problem for Term Rewriting Systems. Technical Report 283, IRIA, March 1978.

[HMM83]   J. Halpern, Z. Manna, and B. Moszkowski. A Hardware Semantics Based on Temporal Intervals. In *LNCS, No 154*, pages 278–291. Springer–Verlag, 1983.

[HMM86]   R. Harper, D. MacQueen, and R. Milner. Standard ML. Technical Report ECS-LFCS-86-2, LFCS, Department of Computer Science, University of Edinburgh, March 1986.

[HO80]   G. Huet and D. Oppen. Equations and Rewrite Rules: A Survey. In R. Book, editor, *Formal Languages : Perspectives and Open Problems*, pages 349–405. Academic Press, 1980.

[Hoa90a] C. A. R. Hoare. Let's Make Models. Draft paper, November 1990.

[Hoa90b] C. A. R. Hoare. Refinement Algebra Proves Correctness of Compiling Specifications. Technical Report PRG-TR-6-90, PRG, Oxford University Computing Laboratory, 8–11 Keble Road, Oxford OX1 3QD, UK, 1990.

[Hob91]   K. M. Hobley. *Specification and Verification of Synchronous Concurrent Algorithms*. PhD thesis, School of Computer Studies, University of Leeds, 1991.

[Hsi81]   J. Hsiang. *Refutational Theorem Proving using Term Rewriting Systems*. PhD thesis, University of Illinois at Champaign-Urbana, 1981.

[HTT88a] K. M. Hobley, B. C. Thompson, and J. V. Tucker. Specification and Verification of Synchronous Concurrent Algorithms: a Case Study of a Convolution Algorithm. In G. J. Milne, editor, *Procs of IFIP WG 10.2 Working Conference on the Fusion of Hardware Design and Verification*. North-Holland, 1988.

[HTT88b] K. M. Hobley, B. C. Thompson, and J. V. Tucker. Specification and verification of synchronous concurrent algorithms: A case study of a convolution algorithm. In G. Milne, editor, *The Fusion of Hardware Design and Verification*, pages 347–374. North-Holland, 1988.

[Hun85]   W. A. Hunt Jr. *FM8501: A Verified Microprocessor*. PhD thesis, University
           of Texas at Austin, Austin, Texas 78712, December 1985.

[Hun89]   W. A. Hunt Jr. Microprocessor Design Verification. *Journal of Automated
           Reasoning*, 5:429–460, 1989.

[Hus85]   H. Hussmann. Unification in Conditional–Equational Theories. In *Procs of
           EUROCAL 85, LNCS 204*, pages 543–553. Springer–Verlag, 1985.

[Jac91]   J. Jacob. The Varieties of Refinement. In *Procs of 4th BCS–FACS Refine-
           ment Workshop*, Wolfson College, Cambridge, January 1991.

[JB88]   S. D. Johnson and C. D. Boyer. Modeling Transistors Applicatively. In G. J.
           Milne, editor, *Procs of IFIP WG 10.2 Working Conference on the Fusion of
           Hardware Design and Verification*, pages 397–420. North-Holland, 1988.

[Jou87]   J-P. Jouannaud. *Rewriting Techniques and Applications*. Academic Press,
           1987.

[Joy87]   J. Joyce. Formal Verification and Implementation of a Microprocessor. In
           Procs of Hardware Verification Workshop, Calgary, Canada, January 1987.

[Joy91]   J. Joyce. Generic Specification of Digital Hardware. In G. Jones and
           M. Sheeran, editors, *Designing Correct Circuits*, pages 68–91. Springer–
           Verlag, 1991.

[Kap84]   S. Kaplan. Fair Conditional Rewriting Systems: Unification, Termination
           and Confluence. Technical Report 194, Laboratoire de Recherche en Infor-
           matique, Orsay, France, 1984.

[KB70]   D. Knuth and P. Bendix. Simple Word Problems in Universal Algebras. In
           J. Leech, editor, *Computational Problems in Abstract Algebra*, pages 263–297.
           Pergamon Press, 1970.

[Ker84]   J. Kershaw. Viper: a Microprocessor for Safety Critical Applications. Memo-
           randum 3754, RSRE, Procurement Executive, Ministry of Defence, Malvern,
           Worcs, UK, December 1984.

[KK92]   D. J. Kinniment and A. M. Koelmans. Modelling and Verification of Timing
           Conditions with the Boyer-Moore Prover. In V. Stavridou, T. F. Melham,
           and R. T. Boute, editors, *Theorem Provers in Circuit Design*, volume A-10
           of *IFIP Transactions*, pages 111–128. North-Holland, 1992.

[Klo87]   C. Delgado Kloos. *Semantics of Digital Circuits*, volume 285 of *LNCS*.
           Springer–Verlag, 1987.

[KM92]   D. Kapur and D. R. Musser. Tecton: a Framework for Specifying and Ver-
           ifying Generic System Components. Presented at the IFIP TC10/WG10.2
           Conference on Theorem Provers in Circuit Design, Nijmegen, The Nether-
           lands (available from D. R. Musser, Rensselaer Polytechnic Institute, Troy,
           New York 12180)., June 1992.

[KMN92]   D. Kapur, D. R. Musser, and X. Nie. An Overview of the Tecton Proof System. In *Procs of a Workshop on Formal Methods in Databases and Software Engineering*, Concordia University, Montreal, May 1992.

[KN84]   D. Kapur and P. Narendran. An Equational Approach to Theorem Proving in First Order Predicate Calculus. Unpublished manuscript, April 1984.

[KSZ86]   D. Kapur, G. Sivakumar, and H. Zhang. RRL: A Rewrite Rule Laboratory. In *Procs of 8th Conference on Automated Deduction*, Oxford, UK, 1986.

[Lap91]   J. C. Laprie. *Dependability: Basic Concepts and Terminology*. Springer–Verlag, 1991.

[Lee88]   M. E. Leeser. Reasoning About the Function and Timing of Integrated Circuits With Prolog and Temporal Logic. Technical Report 132, University of Cambridge Computer Laboratory, Pembroke Street, Cambridge CB2 3QG, UK, April 1988.

[Lee92]   M. E. Leeser. Using Nuprl for the Verification and Synthesis of Hardware. In C. A. R. Hoare and M. J. C. Gordon, editors, *Mechanised Reasoning and Hardware Design*, Prentice Hall International Series in Computer Science, pages 49–67. Prentice Hall, 1992.

[Les83]   P. Lescanne. Computer Experiments with the REVE Term Rewriting System Generator. In *Procs of the 10th ACM Symposium on the Principles of Programming Languages*, Ausin, Texas, January 1983.

[Lew77]   D. Lewin. *Computer Aided Design of Digital Systems*. Computer Systems Engineering Series. Edward Arnold, 1977.

[LFMM92] B. Levy, I. Filippenko, L. Marcus, and T. Menas. Using the State Delta Verification System (SDVS) for Hardware Verification. In V. Stavridou, T. F. Melham, and R. T. Boute, editors, *Theorem Provers in Circuit Design*, volume A-10 of *IFIP Transactions*, pages 337–360. North-Holland, 1992.

[LG86]   B. Liskov and J. Guttag. *Abstraction and Specification in Program Development*. MIT Press, 1986.

[Lin88]   P. A. Lindsay. A Survey of Mechanical Support for Formal Reasoning. *Software Engineering Journal*, 3, 1988.

[LS84]   L. Lamport and F. B. Schneider. The "Hoare Logic" of CSP and All That. *ACM Trans on Programming Languages*, 6(2), April 1984.

[Luo88]   Z. Luo. A Higher Order Calculus and Theory Abstraction. Technical Report ECS-LFCS-88-57, Department of Computer Science, University of Edinburgh, UK, July 1988.

[Mac91]   D. MacKenzie. The Fangs of the VIPER. *Nature*, 352:467–468, August 1991.

[Mar92]   T. Margaria. Hierarchical Mixed-mode Verification of Complex FSMs De-
           scribed at the RT Level. In V. Stavridou, T. F. Melham, and R. T. Boute,
           editors, *Theorem Provers in Circuit Design*, volume A-10 of *IFIP Transac-
           tions*, pages 59–76. North-Holland, 1992.

[MBS92]   D. May, G. Barrett, and D. Shepherd. Designing Chips That Work. In
           C. A. R. Hoare and M. J. C. Gordon, editors, *Mechanised Reasoning and
           Hardware Design*, Prentice Hall International Series in Computer Science,
           pages 3–18. Prentice Hall, 1992.

[MC80]   C. Mead and L. Conway. *Introduction to VLSI Systems*. Computer Science.
           Addison-Wesley, Philippines, 1980.

[MC85]   D. R. Musser and D. A. Cyrluk. *Affirm-85 Reference Manual*. General Elec-
           tric Corporate Research and Development Center, Schenectady, NY 12301,
           August 1985.

[McC89]   W. W. McCune. OTTER 1.0 Users Guide. Technical Report ANL–88–44,
           Mathematics and Computer Science Division, Argonne National Laboratory,
           Argonne, Illinois, USA, 1989.

[Men91]   M. Mendler. Constrained Proofs: a Logic for Dealing with Behavioural Con-
           straints in Formal Hardware Verification. In G. Jones and M. Sheeran, edi-
           tors, *Designing Correct Circuits*, pages 1–28. Springer–Verlag, 1991.

[MG85]   J. Meseguer and J. A. Goguen. Initiality, Induction and Computability. In
           M. Nivat and J. Reynolds, editors, *Algebraic Methods in Semantics*, pages
           459–541. Cambridge University Press, 1985.

[Mil83]   G. Milne. CIRCAL: A Calculus for Circuit Description. *INTEGRATION,
           the VLSI Journal*, (1,2 and 3):121–160, 1983.

[MNP87]   D. R. Musser, P. Narendran, and W. J. Premerlani. BIDS: A Method for
           Specifying and Verifying Bidirectional Hardware Devices. In *Proc of Hard-
           ware Verification Workshop*, Calgary, Canada, January 1987.

[MO81]   Y. Malachi and S. Owicki. Temporal Specifications of Self Timed Systems.
           In H. T. Kung, B. Sproul, and G. Steele, editors, *VLSI Systems and Com-
           putations*, Carnegie Mellon University, Pittsburgh, USA, 1981. Computer
           Science Press.

[MOD91]   Ministry of Defence, Directorate of Standardisation, Kentigern House, 65
           Brown St., Glasgow G2 8EX. *Requirements for the Procurement of Safety
           Critical Software in Defence Equipment: Interim Defence Standard 00–55*,
           interim edition, April 1991.

[Mor90]   C. Morgan. *Programming from Specifications*. Prentice Hall, 1990.

[Mos83]   B. Moszkowski. A Temporal Logic for Multi-Level Reasoning About Hardware. In *Procs of 6th IFIP International Symposium on Computer Hardware Description Languages and their Applications*, Pittsburgh, Pennsylvania, May 1983.

[Mos84]   B. Moszkowski. Executing Temporal Logic Programs. Technical Report 55, Computer Laboratory, University of Cambridge, August 1984.

[MP88]   G. J. Milne and M. Pezze. Typed Circal: a High Level Framework for Hardware Verification. In G. J. Milne, editor, *Procs of IFIP WG 10.2 Working Conference on the Fusion of Hardware Design and Verification*, pages 117–138. North-Holland, 1988.

[MS87]   D. May and D. E. Shepherd. Formal Verification of the IMS T800 Microprocessor. In *Procs of Electronic Design Automation*, pages 605–615, London, UK, September 1987.

[MT91]   K. McEvoy and J. V. Tucker. On Theoretical Foundations for Hardware Design. In K. McEvoy and J. V. Tucker, editors, *Theoretical Aspects of VLSI Computation*. Cambridge University Press, 1991.

[MT92]   K. Meinke and J. V. Tucker. Universal Algebra. In S. Abramsky, D. M. Gabbay, and T. S. E. Maibaum, editors, *Handbook of Logic in Computer Science, Vol 1 Background Mathematical Structures*, pages 189–411. Oxford Science Publications, 1992.

[Mus80]   D. R. Musser. On Proving Inductive Properties of Abstract Data Types. In *Procs of 7th POPL*, pages 154–162, Las Vegas, USA, January 1980. ACM.

[Nor90]   J. Nordahl. Dependability in a Process Algebraic Framework. ProCoS Project Report ID/DTH JNO 4, Department of Computer Science, Technical University of Denmark, DK-2800 Lyngby, Denmark, June 1990.

[NS86]   P. Narendran and J. Stillman. Hardware Verification in the Interactive VHDL Workstation. G.E. Corporate Research and Development Center, Schenectady, NY 12345, USA, 1986.

[ORS92]   S. Owre, J. Rushby, and N. Shankar. Pvs: a Prototype Verification System. Technical report, CSL, SRI International, 333 Ravenswood Ave, Menlo Park, CA 94025, May 1992.

[Ost89]   J. F. Ostroff. *Temporal Logic for Real Time Systems*. Advanced Software Development Series. Research Studies Press, distributed by John Wiley, 1989.

[Pai86]   J. L. Paillet. A Functional Model for Descriptions and Specifications of Digital Devices. In *Procs of Workshop on From HDL Descriptions to Guaranteed Correct Circuit Designs*, pages 19–40, Grenoble, France, September 1986. IFIP WG 10.2.

[Par66]   D. L. Parnas. A Language for Describing the Functions of Synchronous Systems. *Comms of the ACM*, 9:72–75, February 1966.

[PFA⁺85]   J. Poulton, H. Fuchs, J. D. Austin, J. G. Eyles, J. Heinecke, C-H. Hsieh, J. Goldfeather, J. P. Hultquist, and S. Spach. PIXEL PLANES: Building a VLSI-Based Graphic System. In H. Fuchs, editor, *Proceedings of the Chapel Hill Conference on VLSI*, pages 35–60, Rockville MA, 1985. Computer Science Press.

[PN90]   L. C. Paulson and T. Nipkow. *Isabelle Tutorial and User Manual*. University of Cambridge Computer Laboratory, Pembroke Street, Cambridge CB2 3QG, 1990.

[Pnu77]   A. Pnueli. The Temporal Logic of Programs. In *Procs of 18th Symposium on the Foundations of Computer Science*, Providence, November 1977.

[Pnu86]   A. Pnueli. Application of Temporal Logic to the Specification and Verification of Reactive Systems: a Survey of Current Trends. In J. W. de Bakker, W. P. de Roever, and G. Rozenberg, editors, *Current Trends in Concurrency: Overviews and Tutorials, LNCS Vol 224*. Springer–Verlag, 1986.

[Pol88]   R. Pollack. The Theory of LEGO. LFCS draft report, University of Edinburgh, October 1988.

[PS89]   S. Purushothaman and P. A. Subrahmanyam. Mechanical Certification of Systolic Algorithms. *Journal of Automated Reasoning*, 5:67–91, 1989.

[PSE85]   D. Patel, M. Schlag, and M. Ercegovac. νFP: An Environment for the Multilevel Specification, Analysis, and Synthesis of Hardware Algorithms. In J-P. Jouannaud, editor, *Procs of Conf on Functional Programming Languages and Computer Architecture*, pages 238–255, Nancy, France, September 1985. Springer–Verlag.

[Pyg85]   C. H. Pygott. Formal Proof of Correspondence Between the Specification of a Hardware Module and its Gate Level Implementation. Technical Report 85012, RSRE, Malvern, Worcs, UK, November 1985.

[Pyg88]   C. H. Pygott. NODEN–HDL: an Engineering Approach to Hardware Verification. In G. J. Milne, editor, *Procs of IFIP WG 10.2 Working Conference on the Fusion of Hardware Design and Verification*, pages 211–229. North-Holland, 1988.

[Pyg92]   C. H. Pygott. Will Proof Replace Simulation? In C. A. R. Hoare and M. J. C. Gordon, editors, *Mechanised Reasoning and Hardware Design*, Prentice Hall International Series in Computer Science, pages 21–32. Prentice Hall, 1992.

[Rei83]   D. G. Reinertsen. Whodunit? The Search for the New Product Killers. *Electronic Business*, July 1983.

[Rob65]   J. A. Robinson. A Machine–Oriented Logic Based on the Resolution Principle. *JACM*, 12:32–41, 1965.

[Ros91]   L. Rossen. Ruby Algebra. In G. Jones and M. Sheeran, editors, *Designing Correct Circuits*, pages 297–312. Springer–Verlag, 1991.

[Ros92]   A. W. Roscoe. Occam in the Specification and Verification of Microprocessors. In C. A. R. Hoare and M. J. C. Gordon, editors, *Mechanised Reasoning
             and Hardware Design*, Prentice Hall International Series in Computer Science, pages 137–151. Prentice Hall, 1992.

[RW69]   J. A. Robinson and L. T. Wos. Paramodulation and Theorem Proving in
             First Order Theories with Equality. *Machine Intelligence*, 4:135–150, 1969.

[Sam90]   A. Sampaio. A Comparative Study of Theorem Provers: Proving Correctness
             of Compiling Specifications. Master's thesis, Programming Research Group,
             Oxford University Computing Laboratory, 8–11 Keble Road, Oxford OX1
             3QD, UK, September 1990.

[SBE88]   V. Stavridou, H. Barringer, and D.A. Edwards. Formal Specification and
             Verification of Hardware: A Comparative Case Study. In *Proceedings of
             25th Design Automation Conference*, pages 197–205, Anaheim, California,
             June 1988. ACM/IEEE, Computer Society Press. (Reprinted in Formal Verification of Hardware Designs, M. Yoeli ed., IEEE Computer Society Press,
             1990).

[SBN82]   D. P. Siewiorek, C. G. Bell, and A. Newell. *Computer Structures: Principles
             and Examples*. McGraw Hill, 1982.

[Sco69]   D. Scott. A Type Theoretic Alternative to CUCH, ISWIM, OWHY. Unpublished notes, 1969.

[SD84]   C. U. Smith and J. A. Dallen. Future Directions for VLSI and Software
             Engineering. In T. L. Kunii, editor, *VLSI Engineering, Proceedings*, volume
             163 of *LNCS*. Springer–Verlag, 1984.

[Seu90]   M. Seutter. *Glass: A System Description Language and its Environment*.
             University of Nijmegen, Nijmegen, the Netherlands, 1.0 edition, May 1990.

[SG90]   J. Staunstrup and M. Greenstreet.   Synchronised Transitions.   In
             J. Staunstrup, editor, *Formal Methods for VLSI Design*, pages 71–128.
             North-Holland, 1990.

[SGEA91]   V. Stavridou, J. A. Goguen, S. M. Eker, and S. N. Aloneftis. FUNNEL:
             a CHDL with Formal Semantics. In *Proceedings of IFIP TC 10/WG 10.2
             Advanced Research Workshop on Correct Hardware Design Methodologies*,
             pages 117–144, Turin, Italy, June 1991. North-Holland.

[SGG92]   J. Staunstrup, S. J. Garland, and J. V. Guttag. Mechanized Verification of
             Circuit Descriptions Using the Larch Prover. In V. Stavridou, T. F. Melham,
             and R. T. Boute, editors, *Theorem Provers in Circuit Design*, volume A-10
             of *IFIP Transactions*, pages 277–300. North-Holland, 1992.

[SGS⁺92]   V. Stavridou, J. A. Goguen, A. Stevens, S. M. Eker, S. N. Aloneftis, and
             K. M. Hobley. FUNNEL and 2OBJ: Towards an Integrated Hardware Design
             Environment. In V. Stavridou, T. F. Melham, and R. T. Boute, editors,

Theorem Provers in Circuit Design, volume A-10 of *IFIP Transactions*, pages 197–224. North-Holland, 1992.

[She83]   M. Sheeran. *μFP: An Algebraic Design Language*. PhD thesis, PRG, Oxford University Computer Laboratory, 8–11 Keble Road, Oxford OX1 3QD, UK, 1983.

[She84]   M. Sheeran. *μFP: a Language for VLSI Design*. In *Procs of ACM Conference on Lisp and Functional Programming*, pages 104–112, August 1984.

[She85]   M. Sheeran. The Design and Verification of Regular Synchronous Circuits. Draft PRG report, University of Oxford Computer Laboratory, 8–11 Keble Road, Oxford OX1 3QD, UK, 1985.

[She90]   D. E. Shepherd. Verified Microcode Design. *Microprocessors and Microsystems*, 14(10):623–630, December 1990.

[She91]   M. Sheeran. Describing and Reasoning About Circuits Using Relations. In K. McEvoy and J. V. Tucker, editors, *Procs of Leeds Workshop on Theoretical Aspects of VLSI Design*. Cambridge University Press, 1991.

[Sho83]   R. E. Shostak. Formal Verification of Circuit Designs. In *Procs of CHDL 83*, pages 13–30, Pittsburgh, USA, May 1983. IFIP.

[Sie74]   D. Siewiorek. Introducing PMS. *IEEE Computer*, 7(12):42–44, December 1974.

[SMSV83]   R. L. Schwartz, P. M. Melliar-Smith, and F. H. Vogt. An Interval-Based Temporal Logic. *LNCS*, 164:443–457, June 1983.

[SND88]   H. Simonis, N. Nguyen, and M. Dincbas. Verification of Digital Circuits Using CHIP. In G. J. Milne, editor, *Procs of IFIP WG 10.2 Working Conference on the Fusion of Hardware Design and Verification*, pages 421–442. North-Holland, 1988.

[SNGM89]   G. Smolka, W. Nutt, J. A. Goguen, and J. Meseguer. Order-Sorted Equational Computation. In H. Ait-Kaci and M. Nivat, editors, *Resolution of Equations in Algebraic Structures*, pages 299–367, New York, 1989. Academic Press.

[Sor90]   E. V. Sorensen. On the Dependability Prediction of Safety Critical Systems. ProCoS Project Report ID/DTH EVS 4, Department of Computer Science, Technical University of Denmark, DK-2800 Lyngby, Denmark, April 1990.

[SPG81]   A. B. C. Sampaio and K. Parsaye-Ghomi. The Formal Specification and Testing of Expanded Hardware Building Blocks. In *Procs of Computer Science Conference*, Rolla, MO, 1981. ACM.

[ST92]   R. Stephens and B. C. Thompson. Cartesian Stream Transformer Composition. Technical Report CSR-21-92, Computer Science Division, University College Swansea, 1992.

[Sta90a]   V. Stavridou. Specification, Simulation and Verification of a Twisted Ring Counter. Technical Report CSD-TR-637, Department of Computer Science, RHBNC, University of London, Egham Hill, Egham, Surrey TW20 0EX, UK, December 1990.

[Sta90b]   V. Stavridou. Specification, Simulation and Verification of an N-bit Wide Parallel Adder. Technical Report CSD-TR-634, Department of Computer Science, RHBNC, University of London, Egham Hill, Egham, Surrey TW20 0EX, UK, November 1990.

[Suz85]   N. Suzuki. Concurrent Prolog as an Efficient VLSI Design Language. *IEEE Computer*, pages 33–40, February 1985.

[Tho87]   B. C. Thompson. *A Mathematical Theory of Synchronous Concurrent Algorithms*. PhD thesis, Department of Computer Studies, University of Leeds, Leeds, UK, 1987.

[Tho89]   M. Thomas. Development Methods for Trusted Computer Systems. *Formal Aspects of Computing*, 1(1):5–18, January 1989.

[Tho90]   M. Thomas. The End of the Embedded Microprocessor? Unpublished note, March 1990.

[THS92]   *Proceedings of workshop on the Theory of Hybrid Systems*, Technical University of Denmark, Lyngby, Denmark, October 1992. To appear.

[Tid88]   E. Tiden. Symbolic Verification of Switch Level Circuits Using a Prolog Enhanced With Unification in Finite Algebras. In G. J. Milne, editor, *Procs of IFIP WG 10.2 Working Conference on the Fusion of Hardware Design and Verification*. North-Holland, 1988.

[TP91]   G. Thuau and D. Pilaud. Using the Declarative Language Lustre for Circuit Verification. In G. Jones and M. Sheeran, editors, *Designing Correct Circuits*, pages 313–331. Springer–Verlag, 1991.

[TT91]   B. C. Thompson and J. V. Tucker. Equational Specification of Synchronous Concurrent Algorithms and Architectures. Technical Report CSR-9-91, Computer Science Division, University College Swansea, 1991.

[Tur79]   D. A. Turner. *SASL Reference Manual*. University of Kent, UK, 1979.

[USMK83]   T. Uehara, T. Saito, F. Maruyama, and N. Kawato. DDL Verifier and Temporal Logic. In T. Uehara and M. Barbacci, editors, *Procs of CHDL 83*. IFIP, North-Holland, 1983.

[VHD87]   CAD Language Systems Inc, 51 Monroe St., Suite 606, Rockville, MD 20850, USA. *VHDL Tutorial for IEEE Standard 1076 VHDL*, draft edition, May 1987.

[vN46]   J. von Neumann. Planning and Coding of Problems for an Electronic Computing Instrument. In *John von Neumann, Collected Works*, pages 34–235. Pergamon Press, 1946.

[VVCM92] D. Verkest, J. Vandenbergh, L. Claesen, and H. De Man. A Description Methodology for Parameterised Modules in the Boyer–Moore Logic. In V. Stavridou, T. F. Melham, and R. T. Boute, editors, *Theorem Provers in Circuit Design*, volume A-10 of *IFIP Transactions*, pages 37–58. North-Holland, 1992.

[Wag77]   T. J. Wagner. Verification of Hardware Designs Through Symbolic Manipulation. In *Procs of International Symposium on Design Automation and Microprocessors*, pages 50–53, February 1977.

[Wei84]   D. W. Weise. Automatic Formal Verification of Synchronous MOS VLSI Devices. In *Procs of Workshop on Formal Verification*, Darmstadt, West Germany, November 1984. IFIP WG 10.2.

[Win86]   G. Winskel. Models and Logic of MOS Circuits. In *Procs of International Summer School on Logic of Programming and Calculi of Discrete Design*, Markdoberdof, Germany, July 1986.

[Win87]   G. Winskel. Relating Two Models of Hardware. In D. H. Pitt, A. Poigne, and D. E. Rydeheard, editors, *Procs of Category Theory and Computer Science Conference, LNCS 283*, pages 98–113, Edinburgh, UK, September 1987.

[Win89]   T. Winkler. Introducing OBJ3's New Features. Unpublished report, October 1989.

[ZH91]   C. Zhou and C. A. R. Hoare. A Model for Synchronous Switching Circuits and its Theory of Correctness. In G. Jones and M. Sheeran, editors, *Designing Correct Circuits*, pages 196–211. Springer–Verlag, 1991.

[ZHR90]   C. Zhou, C. A. R. Hoare, and A. P. Ravn. A Duration Calculus for Real Time Requirements in Embedded Software Systems. ProCoS Project Report OU ZCC 2, PRG, Oxford University Computing Laboratory, 8–11 Keble Road, Oxford OX1 3QD, UK, June 1990.

Index